JAZZ:
ITS EVOLUTION
AND ESSENCE

Also by André Hodeir
Published by Grove Press

THE WORLDS OF JAZZ

ANDRÉ HODEIR

JAZZ:
its

evolution

and

essence

UPDATED EDITION

With a New Introduction by MARTIN WILLIAMS

Translated from the French by DAVID NOAKES

GROVE PRESS, INC. • NEW YORK

First Black Cat Edition 1961
First Revised Black Cat Edition 1980
10 9 8 7
ISBN: 0-394-17525-5
Grove Press ISBN: 0-8021-4281-8
Library of Congress Catalog Card Number: 79-52101

LIBRARY OF CONGRESS CATALOGING IN PUBLICATION DATA

Hodeir, André, 1921–
  Jazz, its evolution and essence.

  Discography: p.
  Includes index.
  SUMMARY: Discusses the musicians, musical elements, and other factors which have been influential
in the development of jazz music.
  1. Jazz music. 2. Jazz music — Discography.
[1. Jazz music] I. Title.
ML3561.J3H6383 1979 785.4'2 79-52101
ISBN 0-394-17525-5 pbk.

Manufactured in the United States of America

Distributed by Random House, Inc., New York

GROVE PRESS, INC., 196 West Houston Street,
New York, N.Y. 10014

TRANSLATOR'S NOTE

As I noted in the 1956 edition, American jazz specialists who greeted the original publication of *Hommes et Problèmes du Jazz* as a major event would remember the lucidity of André Hodeir's penetrating analytical method. In translating Hodeir's book, I was guided above all by the desire to give as exact an equivalent of his thought and style as possible. Except for a few minor changes of phrase that the author felt were called for by its publication at that time for non-French readers, the text corresponded exactly to that of the Paris edition. As perhaps the first work in which jazz was treated with all the precise methodology and careful presentation that a critic like Hodeir would bring to the study of any art form, the book was unlike any other and has earned for itself a special niche. Except for the omission of the final chapter on the state of jazz at the death of Charlie Parker in 1955, the present edition is a faithful reproduction of the 1956 work. The discography has been revised to indicate where the records are currently available. Finally, I would be remiss not to repeat here the indebtedness I recorded earlier to Marshall Stearns and Wilder Hobson for their helpful suggestions and comments on my translation.

D.N.

TABLE OF CONTENTS

PREFACE TO THE UPDATED EDITION

For those who, like me, have always maintained that jazz is one of the major — though marginal — phenomena of twentieth-century art, it is not at all surprising that jazz bibliography has developed to the extent that it has since the Second World War. To this edifice, whose quality it is not up to me to evaluate, this book constitutes my first contribution of any appreciable value. Written at the beginning of the fifties, it was published in Paris, in 1954, under the title *Hommes et Problèmes du Jazz* (Men and Problems of Jazz). Two years later, David Noakes completed, for Grove Press, its first translation, and it is in this English-language version that the book appears now in an updated edition for which I am writing this preface.

When, around 1951 — about twenty-eight years ago — I was working on some of the chapters that follow, a period of the same length had just transpired since the historic recordings of King Oliver's Creole Jazz Band (1923). Over those twenty-eight years, musicians such as Bix Beiderbecke, King Oliver, Fats Waller, Chick Webb had disappeared; but Louis Armstrong, Sidney Bechet, Duke Ellington, Coleman Hawkins, Johnny Hodges, Billie Holiday, Charlie Parker, Art Tatum, Lester Young — even if they had, on the level of pure creation, passed the zenith of their careers — were still active in 1950. And, while Miles Davis, Gil Evans, Milt Jackson, John Lewis, and Charles Mingus had already manifested themselves, the names of John Coltrane and Elvin Jones remained unknown to us. The jazz scene was accordingly very different from what it has since become. As for the evolution of its language, who could foresee that it would be so devastating?

In 1950–1951, we were just coming out of a "jazz war" that seems quite ridiculous today. One side maintained that the only authentic jazz was that of the Ancients; I was one of those who fought to gain recognition for the merits of the Moderns. These Moderns, at the time, were Charlie Parker, Dizzy Gillespie, Miles Davis. I did not suspect that, upon reaching middle age, I would have my turn to be confronted with this problem of the upsurge of a new school. The destructive furor of free jazz seemed to me sometimes excessive; and perhaps I did not appreciate its true value, although I was aware of it, the desire that inspired men such as Ayler, Sanders, Schepp, and Taylor to explore to their furthest limit certain potentialities that jazz discourse contained, even at the risk of ending up in absurdity and derision. My reticence concerning free jazz testifies, in any case, to the interest that jazz has never ceased to inspire in me. For twenty years, all the music that I have published has been directly influenced by the language of jazz, and I have never seen myself as anything but a jazz composer.

This book, written after the polemics of the late forties, very largely antedates free jazz. Remaining outside the storms of passion, which I touched upon in *The Worlds of Jazz*, it is intended to be devoted to observation and study. That is why records occupy a privileged position in it. Only by means of recordings can there be an objective approach to jazz, that music which exists nowhere and which cannot be analyzed by examining scores. At that time, the shelves of our record libraries contained only 78s; the long-playing disc, which had been invented only recently, had not yet modified the landscape that I wanted to study. Consequently, I refer here to a system of musical examples that almost never exceed three minutes. Applying to such brief recordings (based, in addition to that, on improvisation) the term "works" may seem excessive. The stylistic and technical reference is nonetheless efficacious for purposes of analysis.

It is these same 78s, most of them reissued as LPs, which make it possible today to read the history of jazz. Thanks to them, this history is not a series of dates referring to indecipherable events, but living source material. The interest that the public shows in jazz of the first half of the century is justified by the richness of an art whose many tendencies are more or less well reflected by recorded performances, from Armstrong to Parker and from Ellington to Basie.

This diversity of jazz was such, at the time I wrote this book, that I had tried to reduce it by organizing it into a system of periods — ancient, classical, modern — in order to give a certain rhythmic structure to the account. That is obviously what shows its age the most in these pages. In 1950, when I was studying a kind of music in the full process of evolution, it was clearly imprudent to distinguish between a "classical" period beginning in 1935 and a "modern" period beginning in 1945. Today this "modern" jazz seems very far away, even if it has kept its characteristic traits by comparison with "classical" jazz. Similarly, a finer analysis of certain subtle points would have made it possible to avoid some errors of judgment. Certain formulations (concerning, for instance, the disadvantages of the two-beat measure) seem to me awkward, and I would surely not repeat them at the present time. Nevertheless, the book as it stands has enough unity to dissuade me from undertaking any revision at all. Even though my opinion on some minor questions is no longer exactly the one expressed here, I don't think I should change a word. The reader will find the text in the exact form in which it was published in 1956.

One of the positive aspects of this work, it seemed to me at the time, was that, perhaps for the first time, a volume dealing with jazz was not being presented as a book of initiation or popularization, but as one that had completely different ambitions. It astonished some people that several of my favorite musicians — Thelonious Monk, for example — occupy so small a part of it. But, at the beginning of the 1950s, I was not ready to write the study that I devoted to Monk later (in *Toward Jazz*). Besides, since this book is not an encyclopedia of jazz, it would be futile to look in it for precise references to *all* the great names of history.

The preface of the original edition began with a quotation by Paul Valéry that I can still endorse without any reservation: "As his taste becomes more refined, the admirer of Alfred de Musset abandons him for Verlaine. One who was brought up on Hugo dedicates himself completely to Mallarmé. These intellectual changes generally occur in one direction rather than in the other, which is much less possible." This means that each of us can progress in the assimilation and comprehension of an art form, but that he must follow this path alone. If it has helped some lover of jazz to achieve such "refinement," this book has accomplished its aim.

— ANDRÉ HODEIR
June 1979

INTRODUCTION TO THE
UPDATED EDITION

To come directly to the point, it seems to me that André Hodeir's *Jazz: Its Evolution and Essence* survives its first twenty-four years as one of the most compelling books ever written on the music. And I have no doubt that it will survive twenty-four more — and many more beyond that.

It was certainly a book for its own time. To anyone who did not live through it (and, by now, even to those of us who did) the controversy caused by the innovations of Charlie Parker and his associates may seem a puzzling phenomenon.

Parker's music was even declared to be not jazz at all by one pioneering and influential French commentator. And as a part of the picture, certain American observers and fans retreated to a position that little or nothing of merit had happened in the music since the maturity of the New Orleans style. On the other hand, there were younger enthusiasts for whom jazz started with Charlie Parker and whatever had preceded him was worth scant attention, or perhaps none at all.

Yet here was a critic not only willing to champion Parker's legitimacy but to give us his thoughtful reasons on the matter; willing, indeed, and able to raise and discuss some fundamental questions about the music and its tradition, its soloists, its composers, and its development.

Here was a critic who not only could enlighten us about Parker but who had some highly important things to say about Louis Armstrong and his pivotal position in the history of jazz. And who could give us crucial insight into the accomplishments and the genius of Ellington.

In effect, then, André Hodeir's book was a peace-making effort which in the long run has succeeded superbly, a book which has now persuaded more than two generations of listeners and critics to see the music whole.

And by writing a truly excellent book for its own time, Hodeir demonstrated that excellence, as always, survives its time and assumes a permanent place in our lives.

Some early reactions to *Jazz: Its Evolution and Essence* were interesting. Those fans who already liked Parker generally welcomed the book although I suspect that fewer of them read and absorbed it.

Some early reviewers said, in effect, that they could not understand how, in an aesthetic field, modernists could be declared to be "better" than the tradition. But of course André Hodeir did not say that Charlie Parker was "better" than Louis Armstrong. He did say that he found Parker a better improvisor than Mezz Mezzrow, and he gave us his reasons.

Other reviewers (and some musicians) found André Hodeir's comments occasionally rarified and wanting in an intimate knowledge of the milieu in which the music was produced and of the attitudes of the musicians who produced it. That was a complaint which Hodeir sought to rectify in subsequent stays in the United States. But surely one answer is that Dickie Wells's *Taxi War Dance* solo or Louis Armstrong's on *Big Butter and Egg Man* or Miles Davis's on *Move* are remarkable musical experiences no matter under what circumstances they were produced. And it is their remarkable qualities, which concerned Hodeir, that should lead us to the day-to-day lives of the men who produced them, and not the other way around.

Finally, there were the fundamentalist comments which held one way or another that jazz would remain alive so long as people responded with their feet and not with their heads. I do not quite know how André Hodeir feels about dancing or foot-patting; he does not tell us. But surely the point is that those listeners who are responding *only* with their feet may be missing whole areas of musical pleasure and enlightenment. (And what if jazz attracted *musicians* capable only of responding to the feet — or, as Lester Young once put it, only with their bellies?)

My praise of this book could not be totally unqualified of course. I prefer the original French title of the volume — in translation, *Men and Problems of Jazz.* It may be clumsy English but it is a straightforward yet cautious description of the book's intentions. I do not believe that M. Hodeir quite succeeded in defining Swing for us. Nor does it seem to me just to date all artistry in jazz as beginning with Louis Armstrong. And M. Hodeir can be a severe critic at moments when severity may not be most persuasive.

But enough. It is not a critic's business to impose his opinions on us, but to help us (sometimes force us) to clarify our own.

To say that André Hodeir is one of the few real critics to have written on jazz is not to do him justice. In this book, he proved himself to be the kind of critic that the observers of any artistic pursuit should be pleased to have encountered — indeed, the caliber of critic that perhaps only a truly artistic pursuit could have attracted.

— MARTIN WILLIAMS
Alexandria, Virginia
August 1979

JAZZ:
ITS EVOLUTION
AND ESSENCE

Chapter 1

THE
WORLD
OF
JAZZ

1
Diffusion and Universality of Jazz

Since the Second World War, jazz has spread appreciably and has become considerably better known. The day is past when this music was symbolized for Europeans by the names of Paul Whiteman, George Gershwin, Ted Lewis, Jack Hylton, Jean Wiener, and Clément Doucet, and when the colored star of *The Jazz Singer* turned out to be a white man, Al Jolson, made up in blackface for local color. By now it has become evident that jazz is the Negro's art and that almost all the great jazz musicians are Negroes. People are now acquainted with Louis Armstrong, Duke Ellington, Sidney Bechet, and Dizzy Gillespie; they have been applauded throughout France, in the same concert halls as Gieseking and Menuhin. It is no longer possible, as it was fifteen or twenty years ago, for an alert, reasonably well-informed person to confuse authentic jazz with cheap dance music or pretentious pieces like *Rhapsody in Blue*. In many cases jazz is still difficult to get at, but it can be found.

How strange have been the fortunes of this music, which

seemed destined to remain confined to the banks of the
lower Mississippi! What contemporary observer would have
guessed that the folk music of a small group would become
the language of an entire people fifteen or twenty years later
and, in a few more years, a world-wide phenomenon, with
jazz bands existing simultaneously in Melbourne, Tokyo,
and Stockholm? What does this success mean? It has been
said that jazz is the most fully alive form of dance music
of our time; this is true, but jazz is much more than dance
music. The importance of the movement it has given rise
to may be judged by the number of books and magazines
on the subject published all over the world. Nothing is
stranger, and nothing more reassuring for humanity, than
the universal diffusion of this message first launched by a
people numbering ten million.

We must not delude ourselves, however. Jazz has found
followers everywhere, but these followers are always in the
minority. Everyone remembers the waves of protest that jazz
aroused in the greater part of the French public only
recently. By now, such protest seems to have given way to
a fashionable indifference. People no longer become indig-
nant when they hear Louis Armstrong sing, they smile
politely. A very small number of the newspapers and magazines concerned with the arts feel it their duty to carry a jazz
column. This reticence in the face of such success and these
limitations on an expansion that has been so great in other
respects present a problem we cannot avoid. What are the
causes of these apparent contradictions?

At first, it might seem that jazz is incapable of touching the
masses and is suited only to an elite. This hypothesis would
explain its limited success, but unfortunately it is contra-
dicted by the facts. On the contrary, jazz seems to be accepted
only with the greatest reservations by those regularly referred
to as the elite—that is to say, the small part of the public that
is capable of fully appreciating both classical and modern

artistic masterpieces. There is a simple explanation for this
cultured public's aloofness. Anyone who tries to place jazz
in the perspective of European culture without first revising
his traditional artistic habits has scarcely any chance of understanding it. He can see only its defects; jazz appears to
him in its negative aspects, which are rendered even more
striking by being compared with European art. He is thus
led to reject this music "which is not thought out, not
worked over, not constructed, which has no architecture,
whose harmony is dull and sugar-coated, whose melody
lacks nobility and breadth, whose form and rhythm are
stereotyped," this anti-intellectual music "whose themes are
mostly popular ditties and whose creators are trumpet and
saxophone players."

Such is the conclusion—severe but in many respects well-
founded—reached by the music lover who expects from jazz
the same satisfactions he receives from classical masterpieces.
But isn't there something nonsensical about this attitude?
Would jazz have the slightest interest if its function were
only to bring back to life, in its own way—and hence, necessarily, with less force and purity—the very same musical
emotions that European art cultivates? Obviously, our music
lover is only showing how hard it is for him to enlarge his
horizon. Certain listening habits are so strong that not everyone can free himself from them. In that case, our man has
the right to retort that he can do without jazz; the rich
European musical universe is diversified enough to take up
a lifetime by itself.

2
Jazz As a Complement to Our Culture

When an art involves the most elaborate forms of a culture, often only the most highly educated minds can grasp.

it. When an art is foreign to a culture, it seems, on the contrary, that greater educational conditioning can retard or even prevent an understanding of it. This observation kept me persuaded for a long time that the only way to appreciate jazz was to "acquire a way of feeling like the Negro's." Today I see clearly how illusory such an idea is. Whatever the American Negro's way of feeling is determined by and regardless of whether heredity or environment plays the preponderant role in its formation, it is impossible for a European to identify himself with the Negro, except in a very superficial way. Even if it could be done, the price would be a total renunciation of what is best in European culture. Michelangelo, Vermeer, Bach, Baudelaire, and Kafka have left too profound a mark on us to permit such a monstrous rejection. As great as the merits of jazz may be, this would be too high a price to pay in order to assimilate an art which is not ours by origin.

However, an intermediate position is possible. For us Europeans, the only reasonable solution is to take jazz as a complement to our culture, not as an antidote to the "poisons of intellectualism." What does this music bring to us? Isn't it precisely the kind of music "that can be listened to without burying one's forehead in one's hands," which is what Jean Cocteau called for after the first war? In jazz, "sensorial interests" greatly outweigh "intellectual passion," the simple charm of existence is exalted without much reflection, a sharpened sensuality takes the place of loftiness and the fusion of individualities takes the place of architecture. Consequently, the attitude required of the listener by jazz is completely different from that generally required by classical masterpieces. But whoever knows how to listen to it with the right kind of ear is always paid for his effort. In our time, when the most advanced European art is becoming more and more abstract (Mondrian, Boulez), leaving room for feeling but only in a highly sublimated form, jazz brings

an element of balance that may be necessary and is almost
surely beneficial.

Henri Bernard, a veteran among French jazz fans and a
man of culture besides, has written: "The miracle of the
century is not power failures or airplane crashes or trips
to the moon, but primitive man and Negro folklore."[1] It
would be more exact to write that what gives our epoch its
value is what we have managed to bring into existence. To
be able to take part in the most varied activities of modern
man when they tend to build rather than to destroy, to be
interested in contemporary philosophy without neglecting
sports, to make room for jazz alongside abstract art—that is
what really enriches us. Is it impossible to hear foreign
languages and appreciate their beauty without first disown-
ing and almost forgetting one's mother tongue? On the
contrary, I am convinced that we have the ability to adopt.
differing attitudes of receptivity and comprehension as the
need arises. This does not necessarily force us to judge jazz
in the perspective of European art; instead, it invites us to
broaden our view in order to make room for the only popu-
larly inspired music of our time which is universal and has
not become lost in vulgarity. It is not a question of giving
up what we have, but of acquiring something else.

3
The Jazz Fan

Unfortunately, it must be admitted that such an attitude
is rather rare. The most common position seems to be dic-
tated by the necessity of a choice, even though such a choice
does not absolutely have to be made.

We have seen that the educated man who cannot triumph
over his own culture is not well equipped to appreciate the

[1] H. Bernard: "Claude Luter ou le rossignol délivré des plumes du paon,"
in Jazz-Hot, February, 1949, p. 9.

beauty of jazz. To what type of man, then, does Armstrong's
trumpet or Hawkins' saxophone speak meaningfully? Who
is the jazz fan? Is it the opera subscriber who never fails to
shed a tear over the endlessly repeated misfortunes of Manon
or Tosca? Is it the matron to whom waltzes bring back fond
recollections of her youth, or the shopgirl who swoons when
she hears such popular singers as Georges Guétary or Tino
Rossi on the radio? Obviously, the jazz fan is not any of
these. To be understood, jazz seems to require a fresh, still
unsatisfied sensibility (which may explain why it rarely
takes hold of someone who has already assimilated the beauty
of great European music), a kind of person who is over-
flowing with energy and searching for an outlet. Obviously,
the adolescent is the one who meets these conditions best.
There is therefore nothing surprising in the fact that the
young people of both sexes—but particularly boys rather
than girls—have in a way made jazz their own.

Of course, there is another explanation for this fact. Since
the popularity of jazz is a relatively recent thing, at least
in France, it is logical that only the youngest part of the
public should have discovered its beauty. It can be easily
verified that, past the age of thirty, not everyone is capable
of the effort required to assimilate a new way of thinking
or feeling. This explanation, however, is only partly satisfactory. It ignores a fact to which all the jazz fans of my
generation can testify. Before the war, we all had a few
friends who were dominated by their passion for jazz and
who used to spend most of their pocket money for Louis
Armstrong's and Fats Waller's records. How many of them
have kept the faith? Has more than one out of ten of these
"frivolous fans" enlarged or even kept his record collection?
For the most part, they have succumbed to the routine of
bourgeois existence, which leaves little room for artistic
satisfactions; their love of jazz has not been strong enough
or solidly enough motivated to stand up. They have let

others take their place, and there is every reason to believe that these newcomers will act in the same way.

The explanation is that young people's passion for jazz is based less on a real feeling for music than on another quality which is characteristic of adolescence—enthusiasm. I certainly have no intention of belittling the value of enthusiasm; many great things can be accomplished only through it. But, except in persons of unusual quality, enthusiasm is short-lived. Enthusiasm is the element surrounding the young man who has set out to discover jazz and who can't wait to hear the latest Art Tatum record and to discuss with his friends the most recently published book or the opinion of the critic who is willing to exchange comments with him about the latest issue of the magazine he subscribes to. It is enthusiasm, finally, which transforms the love of jazz into a kind of metaphysical crisis in extreme cases and makes Jelly Roll Morton and Tommy Ladnier be regarded as legendary heroes or saints. But when this enthusiasm dies down, everything collapses in a very short time. The torch is passed on to younger hands; and from year to year, the faces change but the average age of people who go to jazz concerts and read jazz magazines remains the same.

Nevertheless, this description is too general to be accepted literally. As I have said, there are few fans whose infatuation with jazz resists the test of time. Still, there are some, and their existence shows that jazz can bring to a man satisfactions that are not superficial, but profound and in a sense necessary. Although I am not fond of generalizing, I should like to sketch the portrait of such a fan. He is between thirty and forty—rarely older, for jazz has penetrated Europe too recently for there to be more than a handful of real oldtimers. His erudition (by which I mean his knowledge of recordings) is solid, and so are his opinions. In the past, he may have regarded the Greats with religious awe; but his present attitude is marked by a familiarity that is much less respectful. When Cozy Cole and Lester Young play in the city where he lives, he has a drink with one and invites the other to dinner.

Our man generally tends to be conservative. Has he refused to make the effort to understand modern jazz, or have his established habits made it too difficult for any attempt at assimilation to be successful? In any case, nine times out of ten, he considers the jazz of today an ersatz, a deviation, or a sacrilege—an attitude which I condemn, but which I find more congenial than that of so many young fans who, having come to jazz through bebop, have only a rudimentary knowledge of its tradition and reject all old-time and even classical jazz without ever having known what it was like. With all his faults, the veteran jazz fan is valuable to have around. His steadfastness is comforting when compared with the fickleness of the majority, for whom jazz is just an excuse for dancing or a nervous outlet, without any great or lasting value. Best of all, the veteran jazz fan, even when he nears fifty, is able to preserve that rarest of all attributes, to be young at heart. For jazz is a music of young people, made by young people for young people. It is enough to hear the playing of a white-haired jazzman like Sidney Bechet to know that he has remained as young at heart as those who stamp with excitement while listening to him. Thus, unlike the occasionally delirious but short-lived enthusiasm of the frivolous fan, the restrained fervor of the veteran resists the test of time.

At the beginning of his career, there is no way of telling the passing faddist from the fellow who will become a veteran jazz fan. A group of fans may be equally fanatical in appearance; time alone will tell which one has been touched so deeply that his love for jazz will last a lifetime. However sincere or devoted he may seem, no one can say whether a newcomer to jazz is going to belong to one group or the other. Many halfhearted listeners have turned into ardent defenders of jazz, whereas many ardent collectors have suddenly sold their eight hundred records and lost all interest in this music.

4
The Reign of Intolerance

Jazz fans live in a world apart. They receive spiritual nourishment from books and magazines that cannot be fully understood without some previous knowledge; when "Louis" is mentioned, for example, the reader must know that the reference is to Louis Armstrong. With a few exceptions, inhabitants of the jazz world have no contact with the inhabitants of other artistic worlds. Nine times out of ten, if the jazz fan does not scorn "long-hair music," he knows only its most superficial aspects. The fingers of one hand would be almost enough to count those who are interested in both Armstrong and the seventeenth-century Italians, in both Parker and the dodecaphonists. And yet what dissensions rage within this small, closed world! As a general rule, jazz fans are too thoroughly convinced of the superiority of their taste to be able to keep it to themselves. They form little chapels called "hot clubs," whose principal function, though not clearly stated, seems to be the maintenance of perpetual discord between the advocates of traditional jazz and the partisans of modern jazz. Thus, intolerance reigns in this universe. Intolerance is latent even in the normal jazz fan, and it takes only one thing to make it burst into flame—a crowd. The jazz concert is the gathering place for all kinds of intolerance and prejudice. When you add to this the love of sheer noise that is common to all youngsters fresh out of school, it is easy to understand why the public at a jazz concert often is as loud as one at a sporting event. The exclusive partisan of one kind of jazz

wouldn't think of letting his neighbor listen in peace to
an opposing tendency. Is a concert of modern jazz being
organized? It will be disturbed by the advocates of oldtime
jazz, to whom the idea of staying at home sometimes fails
to occur.[2]

Only a step divides intolerance from fanaticism. The most
forbidding fan is the one who feels that he has been initiated
into all the secrets of jazz. He has heard that a Negro audi-
ence is loud and clear in showing its joy, so at a concert
he lets his explode in a great hubbub. He even whistles
instead of applauding, for the sake of authenticity. He has
read in his classics that the well-informed listener claps his
hands on the weak beats. Accordingly, he exercises his
palms. However, since it is hard for him to distinguish the
weak beat from the strong one, he claps haphazardly. The
result is an indistinct rumbling in the hall which adds to
the special atmosphere of jazz concerts. Frequently, enthusiasm grows in direct proportion to the volume of the music.
When Armstrong played in Paris in November, 1952, an
ovation never failed to greet Cozy Cole's use of a little cymbal
that dominated the entire ensemble by its piercing timbre.
This "decibel fanaticism" is a curious form of the
phenomenon.

5

Conceptions of Criticism

For a long time, the intolerance of the jazz fan was bol-
stered by equally intolerant critics, and to a certain extent
it still is. In no other art form, perhaps, have the critics
had so much influence on their public, and this has been
particularly true in France. Since jazz musicians have shown

[2] It must be noted, however, that concerts of modern jazz given by great
Negro stars proceed normally. The prestige of the musicians inhibits any
expression of hostility.

little taste for writing and often lack general culture, the task of enlightening jazz fans has fallen to other amateurs. The criticism of these self-styled "specialists" is responsible for the establishment of a rather fanciful scale of values. Is there anything surprising in that? How could certain kinds of perfection that are purely musical in nature make any impression on an ear which is incapable of recognizing Mezzrow's wrong notes? Can anyone who praises to the sky John Lindsay's or George Stafford's tempo fully appreciate Teddy Wilson's or Charlie Parker's? Nevertheless, this scale of values has the force of law, even today, in the eyes of a sizable segment of the jazz public. Its influence has been reinforced by the success of *Really the Blues,* the book by Mezz Mezzrow and Bernard Wolfe—a success indisputably merited on literary grounds. This vibrant plea in favor of primitive jazz—and of Mr. Mezzrow himself—has caused some shaky ideas to be supported by a number of fence-sitters who failed to distinguish where literary talent and the charm of a captivating personality left off and errors in judgment began. In order to be aware of the possibility of such errors, to say nothing of their extent, the reader should know that American musicians and critics consider Mezzrow an amateur (and his records confirm this evaluation when they are examined carefully). But, naturally, none of this can be guessed simply by reading *Really the Blues.*

During the thirty months, beginning in 1947, when I was in charge of the magazine *Jazz-Hot,* I tried to remove the heavy hand of amateurism which had weighed so long on French criticism. A musician myself, I thought (and I still think) that only a professional can speak about music with any competence. Beside trying to destroy the most arbitrary dogmas, I attempted to build a team of musician-journalists who would be capable of examining the problems of their art with lucidity and of making the ordinary fan understand them. In spite of the work of Jean Ledru, Eddy Bernard,

Henri Renaud, and some others, I realize that this effort resulted in a partial failure. Certainly, the best music critics —one might almost say the only ones—have always been musicians themselves. Who has spoken of Schoenberg with more warmth and competence than Alban Berg? Who has given us a more clear-sighted analysis of *Le Sacre du Printemps* than Pierre Boulez? However, it is characteristic of the European composer to meditate. It is not rare to see him become truly aware of a problem at the very moment when he is in the act of creation. The jazz musician does not meditate. If he happens to listen attentively to the work of another musician, he grasps what it has to offer through intuitive assimilation rather than by reflection. This being so, how can the jazz musician be expected to perform a work of analysis for which his training hasn't prepared him? And even if he could, would he know how to express his essential thought in language that would be clear and precise enough for everyone to understand?

Moreover, this conception of criticism conflicts not only with the habits of jazz fans, who are accustomed to a simple statement of categorical judgments supported by resounding adjectives, but also with their personal reactions, which naturally more closely resemble those of the amateur-critic than those of the musician-critic. It is often for this reason that the musician-critic fails. A certain succession of chords or the voice-leading in an ensemble may appear defective to his ears; but how can he make the amateur aware of this if the amateur does not want to see what is obvious? It took me years to realize that what I thought was "swing" was really only the "hot" aspect of a performance and that swing was intimately connected with getting the notes perfectly in place rhythmically. Since then, I have met hundreds of fans who have yet to grasp this essential point; nearly always, I have found it impossible to get it across to them.

However difficult such an attempt may be, a revision of

values seems necessary. Not that I want to substitute dogmas of my own for the old ones; on the contrary, everything must be subjected to the most radical doubt and reconsidered. Every point established by amateurish criticism must be tested by analysis, every judgment must be thoroughly re-examined.

Of course, analysis alone cannot determine the worth or the worthlessness of a work; but, wherever possible, it should provide a support for personal taste and try to explain precisely what has been grasped intuitively. It is not enough to write that, around 1925, Louis Armstrong introduced a new conception of jazz. It must be shown exactly how this new conception differed from earlier ones, and the terminology used must be as rigorous as possible, even if this means expressing rather complex ideas and thereby running the risk of being called obscurantist or pedantic by the superficial reader. There is a deep interpenetration between what is called "inspiration" and the technique[3] it uses to find expression. It is no doubt arbitrary to separate them in order to try to explain through analysis what should be explained through synthesis. If I choose the former method, it is because the tools of jazz criticism are still too crude. Within the limits of current conceptions, much remains to be done. What I should like is for this book to become, in its small way, the *Discourse on Method* of jazz. I know, long before finishing the volume, that Descartes' achievement is well beyond me; there are many problems that I won't be able to touch. But perhaps some other musician, one more gifted for criticism and more erudite than I, will take up where I leave off and carry this idea further. It would be discouraging to think that jazz is not destined to have, sooner or later, the exegesis it deserves. Fortunately, there is little reason to believe it won't.

[3] I do not use the word to imply "instrumental technique," but rather "technique of thought."

If such an enterprise were to be pursued thoroughly, it would acquire encyclopedic proportions, which are a far cry from the limited dimensions of this book. The fact that I throw the spotlight on Charlie Parker and CONCERTO FOR COOTIE rather than on Lester Young and KO-KO does not imply that the former are superior to the latter, but shows that my aim has been to give the reader the means of judging for himself rather than to offer him a prefabricated scale of values. Criticism should limit itself to being the auxiliary of the individual's personal taste, which is controlled by Valéry's great law of intellectual development which I have already cited. If I happen to express a preference in these pages, let it serve merely as an indication to the reader, a marker showing something about the thing preferred and the person who does the preferring, enabling the reader to measure my taste against his own; but the essential part of my work consists in proposing and illustrating a method— the method of analysis which, for the time being in this field, must precede any constructive synthesis.

Chapter 18

THE EVOLUTION OF JAZZ
AND THE IDEA OF CLASSICISM

Historians have always been tempted to simplify their work by dividing time into clearly marked periods. The major weakness of this system becomes apparent as soon as one thinks of the way in which the limits are confused by events that unavoidably overlap different epochs. It may well seem even trickier to attempt a division of jazz into three, four, or five periods, since it has covered scarcely half a century. The arbitrariness of cutting time up into unjustifiably neat slices is in this case intensified by the thinness of the slices. Since the career of a musician sometimes lasts much longer than the historical period to which it belongs, it is easy to imagine the confusion to which such a procedure can lead. Nonetheless, jazz has been characterized at given times by important movements. It is a good idea for the commentator to be able to refer to them by simply using a phrase. Once their meaning is defined, the words *classic* and *modern* make it possible to avoid a great many periphrases. Obviously, the pros and cons of this subject are pretty well balanced.

I believe a satisfactory solution is impossible without giving up the determination to make tendencies and periods correspond at any cost. For example, 1947 was the great year of Charlie Parker's modern recordings, but it was also

notable for excellent works that were classical or even older
in spirit. Quite independently of date, Louis Armstrong's
work can be identified either with oldtime jazz or with
classical jazz, depending on whether he is surrounded by
oldtimers like Kid Ory or by sidemen who are distinctly
more advanced, such as Earl Hines or Cozy Cole. In any case,
the most vital tendency in 1947 was bebop, and Armstrong's
best work dates between 1928 and 1930, at the very moment
when he was the one who was showing everybody else the
road to follow. It seems reasonable, then, to divide the history
of jazz into periods that correspond to a more or less pronounced preponderance of one school over the others. We
wind up in this way with a division into four or even five
periods, depending on whether or not we choose to divide
the New Orleans epoch. I have finally decided in favor of a
division into five periods (see chart, p. 24).

1
First and Second Periods: New Orleans Jazz

First, there is the epoch of primitive jazz. It runs from
the birth of jazz, to which it is impossible to fix a precise
date (it is generally situated around 1900), to the great
migration that followed the closing down of Storyville, in
1917.[1] We don't know much about this period. There are
no recordings that date before 1917, so we are obliged to
attempt a mental reconstruction of what jazz must have been
like at that time in the light of what contemporaries have

[1] Storyville, "forbidden quarter" of New Orleans, was closed down by
municipal order soon after the United States entered the war. This was an
extremely hard blow to the musicians employed by its cabarets, brothels, and
gambling houses.

said and of recordings that attempt to recapture the spirit
of the period (Original Zenith Brass Band). That is a difficult but not an impossible task, for a number of checks
and counterchecks help us to disperse the shadows in which
this kind of prehistoric period lies hidden from us.

We know more about the second period, that of "advanced
New Orleans" or "oldtime" jazz. The year 1917 saw not
only the migration but also the oldest known recording in
which it is possible to recognize a work of jazz, however
weak it may be: DIXIE JASS BAND ONE-STEP / LIVERY STABLE
BLUES by the Original Dixieland Jazz Band. It would be hard
to overestimate the importance of the testimony records were
to provide from that point on. At first, they were few and
far between and didn't have much musical interest, but they
multiplied and became much more valuable after 1923,
which marks the first important set of recordings in the
history of jazz, that of King Oliver's Creole Jazz Band.
Thanks to records, we are able to describe with some precision the collective language of jazz in the twenties and the
slow development of an individualistic style that brought
with its triumph the division and scattering of the New
Orleans school.

For some time, a contemporary observer might have
thought, around 1927, that jazz was entering a period of
stability in which collectivistic and individualistic tendencies
would be harmoniously fused; but this equilibrum, as it
appears in Armstrong's 1927-1928 recordings, turned out to
be precarious. A few years later, our observer would have
had to agree that what he had taken for the flowering of
classicism was only its preparation, as it was also the swan
song of a style that had seen its day. It couldn't last, because
beginning with this period there came into play other drives
that were destined to become increasingly powerful. It was,
therefore, at the very moment when it was turning out its

A SUMMING UP OF THE EVOLUTION OF JAZZ

AGES (or PERIODS)	DATES	PRINCIPAL CENTERS	PREDOMINANT AND SECONDARY TENDENCIES	LEADERS
Primitive	c. 1900 (?)-1917	New Orleans	original New Orleans style	Buddy Bolden, Bunk Johnson, Em. Perez, etc.
Oldtime	1917-1926	Chicago	advanced New Orleans style	King Oliver, Jelly Roll Morton, Louis Armstrong
Pre-Classical	1927-1934	New York	big band; piano	F. Henderson, J. P. Johnson
		New York	swing style in gestation	Armstrong, Hawkins, Hines, Bix
		Kansas City	growth of the big band	F. Henderson, Ellington, Bennie Moten
Classical	1935-1945	Chicago	vestiges of New Orleans	Noone, Morton, etc.
		New York	swing style	Eldridge, Wells, Hawkins, Young, Fats, Wilson, Tatum, Webb, Cole, Hampton, Goodman
			peak of the big band	Ellington, Lunceford, Basie
			New Orleans Revival (beginning 1938-1940)	Armstrong, Bechet, Morton, Ory, B. Johnson
Modern	1945-...	New York	bebop style	Gillespie, Parker
			cool style	Davis, Konitz, Mulligan
			holdovers: swing style New Orleans big band	Young, Tatum, Garner Armstrong, Bechet Ellington, Hampton
		West Coast	progressive	Kenton, Brubeck

most beautiful works that the New Orleans school lost the lead. It slipped very quickly into an almost complete oblivion, from which it was drawn only by the miracle of the "New Orleans Revival" ten years later. We shall call the jazz of this period (1917-1926) "oldtime" to distinguish it from primitive jazz as we conjecture it must have been performed before 1917.

2
The Modern Period

These first two periods can be marked off rather precisely because, for one thing, they were basically unified, in spite of a New York trend that came into existence right after World War I, combining the New Orleans influence with an extremely rudimentary attempt to form an orchestral language and with a kind of piano playing that sprang directly from traditional ragtime. The same unity does not hold during the following periods. For the sake of clearness, we must now consider the modern period, rather than follow strict chronological order. This period began at the end of World War II, with the first recordings by the Gillespie-Parker team. During its first years at least, the predominant tendency was "bebop." Later, a new form of expression, the "cool" movement, made its appearance and assumed an increasingly great importance. The bop and cool tendencies, therefore, are what is referred to by the term "modern jazz," but this name should not be allowed to disguise the fact that the modern period also includes older varieties of jazz— swing and even the New Orleans style. Finally, a place must be left for the so-called "progressive" tendencies, although they must be considered with a certain amount of caution.

3
Musical Evolution and the Idea of Progress

It may surprise some people that I call the period between
1935 and 1945 "classical." Until recently, if such a term was
used at all, it designated the New Orleans era. This idea was
closely linked to the dogma of the purity of original jazz,
but we shall see that this dogma rests on no serious foundation. A better sense of values and the passage of time make
it possible today to correct this optical illusion. Classicism
implies durability, above all. Isn't a simple glance back
enough to show how outdated most of the works recorded
before 1935 have become? Our record collections, which
are the only impartial witnesses we have, prove that these
works have diminished in value. Even more significantly,
they reveal to us the image of an art still in gestation—hence,
regardless of what people may say about it, still progressing—
an art which, at the time of Louis Armstrong's Hot Five,
was still a long way from having found the equilibrium
that characterizes true classicism.

Perhaps a parenthetical note might serve a good purpose
here. This problem of progress in art[2] has been the subject
of interminable polemics, particularly among jazz specialists.
Some believe that progress is continuous, necessary, and
inevitable; others deny such progress, which they call illusory. They admit the growing complexity of techniques,
but they refuse—not without reason—to regard this as enough
to bring about any real esthetic improvement. The non-
progressionists make much of an argument borrowed from
the evolution of European music. "To believe in progress,"
they say, "is to proclaim Mozart superior to Bach, Beethoven
to Mozart, Wagner to Beethoven, Debussy to Wagner, and
so on—all of which, obviously, is absurd." This argument

[2] We use the word in the sense of *increase of value.*

ignores the fact that Bach is not at the source of the European polyphonic tradition, but that he is, on the contrary, a prodigious culmination of it. Isn't a brief glance at medieval music enough to show that there is not only an *evolution* from century to century, but an almost continuous *progress?* Pérotin was undoubtedly a musician of genius, but he came at a time when everything remained to be done; no one would think of putting his work on the same level as Bach's. An analysis of Machaut's beautiful but arid *Mass* shows by way of contrast how flexible and rich eighteenth-century polyphony was. European music has experienced a period of growth extending over at least five or six centuries; how can jazz be refused a similar period, even though it lasted only twenty-five or thirty years?

A large number of fans like archaic things so much that they have extravagantly praised records made during this period of gestation without realizing that they were applauding rough sketches that represent a valid but clumsy effort to achieve a kind of perfection that other artists attained a few years later. The attempts of Kid Ory to create an expressive language on the trombone were both useful and praiseworthy; the fact remains that Jimmy Harrison and particularly Dickie Wells succeeded where their courageous New Orleans predecessor was doomed to fail.

It seems that the jazzmen of the immediately prewar period, who were so condemned for "puerile progressivism," were actually closer to the truth. In their view, jazz never stopped improving. They naively believed their music better than that of their predecessors, just as they would have judged a 1938 automobile faster and more comfortable than a 1925 model. The principle of this argument could be easily refuted, and, as we have seen, it was refuted. But, although it may have lacked a sound philosophical basis, it was founded on a good appreciation of concrete musical facts. The "moderns" of the time *knew* that their seniors had weaknesses, not only in instrumental technique, but in ear and rhythmic sense as well. What these jazzmen failed to realize was that they themselves had attained a stage of stability, that they themselves had become *classical*. Their attitude was like that of a man who, observing a plant grow for the first time and seeing it become larger and more beautiful week after week, might conclude that it would go on developing like that forever. A broader education would certainly have prevented these jazzmen from making such a mistake in judgment; but how can they be legitimately reproached for not being better educated?

Another argument advanced to support the theory of the impossibility of progress in art is the oversimplified notion that a work of art is nothing but a product of individual genius. This idea does not stand up under examination. The history of art teaches us, on the contrary, that the man of genius is indebted to the past. What he does is part of a tradition. As heir to everything his predecessors have accomplished, he is not absolutely free, not even in the choice of what he wants to do. As André Malraux has said, all art proceeds from an earlier art. Acquisitions are added to acquisitions; they involve some losses and also some renunciations. At first, the acquisitions outweigh the losses; then acquisitions and losses balance, and progress ceases. Ten years after Armstrong created an authentic language for the trumpet, Eldridge developed this language and added to it. But he could do this only by increasing its complexity. He paid for this enrichment by the loss of collective equilibrium; when improvising in a group, Roy continued to play as a soloist. What was natural in the new order killed what had been natural in the old.

Some believers in "continuous progress" persist in proclaiming the inevitable superiority of modern works over earlier ones. They are quite naturally led to consider anything that is not expressed in the most advanced language as being null and void. Such a radical rejection of the past is surely more constructive than mere reverent contemplation of a bygone era, but it is easy to see where such an attitude might lead. It is understandable that the determined modernist should refuse to listen to the current work of any musician of the old school; chances are that such a musician will merely be imitating older men or that he belongs to a generation which has already produced its best work. But to refuse to take the work of the past into consideration is to cut jazz off from its roots, deny it any tradition, and confine it to the fleeting present, which is likewise condemned to disappear without leaving a trace. Doesn't that amount to making out of jazz a monster that destroys itself as it goes along? It is like saying, "The only way jazz can appeal to me is as a passing fancy; and though I like it in its present form, I do so knowing perfectly well that my taste is not very good."

There are sound reasons for preferring a great modern work to a great classical one. The newer work is closer to us and speaks a language to which we cannot fail to respond more directly, once we have fully assimilated it. *Le Sacre du Printemps* is *our* music much more than the *Ninth Symphony*. Isn't it true that those who prefer the Beethoven work confess implicitly their inability to understand Stravinsky's masterpiece? But to prefer something modern and mediocre to a great classical work is the sign of deformed judgment. The extremist attitude taken by many admirers of modern jazz has led them too often to praise rather feeble works. Many of this kind are being turned out these days. I expressed my admiration for modern jazz long before Dizzy Gillespie's recent appearances throughout France unleashed almost everyone's enthusiasm. Several years ago, this new form of expression gave jazz a welcome shot in the arm, but it is impossible to hide the fact that, on the whole, modern jazz has not lived up to the promises of 1945-1947. In all

honesty, aren't we forced to admit that, since Parker's and
Gillespie's great period, the only complete esthetic successes
have been some of Miles Davis' efforts? Whatever the causes
(unfavorable outside conditions, difficulty in expression,
public's hostility, and so forth), contemporary jazz since
1949-1950 seems to have produced hardly anything of more
than secondary importance.[3] For this reason, an exclusive
admiration for the modern period, which so far does not
rank with the richest in jazz history, seems to me just as
nonsensical as the maniacal New Orleans cult.

4
The Classical Period

Having said this much, we can now examine more closely
the period beginning with 1935. One thing to be noted
immediately is that, if any one date marks the end of jazz's
growing pains, this one is it. In that year, jazz found itself
on the threshold of an unprecedented material success; even
more important, it achieved a style that gave it the equilibrium which comes with maturity. This style, which the
Americans called "swing music," was the crystallization and
logical termination of tendencies that had struggled to find
expression during the earlier periods. One sure sign of this
maturity is that the passing years have left no mark upon
even the oldest records in this style. Our modern ear fails
to note any essential fault in them. Take an average record
in any good series of the day—a Fats Waller or a Teddy
Wilson, for example—and you will see that its style has not
aged. Isn't such timelessness a distinguishing characteristic
of classicism? An even clearer indication is given by the
generally high quality of the work produced during this
period. A classical period is by definition a great period.

[3] I am taking only recorded work into account, naturally.

Some people forget that most of the recordings which made jazz great date from this classical period, and particularly between 1937 and 1941, the years when it was at its peak.

It is true that this was also the period of the Goodman type of academic playing and of arrangements with stereotyped riffs; but it was also the era of Ellington's, Lunceford's, Basie's, and Hampton's finest recordings, of Armstrong's second I CAN'T GIVE YOU ANYTHING BUT LOVE, of Hawkins' BODY AND SOUL, of Eldridge's WABASH STOMP. This list is, of course, far from being complete, but it is enough to prove two things: first, that most of the great precursors had become classical figures and were producing their best work; and second, that new leaders were coming up, men in whose work a discerning ear could already tell the direction modern jazz was taking (I am thinking particularly of the first Lester Young recordings). Never before or since have so many great musicians existed side by side, uniting their efforts to found a marvelously rich and diversified school of jazz— and all the more rich and diversified for being both classical and romantic at the same time, for having Eldridge as well as Hodges and Dickie Wells in addition to Teddy Wilson.

5
The New Orleans Revival

Nevertheless, it was during this period in which the major form of jazz was coming out on top that one of the most curious phenomena in the history of jazz took place. The world-wide success of "swing music" had brought about recognition of jazz as a valid art form. As a consequence, jazz of the past was examined in an effort to get at the sources of this music. New Orleans veterans reappeared: Jelly Roll Morton, who had been forgotten for a decade, and Bunk Johnson, a pioneer of the heroic age who was

brought from Louisiana to head a band of old men. Sidney
Bechet, whose career had been somewhat obscure until then,
achieved success. Louis Armstrong began to return to the
music of his youthful days; a few years later, he stopped
playing with big swing bands in order to form a new Hot
Five, with musicians of his own generation. Following these
examples, a number of very young musicians—all of them
white, be it noted—were won over by the pioneers' cult and
tried to revive the atmosphere of primitive jazz. It was the
"New Orleans Revival."

It is clear that the movement was widespread, but its
limitations are also obvious. Much has been written about
the New Orleans Revival. The praises of toothless and
winded cornet players have been sung by zealous partisans
of early jazz, for whom oldtime jazz is necessarily better than
classical, and primitive jazz better than oldtime. Even if
these musicians had been able to recapture the skill and
enthusiasm of their youth, they would still have remained
no more than useful but humble precursors whom many
others had surpassed. It is true that some great soloists lent
their talents to this New Orleans renaissance; and it is thanks
to them that the movement does not appear altogether as a
fossilized vestige of a dead era. It should be noted, however,
that the best recordings of the Revival resulted from a
compromise between the "advanced New Orleans" style,
as it was practiced at the end of the second period, and even
later acquisitions, particularly in the field of rhythm (which
explains the presence of classical-age drummers, such as Sid
Catlett or Cozy Cole, in Armstrong's new Hot Five). Every
time an attempt was made to return to a jazz style absolutely like that of the Golden Age of New Orleans, the
results were inferior to the works that had been used as
models, for there is no getting away from the fact that valid
creation occurs only when accompanied by the joy of discovery. As for the young musicians who lined themselves

up with the veterans, nine times out of ten they acted like amateurish students. Whatever partial successes their likable enthusiasm resulted in, it is regrettable that these youngsters, some of whom were very talented, did not feel an obligation to blaze new trails. The fact that the young Negro musicians took absolutely no part in these efforts limits the importance of the movement considerably. Still, the Revival has served a purpose. It has almost died out in the United States, but in France the most popular bands today are those which play New Orleans style. Through their efforts, we may hope that new segments of the public are constantly being won over to jazz. That is enough to justify them, if not to explain their existence.

6
The Pre-Classical Period, 1927-1934

The period that remains to be studied is the one that joins the classical period (1935-1945) to the end of oldtime jazz, which came around 1926-1927. It is a transitional period, characterized by diverse but complementary tendencies: liquidation of the New Orleans style at the height of its glory, new ideas concerning rhythm, flowering of a kind of individual expression that had appeared at the end of the previous period (Coleman Hawkins, Earl Hines, and especially Louis Armstrong are chiefly responsible for this evolution), and replacement of spontaneous collective music by a worked-out orchestral language (Duke Ellington and, to a lesser extent, Fletcher Henderson and Don Redman get the credit here).

This transitional period, which is a kind of link between oldtime and classical jazz, is far from being the weakest. For one thing, it was Louis Armstrong's greatest time, the period when he recorded most of his key works. By himself, Armstrong would have been enough to raise this period to the

first rank; but, unfortunately, it is impossible to consider
Armstrong by himself, since jazz is a collective creation. We
can see clearly today that, however deeply attached he may
have been to the traditions of New Orleans, Armstrong was
a precursor, ten years ahead of almost all his contemporaries.
His records contain many flaws that are not his fault; in so
many of them, he is just about the only one who really
swings. The tragedy of this genius is that he did not find a
group of musicians capable of understanding and supporting
him until he had passed his prime. If he had come ten years
later, he would have produced a large number of perfect
works; but perhaps the evolution of jazz would only have
fallen that much further behind, since Armstrong seems
to be the only one who could have fathered the classical age.

In spite of Armstrong's solos, the 1927-1934 period, which
he dominated but also kept well ahead of, can be called·
"pre-classical." It witnessed the development of a number
of musical personalities who reached their peak in the
following period; very few of them produced the most important part of their work before 1935. If we had to name
a typical pre-classical soloist—one whose style coincided with
the dominant tendencies of the era and whose principal
activity took place between 1927 and 1934—it would be
trombonist Jimmy Harrison, a very gifted musician whose
premature death prevented him from developing into the
very great soloist of the classical period that he promised to
become, like his contemporary, Coleman Hawkins, and his
younger colleague, Dickie Wells.

7
Jazz's Future Possibilities

Dividing jazz into five periods like this is justifiable because it makes things clearer and establishes a fairly logical
order. The transformation of this music can be followed

from period to period. During the first two, it took form and became organized, but the equilibrium it seemed to reach toward the end of the second was immediately destroyed by the sweep of tendencies that carried it through the pre-classicism of the third period to the classicism of the fourth. From that point on, its historical unity was broken. The homogeneity of the modern period has been lessened by the New Orleans Revival and the persistence of the classical and oldtime schools, which have been both an opposition and an influence, but the period has perhaps been all the richer for this diversity. The classical epoch was also the time when jazz stopped progressing in a straight line. However, its evolution has not come to an end; the present period is to be credited with having subjected everything to re-examination, including, as we shall see,[4] ideas that once seemed fundamental.

The normal evolution of any art form falls into three periods: growth, maturity, decline. On the basis of this brief summary, it might seem that jazz has reached the third stage. At any rate, this is the opinion of Bernard Heuvelmans, an excellent Belgian critic. Another commentator, Boris Vian, sees these fifty years of existence, on the contrary, as a sort of Later Middle Ages that will be fully appreciated only by the men in centuries to come, who will judge them in the light of a subsequent evolution that we cannot make out in advance. This idea is bold; but the history of European polyphony, which extends over more than a thousand years, establishes such a broad precedent that we cannot pass final judgment. Certainly, a very curious similarity between the evolution of jazz and that of European music has often been noted. Beginning at the same point (popular and religious vocal music) and passing through the same stages (instrumental polyphony, accompanied melody, symphonic music, and so on), jazz does indeed seem to have retraced in five

4 Cf. Chapter VIII.

decades the road that European music took ten centuries to cover. However disturbing it may be, this analogy (which must not be taken too literally) does not decisively settle the argument between those who believe that jazz is about to disappear and those who think it has a practically limitless future. Even if we consider only what lies immediately ahead, the future of jazz presents a problem that involves its very essence, and we shall not be ready to discover the answer before getting to the end of this book.

II

FROM THE "PRIMITIVES" TO THE "MODERNS"

Chapter III

BLUES
AND
MILITARY MARCHES

There was a time when it was believed that the original jazz was intrinsically superior to everything that came later. People thought, like Sidney Bechet, that "water is freshest at its source."[a] Everything that got away from the New Orleans tradition, however slightly, was considered a deviation. The whole philosophy of jazz was subordinated to this idea, which had been accepted as a credo, without discussion. New Orleans jazz was pure, other styles were less pure—this was self-evident.

The time has come to subject this notion to the test of radical doubt about which we spoke in the Introduction. The problems of jazz can be rationally reconsidered only in the light of fundamental propositions of tested validity. What I intend to do is examine this one in historical perspective, which is the only way it can be made intelligible.

1
Borrowings of Jazz from European Music

A new form of musical expression is no more capable than a living thing of being the result of spontaneous generation. It is the reflection of a civilization; and one civiliza-

[a] M. Saury: "Huit jours avec Sidney Béchet," in *Jazz-Hot*, November, 1949.

tion owes its existence to others. Once born, an artistic
movement may be strong enough to develop without any
external help. Thus, European musical thought, taken as
a whole, evolved in isolation until the beginning of the
twentieth century, when it began to borrow from exotic
traditions, an advance symptom of the decline of tonal music.
It sometimes happens, also, that artists who belong to
neighboring civilizations borrow from one another and transform their own language more or less profoundly. At times,
these foreign elements fail to fit the genius of a people and
cannot be integrated in its tradition. In such cases, they
result in monstrous graftings, or are simply rejected. But
occasionally their effect is so strong that they get the better
of the tradition they invigorate. What takes place then is a
change of essence. It is in this way, I imagine, that most
new kinds of music are born.

A comparison between the Negro-American music of the
oldest recordings in the New Orleans style and the different
varieties of African music shows immediately that they have
fewer points in common than differences. What can be the
cause of these fundamental, even essential differences? Negro-
American music, from which jazz issued, resulted from a
rupture in the African musical tradition brought about by
the brutal change in environment experienced by the natives
who were seized by slavetraders; it also resulted from the
introduction of new musical elements which enabled the
slaves of Louisiana or Virginia to form a new tradition.
These elements, all of Anglo-Saxon or French origin—hymns,
songs, and, later, popular dances and military marches—gave
jazz some of its principal characteristics: its tonal system, its
form, the four-beat measure, the four-bar unit of construction,[2] a certain kind of syncopation, and so forth. West Indian

[2] The French term is *carrure,* which conveys an idea of squareness of
construction that seems to have no equivalent in a single English word. To
say that jazz has *carrure* means that its melodies are constructed in multiples
of four bars.—D. N.

music, which has rhythmic conceptions and a melodic language that are only vaguely like those of jazz, was created by Negroes whose origin was identical but who were influenced instead by Spanish folklore.

It is generally believed that these non-African contributions were made only at the beginning. This is clearly a mistake. Such external elements may be found in every period of jazz history. Ellington's harmonic ideas, for example, show the influence of Ravel. It is not only themes that jazz has taken from the popular music of the whites. The resulting extension of jazz repertory has caused a transformation in style. Even within the framework of Negro ideas, it is impossible to interpret a military march and a slow ballad in the same way. As we shall see, Hawkins' BODY AND SOUL cannot be analyzed without taking into account a certain feeling that is characteristic of such slow pieces and that appears in many performances which otherwise have little in common with the musical ideas of Broadway. Thus, external influences have affected the evolution of jazz at least as strongly as internal currents.

2
Jazz as a Derivative of African Music

Was there ever an *ideal moment* in its history when jazz was pure, untainted by any influence foreign to its African origin? According to the idea of "original purity" which we have already mentioned, that moment ought to have come about the time jazz was born, that is to say very likely around the beginning of this century. It is interesting to speculate what reaction this idea might have aroused in a contemporary observer whom we shall suppose devoted to purity and sufficiently acquainted with the problems of African music. In the eyes of such an observer, would the then-nascent jazz have seemed a *pure* music? If he used African examples as models, the innovations of the Louisiana Negroes must have seemed particularly unfortunate and he must have felt that only pallid reflections of the ancestral art still survived. Compared with the singers of the Dark Continent,[3] the most authentic of the blues singers would be considered "Europeanized." Don't the blues themselves, with their blue notes, represent quite a deviation from African songs? As we know, these blue notes resulted from the difficulty experienced by the Negro when the hymns taught him by the missionaries made him sing the third and seventh degrees of the scale used in European music, since these degrees do not occur in the primitive five-tone scale. From our hypothetical observer's point of view, these blue notes would be just as *impure* as the "altered notes" of modern jazz seem to the present-day believer in "original purity."

Suppose our observer were to glance at the harmonic system used in the original jazz; it was extremely rudimentary at the time, but already present in rough outline. He would have to deplore the appearance of the *chord*, clearly an intrusion of European origin into Negro-American art—an intrusion which would soon dominate it so tyranically that all improvisation would take place within the framework of a sequence of chords. In authentic Negro music, there are no cadences or chords or tonal functions. The spirit and rules of its polyphony are very different from those governing New Orleans music. Its melodic turns are infinitely simpler. The same intervals are repeated untiringly, without any attempt to look for new effects. Even when based on the blue note, a seventh is a horrible modernism in the perspective of African music.

The same differences are apparent in the domain of

[3] The reader will find it profitable to listen to some of the documentary recordings of African music, of which the catalogues offer quite a choice these days

rhythm. African drummers do not imprison their figurations in the framework of the four-bar unit of construction and the four-beat measure. Furthermore, like the melodists, they like to repeat the same formula indefinitely. Varying the rhythm, therefore, like varying the notes, would strike our observer as the sign of an intellectualized art. He could not see jazz as anything but the denial of a centuries-old, static African conception, with its leaning toward incantation, in favor of another conception, European in origin and based on the development of thought. Listening to the constant variety of Baby Dodds's rhythmic formulas in DRUM IMPROVISATIONS, how could he consider this musician as anything but a civilized man trying, without success, to imitate a primitive?

Even an apparently secondary problem like that of instrumentation might have led our observer to some bitter reflections. The American Negro preferred the perfected instruments of the whites to the primitive instruments of his ancestors. Of course he didn't use them in the same way as Europeans. But borrowing the instruments meant also borrowing musical material, which played a more important role in the formation of jazz than has been recognized. It definitely seems that most of the repertory of the first Negro bands—those that paraded in the streets of New Orleans or rode along them perched on wagons—consisted, not of blues, but of military marches, quadrilles, and polkas. These selections (of which one can get an idea by listening to the recordings of such pioneers as the Original Zenith Brass Band) were scarcely modified rhythmically. Their performances may have had syncopations that recalled the traditional spirituals, but they more closely resembled the concerts given by French brass bands on the village square, right down to the same fluffed notes. The *Negro spirit* that Ernest Ansermet talks about was present only embryonically. The assimilation of foreign elements had scarcely begun. Our observer, of course,

would have been unable to guess the direction in which the
genius of Louis Armstrong would lead jazz some years later.
Would he have seen in all this anything but a childish parody,
the effort of freedmen to imitate their former masters? From
such an observer's point of view, the "pure" African music
of the Negro had undoubtedly been polluted by the introduction of white elements that were obsolutely foreign to its
tradition. Judged by that tradition, jazz, which was the result
of this mixture, ought to have been condemned from the very
first. As an offspring of African music, jazz has all the appearance of a bastard.

3
The Necessity of Borrowing in Order to Evolve

Looking back over half a century, we can realize the narrowness of this point of view. The European element did
in a sense corrupt Negro folklore, but it made it productive
at the same time. Modern conceptions of man's history stress
the profound truth of the almost universal myth of the Virgin
and of the Father of her Son.[4] There is no better explanation
of the birth of jazz. It was the clash of blues and military
marches—the male-female clash symbolized by the old myth
—that launched, to speak like Toynbee, "the transition from
Yin to Yang," transforming an almost motionless folklore
into an art capable of all kinds of evolution. Once the birth
of a new entity is admitted, our observer's point of view is
no longer acceptable. The blue notes that he considers impure have given jazz most of its melodic originality. Use of
the four-beat measure contributed to the creation of something new, called swing. The musical ideas of the pioneers,
as far as we know them, seem rather ridiculous to us, too,
though for quite different reasons. Like our observer, we

[4] Cf. Arnold J. Toynbee: *A Study of History.*

smile at the music of the young Negroes of that time, who have since become the old men in the Zenith Brass Band or in Bunk Johnson's orchestra. But subsequent developments make it possible for us to discern in this music the seeds of a still-distant classicism. We know what fertile plains lay waiting for the American Negro at the end of the rocky trail that led from the crossroads where blues and military marches met.

The problem might be looked at from another angle. One question is enough to define it: Why did the Negroes feel the need to organize brass bands to play the military and dance repertory of the whites in only a slightly different form? What cause could justify their doing so if not the necessity of *borrowing in order to evolve?* Their situation might be compared to that of a country which, at the beginning of its economic development, has to appeal to foreign capital in order to finance its industrialization. Viewed in this way, the Negro-American enterprise did not end in bankruptcy. European borrowings were assimilated and taken full advantage of. From King Oliver to Charlie Parker, American Negroes have created an essentially new music that has only a very superficial resemblance to its white prototype. It is clear, then, that the problem yields the same solution even when approached in this way.

Strangely enough, there are some present-day "observers" who accept everything jazz borrowed from the whites until around 1945 but who now refuse to allow jazz the right to keep on borrowing, even from West Indian music, which has an African origin just as undeniably as jazz does. The Afro-Cuban element is banished even though the polka was tolerated. But the problem is the same in both cases—one of assimilation. It took jazz several years to "digest" military marches; can't it be trusted to do as much again? It would be pretty surprising if the Cuban influence could not be absorbed. Similarly, there has been criticism of the almost

constant use of "altered notes" by Negro musicians of the
younger generation. Admittedly, we are again dealing with
a borrowed rather than an invented element. But in the
name of what faithfulness to the tonal system—which is not
of their creation either—should Negroes deprive themselves
of the possibilities offered by chromaticism and polytonality?

4
Jazz Has Never Been a "Pure" Music

Undoubtedly the essence of jazz lies partially in a certain
Negro spirit, which is the only thing that could have oriented
these continual borrowings in a single direction. The fact
remains that there is no point in its history at which jazz
can be considered a "pure" music as historians might regard
certain kinds of exotic music (but perhaps they are mistaken,
too). To be impartial, should not the purist who regards
the introduction of foreign elements into a national art as
a sign of degeneration conclude that New Orleans jazz is
just as "degenerate" as bop?

Logically, the person who feels the need to throw off the
yoke of European art should not turn first of all to jazz. The
admirable music of Bali, to cite a typically non-European
art, introduces whoever knows how to listen to it into a
world infinitely more different from ours. Nor is jazz the
right thing for someone who likes primitive art above all
else. It will be much more profitable for him to turn to
African music. However, jazz, which is perhaps essentially
the Negro interpretation of elements borrowed from white
music, is closer to our way of feeling than the music of Bali
or the Congo; and this is true precisely because it has a
number of ideas in common with European music, notably
the use of the tonal system. The universality of jazz may
be due in part to these occidental elements, since Western

culture has followed the example of Western civilization in spreading its influence over the entire world. Listening to the unfortunately Europeanized music in the fine Japanese film *Rashomon* makes it impossible to be greatly surprised at the existence of a Hot Club in Tokyo.

Whoever remains faithful to jazz must get out of the habit of regarding it as a "fallen god remembering heaven." In reality, its true aspects are those of a living being which has passed through an infancy, an adolescence, and a prime of life, and which now raises anxious questions about whether or not it is in its declining years. Even if it should pass away, it is sure to leave us an heir, just as European tonal music is doing.

The theory that jazz was once pure but has continually been corrupted by contact with whites has been expressed by many commentators, with only slight variations. For Rudi Blesh,[5] jazz was better in the first period than in the second, and better in the second than in the third. Less logically, Mezz Mezzrow[6] seems to feel that the degeneration of jazz began only around 1930. Other specialists see the first sure signs of white-influenced decadence in the appearance of swing (1935) or bop (1945). Beginning with the same initial proposition, they all have built up a doctrine according to which the superiority of the pioneers over their successors is admitted a priori. They venerate soloists like King Oliver, Kid Ory, and Willie "The Lion" Smith. Since these musicians are as limited in technique. as in creative talent, such veneration can be explained only on the grounds of their supposed purity, even though they are "oldtimers" rather than "primitives." But we have just seen what becomes of the theory of original purity when it is subjected to the test of historical analysis. We are therefore authorized to reconsider our old opinions. True, the effort of the New

[5] Cf. Rudi Blesh: *Shining Trumpets.*
[6] Cf. Mezz Mezzrow and B. Wolfe: *Really the Blues.*

Orleans pioneers to form a new language still deserves respect. Esthetically, however, their work was a failure. It remained for the following generation to reap the benefit of their attempts. We must now show how the jazzmen I call "classical" bore the same relation to these musicians as Molière and Racine bore to such earlier dramatists as Jodelle and Montchrétien. In the next chapter, we shall look at some of the major imperfections shown by celebrated oldtimers.

Chapter IV

A GREAT CLASSICAL FIGURE
AMONG THE OLDTIMERS

(Concerning Eight Recordings of the Hot Five)

1
Their Place in the Evolution of Jazz

On November 12, 1925, in its Chicago studios, the Okeh Company recorded a little five-piece Negro ensemble for the first time. This apparently insignificant event was to have quite a repercussion on the history of jazz. Beginning with this session and continuing until 1928, Louis Armstrong's Hot Five made a long and extraordinary series of recordings.

The eight sides with which the present study will be concerned have as a common denominator only the fact that they were all issued in France the same month. They are: COME BACK, SWEET PAPA (recorded February 22, 1926), GEORGIA GRIND (February 26, 1926), BIG FAT MA AND SKINNY PA and SWEET LITTLE PAPA (June 23, 1926), BIG BUTTER AND EGG MAN FROM THE WEST and SUNSET CAFE STOMP (November 16, 1926), YOU MADE ME LOVE YOU and IRISH BLACK BOTTOM (November 27, 1926). The musicians, as on all the first series of Hot Five records, were: Louis Armstrong (cornet and vocal), Johnny Dodds (clarinet and alto sax), Kid Ory

49

(trombone; replaced by John Thomas on the last two sides),
Lil Armstrong (piano), and John St. Cyr (banjo). In addi-
tion, May Alix takes the vocal on BIG BUTTER and SUNSET
CAFE.

It would be unwarranted to judge the whole series of
Hot Five recordings on the basis of just these eight sides,
which are not even among the most successful. Nevertheless,
some general characteristics may be made out in them. They
give a fairly precise idea of the band's style. Its strong points
may be balanced against its weaknesses. And perhaps nowhere else is the need for a revision of values more pressing
than here, for the most extravagant praise has been lavished
on these records for years.

Still, opinion is divided as to their true value. When they
were issued in France, I happened to listen to them in a
mixed group of musicians and jazz fans. Reactions varied
tremendously. Most of the fans—and especially the younger
ones—listened respectfully and admired everything, as had
been recommended by the books that had helped them become acquainted with jazz. The professional musicians—
and, curiously enough, again it was especially the younger
ones—adopted exactly the opposite attitude. Except for Armstrong's contribution, nothing pleased them. Since they had
lost all contact with the old style of jazz, they did not for
one moment feel the emotional appeal of this music and
saw only its defects. Their most frequent reaction was
hilarity. These extremist positions, it must be said, are very
common in the world of jazz.

Compared to the older New Orleans style, this music is
characterized by the triumph of the individual personality
over the group. The 1926 Hot Five's playing is much less
purely collective than King Oliver's. In a sense, the improvised ensembles are cornet solos accompanied by impromptu
countermelodies, rather than true collective improvisation.
This judgment is based on the very essence of the works,

and not merely on the cornet's closeness to the microphone.
Listen to them carefully. Isn't it obvious that Armstrong's
personality absorbs the others? Isn't your attention spontaneously concentrated on Louis? With King Oliver, you
listen to the *band;* here, you listen first to *Louis.* Also note
that the clarinet in the Hot Five has lost much of its former
importance. In brass bands during the first years of the century, it attracted attention by dancing high and clear over
the brasses. In King Oliver's band, it became one element
in a more complex polyphonic ensemble. In these recordings,
it has been relegated to the background. This decline in
the clarinet's role has continued up to the present, when
many people no longer consider it a jazz instrument.

2
Their Rhythm

So far as I am aware, the question of how perfect oldtime
jazz was rhythmically has never been seriously studied. It
deserves to be. I know that many fans are inclined to sneer
at technical questions. But this is not a purely technical
problem; it concerns the very essence of jazz. Moreover, is
a problem ever solved by being neglected, or by not being
recognized as a problem?

I am convinced that what we call swing did not appear
overnight. Perhaps it took a combination of extraordinary
circumstances to give full expression to this element, which
had been latent since the very beginning of music. I wouldn't
go so far as to state that Louis Armstrong was the one who
"invented" swing, but listening to these records might make
one think so. Actually, I believe that the rhythmic sense of
jazz musicians continued to grow finer as their art took
shape. This sense matured slowly. Armstrong arrived at just
the right time to pick the tastiest fruit of Negro-American
music.

Fifteen years of perfected rhythm have brought our ears to the point where they can no longer tolerate the rhythmic weaknesses of the precursors. For many of us, these weaknesses cover up what is valid in their art from other points of view. Thus, accustomed to a complete rhythm section, we are disconcerted by the absence of bass and drums which is one of the striking characteristics of the Hot Five. After hearing these records, a musician told me that he thought it impossible to play with real swing without the backing of these two instruments, or at least one of them; and when I pointed out to him that some of Fats Waller's piano solos swing far more than many orchestral recordings, he answered aptly, "That's because Fats uses his left hand to suggest the presence of a bass fiddle."

This raises a question that is touchy but unavoidable: Does the Hot Five's music swing, or doesn't it? It seems to me that it swings only partially—only to the extent that rhythmic mistakes, which are fairly numerous in these records as in all jazz of the period, do not get the better of the "vital drive."[1] In 1948, an English magazine carried a controversy about Louis Armstrong that included, among some perfectly unjustified criticism, the following remark of Stéphane Grappelly: "It is certainly true that Armstrong's first records lack swing; *and Rees is right to criticize the musicians Armstrong chose to play with him.* I have always held this mistake against him."[2] This opinion was far from being welcomed by the fans. Nevertheless, the point is well taken, except to the extent that it fails to consider the very small possibility Armstrong undoubtedly had of improving his choices. In respect to swing, Louis cannot in any case be compared with his sidemen in the early Hot Five, whose rhythm is extremely weak. Listen to Johnny Dodds's alto solo in COME BACK, SWEET PAPA. Isn't it an excellent sample

---

[1] Cf. Chapter XIII, "The Evolution of Rhythmic Conceptions."
[2] Cited by Boris Vian: "Revue de Presse," in *Jazz-Hot*, May, 1948.

of not getting the notes in the right place, rich in rhythmic faults and anti-swing if anything ever was? Now listen to the next chorus, in which Louis is perfect; he seems to want to give his clarinetist a lesson in swing. Compared to Armstrong's Kid Ory's break invites the same remark; rhythmically, it's the difference between night and day. I would recommend that all jazz fans make the necessary effort to *feel* this difference, which is obvious to any jazz musician even if his own playing does not show much swing.

A bit further on, Dodds and Armstrong play the verse in sixths; hence, they ought to play exactly together. Does Dodds try to make his part fit in with Louis's? He almost never succeeds. Similarly, in SWEET LITTLE PAPA, he does not get the notes of his breaks in the right place. Under such conditions, how can there be any question of his swinging? In the same record, starting with the exposition, Kid Ory uses a corny kind of syncopation—the kind jazz musicians scornfully call "polka style." Compare this passage with Armstrong's re-entry, which follows immediately. How stiff Kid Ory is and how heavily he leans upon the beat, whereas Louis seems to soar above it in an easy, relaxed way! Yet the construction of their phrases is almost the same. Besides, in all justice, it must be said that Kid Ory has better moments (cf. his break in SUNSET CAFE). Sometimes John St. Cyr also uses corny syncopation (as in his accompaniment to the vocal of YOU MADE ME LOVE YOU), but he appears to be a much more gifted musician than Ory and Dodds, to judge by the suppleness of his 4/4 beat, particularly in GEORGIA GRIND. It is likely that St. Cyr paved the way for modern guitarists. Finally, there is Lil Armstrong grinding out notes at the keyboard. Whether she sings or plays, it is clear that she and swing never got along well together.

Fortunately, Louis is there. With him, there can be no question of getting the notes in the wrong place or of "polka syncopation." He is ten years ahead of the rhythmic ideas of his sidemen. This is particularly noticeable in the initial ensemble of IRISH BLACK BOTTOM, where he is the only one who doesn't use corny syncopation. His playing is absolutely perfect, supple, and easy. He swings as much as Lester Young in I WANT TO BE HAPPY, as Lionel Hampton in FLYING ON A V-DISC, as the Basie band in the final choruses of SENT FOR YOU YESTERDAY; and he does this in spite of sidemen who might have paralyzed him. Perhaps the most amazing thing is that Dodds and Ory did not make more progress with such a master, that they did not try to adopt his rhythmic ideas. It is easy to imagine how happy Armstrong must have felt when he could record with Earl Hines and Zutty Singleton, two musicians who assimilated his lesson very well and very early. In fact, there is no possible comparison between these recordings and the rhythm of NO ONE ELSE BUT YOU, to take only one example.

3
Their Ensemble Playing

Fortunately, Dodds and Ory are only extras. As we have seen, the listener's attention is inevitably concentrated on Armstrong, even in the ensembles, which consequently resemble accompanied solos.

These ensembles are fairly numerous. They take up about one third of the playing time, the other two thirds being divided between instrumental solos and vocals. Except for a few unimportant passages, the ensembles are improvised. In them Armstrong uses the same economical, concentrated style that he generally employs in his individual improvisations of the period. There is no lyricism here. The great, soaring flights of BASIN STREET BLUES or TIGHT LIKE THIS belong specifically to his language as a soloist. They would be out of place in an ensemble. Moreover, in 1926, Armstrong may not have been ready to imagine such flights. Except in the chorus of BIG BUTTER and a few other passages, his phrasing as leader and as soloist is identical. This can be heard in the fourth chorus of YOU MADE ME LOVE YOU, where Louis plays the first half as a solo and the second half with the others. The beautiful paraphrase begun in the first sixteen bars continues with relentless logic in the following sixteen, in spite of the clarinet's and trombone's intrusion, which neither helps nor hinders because Louis's part is too fascinating for the others to attract any attention.

In general, these others are pretty uneven. Johnny Dodds, who shows an undeniable sense of the collective style at times, commits gross errors at other times. Some of his phrase endings in the ensembles of COME BACK, SWEET PAPA and BIG FAT MA are spoiled by his playing in unison or octaves with the cornet part; such contrapuntal platitudes must be deplored. Note that it would have been quite simple for him to avoid them, since Louis wisely sticks right to the theme. In other places, his rudimentary technique does him a disservice; I can't help feeling uncomfortable when I listen to his fumbling in BIG BUTTER. Kid Ory shows himself to be a better musician than Dodds. His sense of counterpoint seems much surer; he doesn't commit comparable mistakes. On Dodd's behalf, it must be said that his part is more difficult than Ory's in execution and conception. The trombonist, in fact, is helped considerably by the harmonic basses of the theme, and he therefore improvises a great deal less.

4
Their Solos

The cornet solos are, of course, far and away the most interesting. We are dealing here with a twenty-six-year-old Louis, one who had not yet smacked the world in the face with his introduction to WEST END BLUES but who already towered over his contemporaries, one who had not apparently abandoned the traditions of King Oliver and Bunk Johnson but who had created a much richer idea of rhythm and who had used his brilliant technique to make individual improvisation more and more an expression of his personality.

On these eight sides, Louis's solos are moving, balanced, and musically rich, but they are so simple in form and expression that many listeners hesitate to rank them as highly as the more showy, dramatic, and variable solos of the following period. Choosing between them can only be a matter of personal preference. For my part, I think that, even though Armstrong's personality had not yet emerged completely, it is sufficiently in evidence to invalidate the rather widely held opinion that these records are minor works. I would even say that, except for a few clichés (such as the upward chromatic progression which ends the opening ensemble of IRISH BLACK BOTTOM), these solos are free from the weaknesses that sometimes tarnish the output of the great trumpeter after 1930.

Each chorus merits detailed analysis. I have already mentioned the beautiful paraphrase of YOU MADE ME LOVE YOU, which is so striking in its harmonious simplicity. SUNSET CAFE is full of finds, particularly the ascending arpeggio that ends the verse and the final chromatic descent. The chorus of SWEET LITTLE PAPA is outstanding especially because the performance is so dynamic; it is tremendously alive. But, without any doubt, the most successful of all is BIG BUTTER AND EGG MAN. In this record, Armstrong manages to transfigure completely a theme whose vulgarity might well have overwhelmed him; and yet his chorus is only a paraphrase. The theme is not forgotten for a moment; it can always be found there, just as it was originally conceived by its little-known composer, Venable. Taking off melodically from the principal note of the first phrase, the soloist begins with a triple call that disguises, behind its apparent symmetry, subtle differences in rhythm and expressive intensity. This entry by itself is a masterpiece; it is impossible to imagine anything more sober and balanced. During the next eight bars, the paraphrase spreads out, becoming freer and livelier. Armstrong continues to cling to the essential notes of the theme, but he leaves more of its contour to the imagination. At times he gives it an inner animation by means of intelligent syncopated repetitions, as in the case of the first note of the bridge. From measures 20 to 23, the melody bends in a chromatic descent that converges toward the theme while at the same time giving a felicitous interpretation of the underlying harmonic progression. This brings us to the culminating point of the work. Striding over the traditional pause of measures 24-25, Armstrong connects the bridge to the final section by using a short, admirably inventive phrase. Its rhythmic construction of dotted eighths and sixteenths forms a contrast with the more static context in which it is placed, and in both conception and execution it is a miracle of swing. During this brief moment, Louis seems to have foreseen what modern conceptions of rhythm would be like. In phrasing, accentuation, and the way the short note is increasingly curtailed until finally it is merely suggested (measure 25), how far removed all this is from New Orleans rhythm!

This astonishing chorus is a perfect example of the phenomenon of "transformation without sacrifice of fidelity" in which subsequent jazz has abounded. Even more important, it is perhaps the first example of a typically individual esthetic conception to be found in the history of recorded jazz.[3] All things considered, the timid solos that had previously appeared in recordings done in the New

---

[3] Naturally, this does not include piano solos, although even they were, for the most part, rather formless.

Orleans style were only fragments of collective improvisation removed from their polyphonic background. Couldn't King Oliver's famous solo in DIPPER MOUTH BLUES and Johnny Dodds's in CANAL STREET both have been extracted, as is, from ensemble choruses? Neither of these musicians can be said to have fully freed himself from the framework of collective jazz. With his chorus in BIG BUTTER, Louis Armstrong begins using without effort the language of the individual soloist. This solo makes sense in the way a melody should. Rejecting orchestral formulas in which most improvisations were swallowed up, it stands as a finished example of an esthetic conception that other solos of that time merely suggested in a confused way. It has a beginning, a middle, and an end; it follows a progression that is unlike an ensemble's. The phrase extending from measures 9 to 16 and the one at the end of the bridge are essentially a soloist's phrases. It is not unreasonable to believe that this improvisation of a genius opened a new chapter in the evolution of jazz. For that matter, the sensational effect it had is well known.

The greatest artists have their weaknesses. It would not be honest to skip over them after spending so much time discussing those of others. Doubtless, we should not pay much attention to the barely perceptible wavering at the end of the BIG BUTTER chorus; can't we suppose that it was due, ironically enough, to Louis's being obliged, as leader, to let the vocalist know it was time for her to come back on? But his phrasing in the exposition is not beyond reproach. If concern for fidelity to the theme is what led him to use corny figures (measures 10, 11, and 19), he was being overconscientious. The chromatic ascent that ends the opening ensemble of IRISH BLACK BOTTOM is a cliché unworthy of a great musician. Finally, Armstrong fluffs rather frequently in these records (especially in SWEET LITTLE PAPA).

None of these items are particularly important, but they were worth noting.

I have just used the word *genius*. It is not something I do often. I am not one of those who believe that the Negro race has produced more geniuses in thirty years than Europe has in ten centuries. There are artists of genius in the world of jazz, but there as everywhere else they are extremely rare. Louis Armstrong is one of them. The mystical foolishness that ranks jazz as the only music worthy of interest has led its victims to multiply the number of jazz geniuses. I remember reading more than once that Johnny Dodds and Kid Ory were among these luminaries. Hundreds of fans are convinced that this is so. Alas, how far they are from the point! It is not a question of disparaging Dodds and Ory, but simply of setting things straight. The shortcomings of these two musicians are not merely technical; both are deficient musically as well. If a soloist shows that he is incapable of playing two syncopations in time, can he be considered a genius *as a jazzman?* In that case, the logical conclusion would be that rhythm, and therefore swing, are inconsequential elements in jazz. Who would argue in favor of such a paradox?

It will be objected that Johnny Dodds plays slow blues very well This is true, but the blues are not the whole of jazz. As long as a fan remains unaware of the serious rhythmic imperfections that mar the playing of men like Ory and Dodds, he will be equally unaware of the rhythmic perfection of others like Basie, Hampton, Hodges, and Lester Young, and he will not be able to appreciate them fully. A novice to whom I played the beginning of SWEET LITTLE PAPA confessed that he could not tell the difference between Armstrong's and Ory's rhythm. His sincere effort to understand the weaknesses of one and the perfection of the other was a thousand times more likable than the shoulder-shrugging of more advanced fans, whose prejudices prevent them from taking the step that would lead them to objectivity. Just as a reflection of taste, their reactions surprise me. Do they really think that Dodds has a good tone on the alto in COME BACK, SWEET PAPA? Do they believe that Kid Ory expresses musically interesting ideas in his solos in SWEET LITTLE PAPA and BIG FAT MA? Do they see anything that can compare, for example, with Johnny Hodges' solo in THE MOOCHE or with Dickie Wells's in BETWEEN THE DEVIL AND THE DEEP BLUE SEA?

It takes a lot of imagination and the best will in the world to discover genius in the badly formed phrases of Johnny Dodds. However, the sincerity of this pioneer jazzman is beyond doubt, and he does not deserve the scorn that has been heaped on him by the enemies of oldtime jazz. Mediocre as he may seem on these records, Dodds is gifted with a real personality, whereas Artie Shaw, for example, doesn't have any, in spite of his technical precision and perfect execution. What makes Johnny Dodds admirable is the emotion he communicates. His chorus in GEORGIA GRIND contains some childish attempts at "virtuosity" (!), but its very simple melodic line is not without beauty. His rough tone means more to me than the overpretty sound of many modern clarinetists. It is difficult to forget his rhythmic weaknesses, his miserable introduction to SUNSET CAFE, and his suicidal break (obviously learned by heart) in SWEET LITTLE PAPA. In all fairness, however, it must be recognized that these records—and those of the Hot Five and the Hot Seven in general—do not represent him at his best. Curiously enough, it seems that Armstrong's presence, far from stimulating him, bothers and even paralyzes him. With King Oliver (before Armstrong had really found himself), Dodds seemed to be much more at ease. With his own Bootblacks, recording during the same period as the Hot Five, and with Jelly Roll Morton, he also shows up better, although still without giving evidence of a praiseworthy sense of rhythm. Finally, Dodds is at his best in slow blues, and these eight sides are all in a more or less moderate tempo. Moreover, only GEORGIA GRIND is based on the classic twelve-bar blues.

As a soloist, Kid Ory is obviously very weak. He has no melodic inventiveness, or, if he does, he lacks the necessary technique to express it. It would be impossible to dream of better examples to illustrate this than his solos in SWEET LITTLE PAPA and BIG FAT MA, which lack any individual character and are nothing but wholly inexpressive ensemble playing. His chorus in the blues, GEORGIA GRIND, is certainly more satisfactory; but the trombone was not really raised to the rank of a solo instrument until later, by Jack Teagarden and Jimmy Harrison. Concerning the solos of John Thomas and Lil Armstrong, the less said the better. As for John St. Cyr, whose accompaniments are generally excellent, he takes one perfectly useless break in SWEET LITTLE PAPA. It requires a singular attraction to the archaic to enjoy his banjo solos. That leaves the vocals. They are of two kinds, and have nothing in common. On one hand there are those of May Alix, and on the other there are Louis's. Of the former there is little to say except that they are among the ugliest and most grotesque things that the vigilance of man has allowed to be preserved on wax. There is little to say about the latter, either, but for diametrically opposite reasons. His GEORGIA GRIND vocal, which is centered around the tonic, is a very beautiful example of psalmodic blues. Sometimes Louis expresses more swing by speaking than his sidemen show in their playing. I imagine they must have found this somewhat discouraging.

Made by a group that was so far from being ideally homogeneous, these recordings could not have been brought off much better than they actually were. It may be stated without fear of contradiction that in them Louis Armstrong simply does not play the same kind of jazz as his musicians.

The chasm between them is unmistakable. It brings to mind
Charlie Parker playing with "Jazz at the Philharmonic." The
records of the Hot Five show us a great innovator working
within the framework of a tradition which had given him
his start but which his own evolution had already rendered
obsolete. There is nothing to be surprised at, then, if these
recordings are to a certain extent failures. They would have
been better, however, if Armstrong had not hesitated to
reduce even further the role of the others. Why did Lil Armstrong and Kid Ory take solos? Why did May Alix sing an
entire chorus in BIG BUTTER AND EGG MAN? Worse yet, why
did she have to return immediately after the cornet chorus?
What a letdown for the unlucky listener! No sooner had a
mighty peak of jazz been attained than this catastrophe had
to strike. It takes a lot of Armstrong choruses to make up
for such errors.

Just as they are, the Hot Five recordings, which are not
unfairly represented by these eight sides, constitute the
most impressive, if not the most authentic, evidence of what
the New Orleans style was like in its Golden Age. Beneath
an apparent equilibrium, there are already signs of the
powerful creative urge which, through Louis Armstrong's
perfect rhythm and settled individual style, was going to
lead to classicism. More than a quarter of a century later,
these records, which are faded in some spots but as fresh
as ever in others, show clearly that Johnny Dodds and Kid
Ory may have been precursors but Louis Armstrong was
the first great classical figure of jazz.

Chapter V

THE ROMANTIC IMAGINATION
OF DICKIE WELLS

Does life begin at forty? That's what the title of a prewar comedy asserted. The jazzman does not bear out this optimistic philosophy, for it seems that his life—his musical life, of course—usually comes to an end around that age. Some striking exceptions, such as Sidney Bechet, do not invalidate what I believe could be stated as a general rule. All you have to do is go over the principal musicians now in their forties. Is it not perfectly clear that, although some of them may have a great deal of talent left, their current work is only a pale reflection of their former splendor? They are the survivors of the men they were rather than the same men living on; or, if they are the same, they are carried along only by an ever-diminishing momentum.

The European composer, at least under favorable circumstances, moves toward purity without losing his essential driving force and grows greater with meditation. By comparison, the jazzman may well be thought to be at a disadvantage. His fate is too precariously tied up with his youth for him not to feel bitter regrets as he grows old, if he sees clearly what is happening. Is the cause of this almost inevitable decline physical or psychological? Does it come from a stiffening of the muscles or a loss of breath power that diminishes the ability to swing? Or does it come from the impossibility of continually finding something new, which results in the boredom of repetition and a loss of the necessary joy in playing? It is probably a combination of both. Such as it is, there is something pathetic in a destiny that corresponds to the development of the human body rather than to that of the mind and spirit.

Dickie Wells entered his forties quite a few years ago. He was born in Centerville, Tennessee, on June 10, 1907, and began his musical career at the age of fifteen in the obscure Booker Washington band. Around 1925, he went to New York, where he worked with Charlie Johnson and later with the Scott brothers. After playing with Luis Russell in 1931, he stayed for a few months with Elmer Snowden and Bennie Carter before joining Fletcher Henderson's orchestra in 1933. After that famous group disbanded, he joined Teddy Hill's band and came to Europe with it. It was in Paris, in 1937, that he made records under his own name for the first time. Upon his return to the United States, he was signed by Count Basie, with whom he remained until after the war, when he joined Sy Oliver's orchestra. After some further peregrinations, including another stay in Europe (1952), he was to be seen not too long ago at the Savoy in Boston—leading, of all things, a Dixieland band!

1
The Early Days of Dickie Wells

As far back in his past as records permit us to look, Dickie Wells has always been an innovator with a powerful personality. The earliest recordings of his that we have—HAPPY HOUR and SYMPHONIC SCREACH, made with Lloyd Scott in 1927—show him surrounded by depressing musicians: a clarinetist (Cecil Scott, no doubt) to whom even Johnny Dodds could have shown a thing or two about getting the

notes in the right place rhythmically, a trumpeter striving
in vain to imitate Red Nichols, and a rhythm section that
would disgrace an amateur hour. Caught in this Gehenna,
the nineteen-year-old trombonist improvises on the first side
a break which suggests that he might really be able to swing,
and on the second he turns out a first-rate solo that reveals
unusual temperament.

Try to imagine the time when these recordings were made
—January, 1927. Jack Teagarden and Jimmy Harrison had
scarcely rescued the trombone from the oom-pah of tailgate
style. Stimulating each other to greater efforts but with different ability, they were trying to enlarge their instrument's
field of action and to make it a vehicle for expressive melodic
thought. Whatever may be thought of their respective work,
it must be admitted that they created a kind of classicism
from which Dickie Wells, a born romantic, profited greatly.
Yes, the Dickie Wells of SYMPHONIC SCREACH owes a lot to
his elders Jimmy Harrison, Teagarden, and also Charlie
"Big" Green. Even without them, he would undoubtedly
have made the trombone expressive; but undoubtedly it
would have taken him longer to do so. In spite of this, his
solo in SYMPHONIC SCREACH is already marked by a personal
style. The tone is denser, the accent more somber and grandiose, and the phrasing more supple than Harrison's.

Nearly three years later, we find Dickie Wells again with
Cecil Scott, who had by then succeeded his brother as leader
of the band. The group had improved noticeably, thanks
largely to the presence of two young trumpeters named Bill
Coleman and Frankie Newton. Although the rhythm section
does not set him off to advantage, Dickie Wells shows in the
course of a twenty-four-bar exposition that he had made real
progress rhythmically; he does not always get the notes
perfectly in place (cf. the end of the first sixteen-bar group),
but he does not use corny syncopation in the principal
phrase and he swings well. The whole of this solo, starting

with the initial glissando toward the upper register, is resolutely ahead of its time. In SPRINGFIELD STOMP, Dickie Wells
improvises a series of breaks of which at least one reveals
his individual tendencies by its mobility and vehemence;
but it is with BRIGHT BOY BLUES that the constricting framework of the traditional trombone chorus is broken for the
first time, at least on records. Very likely following the path
blazed by Armstrong (though it was undoubtedly his own
path as well), the twenty-two-year-old Wells here creates a
chorus that places him in the front rank of jazz musicians,
right up there with Hodges, Hawkins, and Hines. The personality asserted here is an authentic one, and the style no
longer retains any elements borrowed from predecessors.
There is much more than a suggestion of his idea of using
contrasts (changes in register and, to a lesser extent in this
particular record, rhythmic diversity), and it is this idea,
along with his beautiful, deep tone and the fact that no
other trombonist has so much melodic inventiveness, which
has made it necessary even for those who hate all superlatives
to call him the most remarkable musician on his instrument.

2
The Elements of His Style

Dickie Wells's tone, which is full of well-controlled emotion of high quality, would be enough by itself; I mean that,
like Armstrong or Hodges, he is one of those jazzmen for
whom melodic inventiveness is a supplementary and almost
superfluous gift, since they manage to express themselves
completely by their tone. All they have to do is blow into
their instruments to achieve something personal and move
the listener. Dickie Wells gets this expressive quintessence
out of the most thankless instrument of all. When played
without majesty, the trombone easily becomes wishy-washy

and unbearable. Dickie Wells is majesty personified, in style and particularly in tone. Of course, he does not neglect his instrument's special possibilities. He rather often uses the slide, which is its principal element; his famous chorus in SWEET SUE, with Spike Hughes, is only one example among many. But he uses it like a born nobleman, with perfect taste and an aristocratic nonchalance that is as far removed from the deliquescence of Lawrence Brown as from the triviality of Kid Ory.

Dickie Wells has an admirable knowledge of how to bring out the full value of his tone by inflection and vibrato. This is where his discreet use of the slide is especially marvelous. A record like Spike Hughes's ARABESQUE is particularly instructive in this respect, and I'm sorry not to be a trombonist so that I could make a profitable instrumental analysis of it. Wells frequently uses what might be called *terminal vibrato*. The note (usually isolated or at the end of a phrase) is level at first, but after an instant it begins to vibrate more and more intensely up to its brutal end. Graphically, this might be expressed as in Fig. 1.

FIG. 1

This method is certainly not new, and there are others who sometimes use it equally well (I will mention only Louis Armstrong, who uses it even more as a vocalist than on the trumpet); but it is so perfectly integral a part of Dickie Wells's playing that it seems hard not to recognize it as an important element. We will note later how it plays a role in the very construction of many of his choruses. For the moment, let me simply cite the two records that I believe to be the best examples of his use of terminal vibrato: MUSIC

AT SUNRISE, with Spike Hughes, and PANASSIÉ STOMP, with
Count Basie. The latter also brings out another distinguishing trait of Dickie Wells's style, the *ornamented note*. It is
fairly close to what is called a *mordent* in classical music
(that is, the quick alternation of a principal tone with an
auxiliary one). What it involves is a small group of neighboring notes played legato, and the note being ornamented
is usually high (HOW COME YOU DO ME, with Spike Hughes)
or at least higher than the note that follows (fig. 2). Ornamented notes occur rather frequently in Dickie Wells's
choruses, even in rapid tempos.

FIG. 2

Like all great jazz musicians, Wells is a skillful instrumentalist as well. He never shows off his virtuosity (a childish
thing to do, anyway, since the trombone does not have the
trumpet's brilliance, which excuses some trumpeters' abuses
of their instrument's virtuoso possibilities); but whenever
the occasion demands it, he shows a mastery that is not at
all usual for his time. In Teddy Hill's MARIE, his chorus
is very amusing and easily handled in spite of a very lively
tempo. I know of only one recording in which his technique
is faulty—the Spike Hughes version of SWEET SUE, where he
plays some notes off pitch. This is unimportant in view of
the high level maintained in the rest of his solos.

Dickie Wells is not only an expressive and moving soloist
with a good instrumental technique. He is also one of those
who swing the most. His ease and rhythmic precision are
all the more extraordinary because one rarely hears his equal
even on instruments that are less heavy and less difficult to
handle than the trombone. Perhaps not enough attention

has been paid to the fact that the shape of some instruments makes them less adaptable to swing than others; for every ten trumpeters who swing, it is hard to find one trombonist. It is certain that in records like Spike Hughes's FIREBIRD, AIR IN D FLAT, BUGLE CALL RAG, and HOW COME YOU DO ME, Teddy Hill's HERE COMES COOKIE, Basie's TEXAS SHUFFLE, and his own BETWEEN THE DEVIL AND THE DEEP BLUE SEA, Dickie Wells plays with more intense swing than any but a few trumpeters have attained. Sometimes, in the manner of Lester Young, he even sacrifices everything else to swing, concentrating all his rhythmic powers on one or two notes repeated at greater or lesser length. Examples of this procedure may be found in Basie's TEXAS SHUFFLE and even in a record that goes back as far as 1933, Spike Hughes's BUGLE CALL RAG.

3
Symmetry and Contrast

We have just reviewed briefly the principal elements in Dickie Wells's playing. Now let us consider how he uses them to serve his musical thought, and how this thought is organized. This involves one of the most delicate subjects in the study of jazz—that is, the construction of choruses. The question has scarcely been touched, and we cannot deal with it in detail here. Let us merely note that, because of its clarity and simplicity, the work of Dickie Wells lends itself pretty well to the succinct analyses we are going to devote to it.

It seems incontestable that Wells is one of the most perfect constructors of choruses in the history of jazz. He has not only a sense of contrast, as we have already observed, but also—and perhaps to an even greater extent—a sense of balance. I mentioned near the beginning of this chapter that he is a born romantic. I believe this is true in a certain sense, for few musicians have his vivid imagination, his sweeping ardor, his impetuous effervescence, and his profoundly dramatic accent; but these expressive qualities, which make him one of the most sensitive soloists, are supported by a firm foundation in his sense of *balance*, and this is what distinguishes him from equally admirable but less well organized musicians (Roy Eldridge, for instance).

The art of Dickie Wells seems to be governed by two essential ideas, *symmetry* and *contrast*.[1] They may appear contradictory; but all you have to do to be convinced of the necessity of both is to imagine what a musician's playing would be like if either one were missing. A style based on contrast alone would be incoherent, and one that is too symmetrical would be monotonous. In varying degrees, these two qualities are found linked together in the work of all great musicians; but no one unites them better than Dickie Wells.

He often shows this desire for symmetry right at the start of a solo. His choruses frequently begin with a kind of *doublet*—that is, a short phrase that is repeated, either identically or transposed, after a brief pause. This procedure, which the great trombonist seems to be particularly fond of, has the excellent effect of *airing out* the first bars of a chorus, permitting a subsequent gradation of contrasts that would risk decreasing the tension if presented in the opposite order. This initial doublet is found in some of his best solos: Spike Hughes's SWEET SORROW BLUES (in which the phrase includes a very expressive inflection) and Basie's LONDON BRIDGE IS FALLING DOWN, TAXI WAR DANCE, and MISS THING, among others.

---

[1] By *symmetry*, I mean the rhythmic or melodic repetition of a given motif; by *contrast*, the violent opposition of upper and lower registers, of forte and piano, of motion and repose.

Another favorite procedure of Dickie Wells is what might be called the *entry note*. It is an isolated note that does not appear to be attached to the chorus; on the contrary, it seems quite independent of what follows. It shows up at the beginning of some solos, serving no apparent melodic purpose, as if the musician had just wanted to check the pitch or tone of his instrument. However, its musical meaning cannot be denied. To my way of understanding, it serves as a link; by means of this simple note, Wells skillfully manages to form a connection between his chorus and the preceding one. Such a connection is too often neglected by most improvisers, who don't care what relation their variation has to the one before. Moreover, this entry note is nearly always expressive. Wells makes up for its apparent melodic insignificance by using a warm and moving vibrato (generally of the "terminal" type mentioned earlier). Interesting examples of the entry note may be found in Teddy Hill's WHEN THE ROBIN SINGS HIS SONG AGAIN and particularly in HOT CLUB BLUES, where it is immediately followed by a doublet (a rather infrequent but very effective combination). Naturally, none of this is systematic; and Dickie Wells does not refrain from using other kinds of entries. One of the most original is surely his glissando break in Teddy Hill's A STUDY IN BROWN.

His taste for symmetry is again reflected in the way he breaks up his choruses, but it is animated by an inventive imagination that prevents him from making his divisions too uniform. Examples of choruses cut up in four-bar divisions are fairly rare (Spike Hughes's AIR IN D FLAT is one, and so is Basie's DOWN FOR DOUBLE). Actually, Wells's sense of symmetry is manifested in more subtle ways, because they are closely connected with the ways in which he shows his sense of contrast. In the chorus of SWEET SORROW BLUES, for example, after the initial doublet, the phrase develops and comes to a drop into the lower register, then drops again (symmetry) but this time in the middle register (contrast). Similarly, in the chorus of Spike Hughes's HOW COME YOU DO ME, the repetition of certain motifs (symmetry) is set off by their rhythmic disjunction (contrast).

It definitely seems that Wells's taste for contrast exceeds his taste for symmetry and is the dominant element in his style.[2] There is scarcely a single solo in which it is not manifested, in one way or another. Let us take his chorus in Spike Hughes's PASTORAL as an example. Wells takes sixteen bars in a moderate tempo. The first eight are rather static; they open with a repeated note, and the ensuing melodic development is very calm. On the other hand, the following eight bars are much more animated; Wells uses a staccato phrasing that forms a sharp break with what went before. In Hughes's BUGLE CALL RAG, Wells starts by swinging on a repeated note, then suddenly takes off into the upper register, and accentuates the tension of the phrase by inflection before going into a very mobile final drop. The first eight bars of his solo in Fletcher Henderson's KING PORTER STOMP (Vocalion version) are constructed in very angular fashion, with very dry notes that are "shot out"; the other eight bars begin with an upper-register held note that is taut in sonority but still forms a perfect rhythmic contrast with what went before. On the other hand, Dickie Wells knows how to use a calm vibrato to create a feeling of relaxation at the end of a violent episode (as in Basie's TEXAS SHUFFLE). A tranquil, intimate chorus with little contrast, such as the one in DICKY'S DREAM (also made with Basie), must be considered an exception. Actually, his taste for contrast is so great that he will even oppose his chorus to the preceding one. We have a striking example of this in Hughes's SOMEONE STOLE GABRIEL'S HORN, where Wells fol-

[2] This does not invalidate my earlier statement that balance is Wells's principal quality.

lows the sax's very regularly divided solo with its exact rhythmic and plastic antithesis, full of glissandos and irregularly broken up.

Let us now examine the style of Dickie Wells from a strictly rhythmic point of view. His choruses may often be divided into regular sections, but within these sections he exercises a rare amount of rhythmic imagination. He uses notes of greatly varying length and combines them very freely. In Spike Hughes's FIREBIRD, for example, he plays on the beat, in the manner of the New Orleans trombonists (though naturally he is incomparably better about getting the notes in the right place and about swinging). In Basie's LONDON BRIDGE, he plays a long series of quarter notes on the beat, ending with two syncopated notes (one of Louis Armstrong's favorite procedures). On the other hand, in Hughes's MUSIC AT MIDNIGHT, he uses much less regular rhythms, such as a triplet of syncopated quarter notes. His chorus in Basie's TAXI WAR DANCE contains an unusual number of short notes (eighths), whereas welcome contrasts between long and short notes give his PANASSIÉ STOMP solo rare rhythmic suppleness. Another rhythmically interesting chorus is the one in Teddy Hill's MARIE. Although the tempo is very fast, Dickie Wells comes on with a series of eighths; then he slows up somewhat with a mixture of eighths and quarter notes, and even some half-note triplets that form a curious contrast to the work of the rhythm section (three against four); and he ends very humorously with a break made up of eighth notes again. In Spike Hughes's AIR IN D FLAT, the diversity of rhythmic values counterbalances the symmetry of four-bar division; each of these four phrases stands in rhythmic contrast to the others.

To see the freedom and rhythmic diversity of Wells's phrasing, it is sufficient to study a simple eight-bar phrase taken from I FOUND A NEW BABY, which he recorded in France in 1937. Notice (fig. 3) the long, vibrated note—it

FIG. 3

might be compared to an entry note—in the first measure;
the syncopated phrase that follows; the descending phrase,
straddling the bar line between the fourth and fifth measures, which is also syncopated but with longer, dislocated
notes (dotted quarters), and which comes to rest on the
second beat of the fifth measure (note here that the glissandos further amplify the feeling of rhythmic uncertainty
caused by the dislocation of the syncopated notes); and
finally the very classical descending phrase of measures 6-8,
which might almost have been taken from an Armstrong
chorus. Here again, it would be a mistake to believe that the
phrase is any the less cohesive for showing imaginative
variety. Moreover, Dickie Wells is perfectly capable of developing a chorus according to the strictest rhythmic progression. Even in the tight quarters of an eight-bar bridge,
he can begin statically, step things up, and finish by playing
eight to the bar. His short solos in Teddy Hill's HERE COMES
COOKIE and WHEN THE ROBIN SINGS HIS SONG AGAIN are almost
twin-like examples of this. It will be observed, especially in
the second, that Wells has a tendency to "swallow" the sixteenth notes of his dotted-eighth-and-sixteenth groups; this
fits in very nicely with his particularly supple and nonchalant
way of swinging.

Melodically, there is the same alternation between imagination and conformity. Although Wells has a predilection
for changes in register (those of A STUDY IN BROWN are
typical), he has nothing against staying in the upper register
(as in Spike Hughes's FANFARE) or in the middle range. He
rarely tries to make an effect with a high note, although

examples that might be noted are the high F in Basie's DOWN
FOR DOUBLE and the somewhat unfortunate glissando in the
Kansas City Six's I GOT RHYTHM. Much more interesting is
his liking for wide intervals (something few trombonists
have, I believe), which is demonstrated on this same side,
notably during his first bridge (fig. 4). (Note also, in this
excerpt, the great rhythmic originality expressed by the
triplet of half notes in measure 19 and the triplet of syncopated quarter notes in measure 22.)

FIG. 4

A great deal more remains to be said about such an
astonishing musician, but that would take us beyond the
limits of a study like this. Before concluding, however, I
should like to go over what I consider his most interesting
records. In roughly chronological order, they are as follows:
Lloyd Scott's SYMPHONIC SCREACH and Cecil Scott's BRIGHT
BOY BLUES, which I discussed near the beginning of this
chapter. Luis Russell's GOIN' TO TOWN, which is a kind of
recorded synthesis of all Wells's principal characteristics:
attack, glissando, vibrato, "bite," and freedom of rhythmic
construction. Nearly all the Spike Hughes series, and particularly HOW COME YOU DO ME, which swings extremely well
in a moderate tempo and shows off other aspects of Wells's
playing, such as the ornamented high note, dislocation and
rhythmic contrast, and harmonious construction; FANFARE
(vehemence); SWEET SORROW BLUES (simplicity); ARABESQUE
(ease); AIR IN D FLAT (balance in spite of contrasts); and
BUGLE CALL RAG (modernism of style). Teddy Hill's HERE

COMES COOKIE, MARIE, and A STUDY IN BROWN. Count Basie's
TEXAS SHUFFLE, PANASSIÉ STOMP, LOVE JUMPED OUT, JIMMY'S
BLUES, NOBODY KNOWS, and particularly HARVARD BLUES
(Okeh version), the orchestra's masterpiece in a slow
tempo. Finally, under his own name, BETWEEN THE DEVIL AND
THE DEEP BLUE SEA, which has a bridge that is a little gem,
and the admirable DICKY WELLS BLUES, which would be one
of the truly great jazz records if the rhythm section were
up to the level of the soloist—it is, alas, very far from it!—
and if even Wells himself had not weakened somewhat in
the last two choruses.

There is perhaps no way to conclude except by returning
to our starting point, which was not exactly optimistic. It
is unpleasant to observe the decline of a musician one likes.
Many people refuse to do so. Nevertheless, the sincere critic
must face the facts. How can the fact be avoided that Wells's
solos, even with Basie, became increasingly rare toward the
end of the war and kept diminishing in quality? I am thinking of TUSH (with Earl Warren, April, 1944) and FOUR
O'CLOCK DRAG (with the Kansas City Six at about the same
time), both of which are among his weakest choruses; the
second, a slow blues, gives the painful impression that Wells
has lost the feeling and has to force himself to play.

A few years ago, it was still possible to think that these
were simply lapses. But Dickie Wells came to Europe in
1952. We hoped to hear the brilliant soloist again; instead,
all we heard time after time was a worn-out, diminished,
unrecognizable Wells. The fate that condemns nine jazzmen
out of ten to end up as caricatures of their past greatness
has caught up with the great trombonist. Under these circumstances, it is best to forget the Wells of today in order
to remember the marvelous soloist he was before the war.

Chapter VI

A MASTERPIECE:
CONCERTO FOR COOTIE

1
Ups and Downs of the Concerto

Some pieces of music grow old; others stay young. At times we can hardly believe it possible that once we actually enjoyed listening to a page of music or a chorus that now seems overwhelmingly long on faults and short on merits. To make up for this, some works seem more and more attractive to us as time goes by. For one thing, we are more difficult to please at thirty than we were at twenty. Instead of liking a hundred records, we no longer like more than five or six; but perhaps we like them better. Judging by my own experience, there can be no doubt that the test of time has favored Ellington's CONCERTO FOR COOTIE—more, perhaps, than any other work, and this is a sure sign of merit. It has become clear to me that this piece is one of the high points in Ellington's output, which has been vast and rich in flashes of genius, but unequal and occasionally disappointing. I would even say that it offers a striking epitome of certain essential aspects of his work.

The concerto formula—that is, a composition centered around a single soloist accompanied by large orchestra—is widely used these days. There is almost no repertory that does not include a certain number of arrangements conceived with an eye toward the possibilities, the style, and the ambitions of such and such a popular soloist. In 1940, even though it wasn't exceptional, the concerto was rarer. It was only four years before then that Ellington had recorded his first concertos, one of which, ECHOES OF HARLEM, had already been designed for Cootie Williams. Admittedly, the appearance of these compositions did not constitute an innovation in the form. Before Ellington, Armstrong had recorded solos that had all the concerto's appearances. But the Ellington style of concerto, from the very beginning, not only introduced a markedly different musical climate but also laid the foundation for an infinitely richer conception. In it, far from merely serving to set off the soloist as in Armstrong's records, the orchestra worked in close collaboration with him. Naturally, it would be impossible to state positively that Duke Ellington and his group grasped from the beginning all the possibilities that this kind of composition offered, but it seems probable all the same. In any case, the fact is that, after several years of varyingly successful experiments (the detestable TRUMPET IN SPADES, in which Rex trumpeted to such poor advantage, comes to mind), the orchestra recorded, on March 15, 1940, this CONCERTO FOR COOTIE, which still strikes us, a decade and a half later, as the masterpiece of jazz concertos and as being, along with KO-KO, the most important composition that Duke Ellington has turned out.

The concerto formula is not faultless; to be more precise, it invites esthetic lapses that the arranger and the soloist do not always manage to avoid, even when they are fully aware of the lurking danger. Fear of monotony engenders an abusive use of effects; the difficulty a soloist has in improvising freely against too melodically and harmonically rich an orchestral background leads to the greatest possible reduction of the orchestra's part. In this way, a kind of by-product of the concerto is produced, with a virtual elimination of all dialogue between the soloist and the orchestra, which is actually the basic reason for the form's existence. On the other hand, the fact that the arranger conceives the concerto in terms of a single soloist—of such and such a special soloist—makes it possible to attain most easily in this form that cardinal virtue of any work of art, unity. Perhaps it will be objected that this is a classical composer's idea, but I think I have had enough experience with jazz to affirm that the notion of unity is just as important in this music as in European music. Is it possible to believe that a record joining the talents of Armstrong and Parker, even at the top of their form, would constitute a composition, in the real sense of the word? Certainly not. We could go further and say that, in actuality, such a confrontation would immediately be recognized as unfruitful. Neither Armstrong nor Parker would really be in top form; it is much more likely that neither would be able to play at all. True, I have purposely taken an extreme example; but records have given us many specimens of similar though less extreme confrontations, and I don't remember a single successful one in the lot.

In the light of this, it is easy for me to say in what way CONCERTO FOR COOTIE rates my qualification as a masterpiece. CONCERTO FOR COOTIE is a masterpiece because everything in it is pure; because it desn't have that slight touch of softness which is enough to make so many other deserving records insipid. CONCERTO FOR COOTIE is a masterpiece because the arranger and the soloist have refused in it any temptation to achieve an easy effect, and because the musical substance of it is so rich that not for one instant does the listener have an impression of monotony. CONCERTO FOR COOTIE is a masterpiece because it shows the game being played for all it is worth, without anything's being held back, and because the game is won. We have here a real concerto in which the orchestra is not a simple background, in which the soloist doesn't waste his time in technical acrobatics or in gratuitous effects. Both have something to say, they say it well, and what they say is beautiful. Finally, CONCERTO FOR COOTIE is a masterpiece because what the orchestra says is the indispensable complement to what the soloist says; because nothing is out of place or superfluous in it; and because the composition thus attains unity.

2
Structure of Concerto for Cootie

CONCERTO FOR COOTIE should not be considered as an ordinary arrangement. Its unusual structure, the polish of its composition, the liberties with certain well-established rules that are taken in it, the refusal to improvise—these characteristics are enough to place it rather on the level of original composition as this term is understood by artists of classical training. CONCERTO FOR COOTIE is not derived from any earlier melody. True, DO NOTHIN' TILL YOU HEAR FROM ME uses the same melodic figure; but this song, composed by Ellington, is several years later than the orchestral work. There can be no doubt that it was adapted from it.[1] Do NOTHIN' is in a way the commercial version of the guiding idea behind CONCERTO FOR COOTIE. Indeed, it retains only the initial phrase. We wouldn't even have mentioned the song here but for the fact that this phrase had to be revised to conform to the traditional framework of the thirty-two-bar song. We shall be able to appreciate the original better by comparing it with this popularized version.

This initial phrase, which constitutes the principal théme of the CONCERTO, undergoes numerous transformations in

[1] DO NOTHIN' was recorded by the Ellington band, with a vocal by Al Hibbler, in 1947.

the course of the composition. We shall call it theme *A* at its first exposition, *A'*, *A''*, and *A'''* in what follows. Figure *B*, which comes between the second and third exposition of *A*, serves merely as an episode; actually, it comes where the bridge would have if DO NOTHIN' had preceded the CONCERTO. On the contrary, theme *C* is extremely important. Played in a new key—and one that is not even neighboring—it completely changes the lighting and atmosphere of the composition. The lyricism of its lines, its range spread over a whole octave, and its being diatonic form a perfect contrast with the restraint of the first theme, which is static, chromatic, and confined within the limits of a fourth except for its last phrase. Finally, the re-exposition of *A* is immediately followed by a final coda that borrows its components from Ellington's MOON GLOW, put out in 1934 by Brunswick. Here, in outline form, is how these various elements are joined together:

Plan of CONCERTO FOR COOTIE

Introduction	8 bars
I. *Exposition* (F major)	
Theme *A*	10 bars
followed by *A'*	10 bars
followed by *B*	8 bars
followed by *A''*	10 bars
followed by a modulatory transition	2 bars
II. *Middle section* (Db major)	
Theme *C*	16 bars
followed by a modulatory transition	2 bars
III. *Re-exposition and coda* (F major)	
A'''	6 bars
Coda	10 bars

For a number of reasons, this construction is the furthest thing from being customary in jazz. The notion of variation scarcely subsists in it at all. As for the concept of chorus, it has disappeared without a trace. For that matter, since improvisation doesn't play any active role here, there would have been no reason for Ellington to preserve the traditional division in choruses. It was logical to adopt a more flexible structure, one more closely related to the "composed" nature of the piece. The mold chosen calls to mind the da capo form of the eighteenth-century Italians, although the recurrence of *A* after the middle section. *C* is hardly more than suggested.

Another surprising thing is the use of ten-bar phrases, an unprecedented practice in the history of jazz arrangements. This innovation is even bolder than it seems at first encounter. The initial phrase, as it appears in the printed edition of DO NOTHIN', does indeed comprise eight bars. The two extra bars of *A* and *A'* could therefore be considered as little orchestral codas added as an afterthought, constituting a kind of rebound of the phrase played by the soloist, even though they fit in—it would not be enough to say merely that they follow—so perfectly that the ear is aware of no break. But a closer analysis of the phrase's articulation reveals that its final turn in the DO NOTHIN' version is completely different from the original ending. The new turn is, for that matter, pretty weak, and there can be no doubt that it was added in order to re-establish a rhythmic equilibrium of the conventional kind that the CONCERTO, a free composition, deliberately ignored. Notice (fig. 5) that in CONCERTO FOR COOTIE the final note comes one bar sooner than is customary. Ending a phrase like this on a weak measure was, in 1939, absolutely revolutionary, and yet no one seems to have noticed it, because the band takes up the phrase right away and goes ahead with it as naturally as can be. The listener who hasn't been forewarned is not aware that the real phrase ends in the sixth measure, and the forewarned listener doesn't react much differently. It would

FIG. 5

Top line: the melody of SO NOTHIN' TILL YOU HEAR FROM ME as published by Francis Day.

Middle line: the initial phrase (A) of CONCERTO FOR COOTIE.

Bottom line: the same phrase as played in its second exposition (A')

N. B.—The vertical arrows indicate measures that reproduce the ones above exactly.

almost seem as though seven-bar melodies had been heard since the beginning of jazz.

The second exposition of A—that is, A'—fits in with the traditional rules; the twofold repetition, in the sixth measure, of a group of four eighth notes is enough to create anew the usual symmetry. The little orchestral coda remains, though, making the section cover ten bars. A", on paper, differs from A only in these last two measures, which prepare the transition to C. However, the performance gives the phrase quite a different aspect. In addition to the question of sonority, which we shall consider later, it must be noticed

that Cootie here gives back to the notes their rhythmic
values, which he had deliberately distorted during the first
exposition of the theme. Finally, A''' is a merely suggested
restatement of A. After four bars, which include a melodic
variant, there is a sudden branching out to the coda—a
conclusion for which the way has been prepared by the
changing harmonies that underline this restatement.

3
Simplicity and Subtlety of the Harmony

The harmonic language of CONCERTO FOR COOTIE is, on the
whole, extremely simple. Apart from the introduction, the
general climate of the piece is as resolutely consonant as
KO-KO, Ellington's other masterpiece of that period, was the
opposite. In the CONCERTO, dissonance plays a secondary role;
it does not constitute the foundation of the harmony. It
does not serve to create a feeling of tension, but operates
as a means of adding color.   Nonetheless, the many dissonances to be found in the work are not there for nothing:
there can be no doubt that their suppression would weaken
it considerably. It is they, certainly, that by contrast make
the consonances sound so bright and fresh. This over-all
harmonic simplicity doesn't rule out subtlety of detail. Certain passages have presented problems to the best-trained
ears. The little phrase in contrary motion in the seventh
and eighth measures of the coda, which is harmonically a
real gem, would provide a test in musical dictation for the
greatest specialists in this ticklish sport; but I want to call
attention merely to its musical beauty, which I like to think
any listener will appreciate.

Another exceptional passage is the measure just before
the exposition of theme C. I doubt that there are many

examples of modulations more striking than this one, not only in jazz but in all music. On paper, it seems extremely simple, and no doubt it actually is. Listening to it, one has to admire the abruptness and rigor of this turning; and its effect is all the more astonishing because Ellington has put before it a two-beat rest that constitutes—taking into consideration the completely inconclusive phrase just preceding it—the most effective break you could ask for between one part of a piece and another that you would have expected to follow without any break at all. To call this a stroke of genius is, for once, not to misuse the phrase.

It would be possible to mention a number of other harmonic finds. In spite of its ambiguous character and a certain acidity that does not lack charm, the introduction is not the most successful part of the composition. I prefer certain details in the purely accompanying part: the saxes' dissonances behind phrase *A'* or a complementary phrase like the one in the eighth measure of *C*, which has a melodic, harmonic, and instrumental savor that is truly penetrating. Atttention should also be called to the occasional use of blue notes in some of the trombones' punctuation of phrases *A* and *A"*. Although, basically, CONCERTO FOR COOTIE has no more connection with the blues than Hawkins' BODY AND SOUL, these blue notes are by no means out of place; the faint touch of the blues that they introduce fits into the atmosphere of the piece perfectly.

There remains the added-sixth chord, which is put to considerable use here. This harmonic combination, which generally raises my hackles, fills me with joy in the CONCERTO. It is true that Ellington sometimes uses it in a regrettably Gershwin-like way, but that certainly is not the case here. Why? I couldn't say for sure; that sort of thing is more easily felt than explained. Perhaps the consonant climate of the piece accounts for a large part of it; perhaps the general feeling and the orchestration itself play a decisive role. What must be remembered is that no chord, however flaccid, is inherently ugly; the only thing that counts is the use made of it.

4
The Orchestra at the Soloist's Service

There is no point in dwelling on the orchestra's role in CONCERTO FOR COOTIE. What we have already said is enough to define it. In this piece, as in most jazz concertos, the orchestra never dominates the soloist; it introduces him, supports him, continues where he leaves off, provides a connection between two of his phrases—in a word, it is at his service. Notice that the orchestra states no theme; when it happens to sketch one of the main motifs, it does so as a reply, not as a statement. The soloist always takes the initiative. Like a good servant, the orchestra is satisfied with approving. Even the admirable modulation that precedes the entry of *C* is not, from a structural point of view, anything but the opening of a door; once the guest of honor is shown in, the servant fades away into the background.

Still, this servant, though he may not obtrude, says exactly what must be said, and his clothes may not be sumptuous but they are exceptionally elegant. The orchestra's bearing is equaled in sobriety only by the orchestration. In both respects, CONCERTO FOR COOTIE is a model of discretion and authenticity. It displays an economy of means that is the sign of real classicism. To me, the little syncopated figure that is given alternately to the saxes and the brasses to punctuate each exposition of *A* is infinitely more valuable than the overloaded backgrounds that the big modern band does not always know how to do without; it achieves a maximum of effectiveness without using more than two chords, although it is true that these are renewed each time. Judged by the same standards, the orchestral background of *B* is possibly even more successful. And what is there to say about the countermelody of *C*, where the saxes, in their chromatic movement, support Cootie's lyric flight so majestically?

Another cause for admiring astonishment is the incomparable co-ordination between the harmony and the orchestration. In order to express the nuances of a clear harmony in which there are nonetheless plenty of half-tints, the composer has everywhere hit upon just the instrumentation called for. Orchestral color and harmonic color blend in a way that delights the amateur in me as I observe what this combination brings to the piece and that impresses the professional in me as I remember how rare such a combination is. Actually, this blending is the principal virtue of an orchestration that doesn't offer any sensational innovations but that can still boast some captivating details. I shall mention only the orchestra's big descent at the end of *A'* (cf. fig. 5), in which the principal motif, taken by the clarinet, does not emerge clearly from the cloud of enveloping chromatic lines but is delicately suggested; the imitation of the theme is guessed at rather than actually heard.

If I have stressed the lesson in simplicity that the CONCERTO presents in both its harmony and its orchestration, it is because that is precisely what the piece has to teach. However, it is all too easy to confuse what is simple with what is merely simplified. CONCERTO FOR COOTIE demonstrates the possibility of achieving a real orchestral language while observing the strictest economy of means. It constitutes, indeed, a summit that few musicians have reached. In this respect, Duke Ellington here makes one think of Mozart. I don't know whether the jazz fan will appreciate the significance of such a comparison, but I feel safe in making it because this composition deserves to be considered not merely as a specimen of jazz, which is only one kind of music, but as a specimen of music, period.

5
Strong and Weak Points of the Performance

We have just considered the orchestral part of the CONCERTO in its conception. But we must not forget that the conception of a work of jazz cannot be separated from its execution. When Ellington wrote the trumpet part, he wasn't thinking of anyone but Cootie, and similarly he didn't design the work as a whole for any orchestra but his own. Whether the CONCERTO was composed by one man or by a whole group is a good question. It has been and will continue to be asked, although the answer can be provided only by those who were present when the piece was created, either as participants or witnesses. The only thing we can be sure of is that the whole band, then in its great period, took part in the performance. Wallace Jones and Rex Stewart were on trumpet, Joe Nanton, Juan Tizol, and Lawrence Brown on trombone, Barney Bigard on clarinet, Otto Hardwicke, Johnny Hodges, Ben Webster, and Harry Carney on sax, Duke Ellington at the piano, Fred Guy on guitar, Jimmy Blanton on bass, and Sonny Greer on drums; and we mustn't forget, of course, Cootie Williams on solo trumpet. Listing these names and remembering that we are now going to talk about performance brings us right to the heart of jazz. Let us accordingly abandon the very general approach we adopted when talking about the problems offered by the harmonic and orchestral aspects of the piece.

I don't know exactly when the CONCERTO was composed or when it began to be performed, so it would be hard for me to prove that it was not completely broken in when it was recorded, but this seems likely. If so, perhaps the record would have been the better for being put off until after enough performances to correct the occasional lack of preciseness of which the band is guilty. But it is not certain that the result would have been very different. Even at that time,

the Ellington orchestra was frequently somewhat easygoing
in its performance as a group; it rarely had Lunceford's kind
of precision. On the other hand, there is no way of knowing
whether Cootie would have played his part with the same
spirit after another twenty run-throughs; his fire might have
died down along the way, and it must be admitted that this
would have been completely regrettable. For that matter,
the flaws I have referred to are notably few; they are venial
and easily overlooked. If they cause regrets in spite of this,
it is because they are the only thing to be criticized in a
record that otherwise calls only for praise. But you would
have to be particularly narrow-minded to let the beauties
of this piece be obscured by paying too much attention to the
fact that the saxes, for example, scurry after one another
in the scale leading to the coda. Alongside these slight defects, the playing in CONCERTO FOR COOTIE actually has many
solid virtues. The balance among the players and their fine
sound in both loud and muted passages are highlighted by
an excellent recording technique. Nuances are performed
with sensitivity and taste. The band seems to be one man
following or, even better, anticipating the leader's wishes.

The tempo of CONCERTO FOR COOTIE is "slow moderato,"
a difficult one to keep to, but just right for the piece. There
are few records in which the rhythm section of the band
plays in quite such a relaxed way, and by the same token
there are few in which the band phrases with as much swing.
Naturally, this is not a torrid record like Hampton's AIR
MAIL SPECIAL. That kind of exaltation, which has its own
appeal, is only rarely Duke Ellington's line. But CONCERTO
FOR COOTIE is a perfect example of a performance that is full
of swing in a gentle climate.

The rhythmic success of the performance is based largely
on Jimmy Blanton's playing, of which this is certainly one
of the best recorded examples. It is fascinating to follow the
bass's admirable part, curiously aired out as it is with whole

bars of silence. At each exposition of theme *A,* Blanton
stops playing, only to put in a discreet but effective reap-
pearance at the fifth bar. Such details might constitute the
whole attraction of an ordinary record. Here, they almost
pass unobserved. I remember that, when I once put Pierre
Gérardot on the spot by asking whether the tempo of CON-
CERTO FOR COOTIE was slow or medium, he had to stop and
think a moment before being able to answer. If I had asked
him such a question about some run-of-the-mill record that
had just appeared, he would doubtless have replied right
off; but the CONCERTO, for him as for me, was in a world
apart from the jazz of every day.

6

An Authentic Composition and the Interpreter's Part in It

The time has come to turn to the soloist's part and ask
questions about it just as we did about the orchestra's role.
We have just seen that one of the essential characteristics
of CONCERTO FOR COOTIE is the elimination of improvisation.
There is nothing arbitrary about this; it was imposed upon
Ellington by circumstances. As we have already said, partly
because it is a kind of concert music but even more because
of its very form, the jazz concerto (at least when the orchestra plays more than a merely passive role) seems to require
of the soloist greater circumspection than he usually shows
in a simple chorus-after-chorus performance. It is appropriate to mention that most of the concertos that came before
this one were already notable for the extent to which they
had been worked out. No one would believe, for instance,
that Barney Bigard's part in CLARINET LAMENT was spontaneously improvised from one end to the other in the studio.
Nevertheless, a large part was surely left to the moment's
inspiration. CONCERTO FOR COOTIE has every appearance of

being the first jazz record with an important solo part in which improvisation does not figure at all.

Does that mean that we have here a European-style concerto, a composition worked out in private, then written down, and finally rehearsed and performed? Yes and no. Undoubtedly Ellington realized that such a piece had to be thought out from the first to the last, right up to and including the solo part. Whether this part was put down in black and white or memorized makes little difference. The only thing that counts is its character, which, as far as the melody is concerned, is that of something fixed and final. There seems nothing unwarranted in saying that one performance must have differed from another only in minor expressive details that are left to the interpreter in other kinds of music as well. It remains to be determined whether the trumpet part, of which at least the actual notes were decided on before the recording, is the work of Cootie, of Duke, or of several hands. The question is not easy for anyone who wasn't there when the composition was created. It is hard to believe that a piece of music so perfectly unified as to be almost without parallel in the whole jazz repertory should not be the work of a single man; and that man would have to be Duke Ellington. True, anyone who is familiar with the way that famous band works would have to think twice before positively rejecting the possibility of a collective effort; but, all things considered, this kind of gestation seems unlikely. Pending definite information to the contrary, we shall regard CONCERTO FOR COOTIE as a real *composition* as European musicians understand this word.

However, if the notes of this trumpet part were decided on before the recording, it was still only the notes that were. This feature is what takes us far away from European conceptions. Ernest Ansermet had the right idea when he observed, more than thirty years ago, that even though the work of jazz may be written down, it is not fixed. Unlike the

European concerto, in which the composer's intention dominates the interpreter's, the jazz concerto makes the soloist a
kind of second creator, often more important than the first,
even when the part he has to play doesn't leave him any
melodic initiative. Perhaps Cootie had nothing to do with
the melody of the CONCERTO; he probably doesn't stray from
it an inch; and still it would be impossible to imagine CON-
CERTO FOR COOTIE without him.

We here touch upon one of those mysteries of jazz that
classical musicians have so much trouble in recognizing but
that are basically simplicity itself. For the European musician, sound is a means of expression that is distinct from the
creation of a work; for the jazz musician, it is an essential
part of this creation. That difference is enough to create a
gulf between two conceptions that in other respects seem
to work together in the piece we are talking about. No interpreter of European music, whatever his genius, will tell us
as much about himself as Cootie does in these three minutes.
It is the expressionist conception of jazz that allows the interpreter to substitute himself for the composer, to express his
personality completely, to make himself a creator. Some
people condemn expressionism of any kind, regarding it as
a debasement. To do so is to condemn almost all jazz. Although many soloists may have abused the possibilities offered them, the greatest have managed to stay within certain
limits; but these limits themselves are broader than some
ears, convinced of the absolute superiority of European art,
can tolerate in a musical manifestation that is judged, a
priori, to be inferior.

Don't misunderstand me: I don't in the least claim, like
most specialized critics, that jazz is *the* music of our time.
On the contrary, I want very much to stress, even though I
were to be accused of "racial prejudice," that, to me, the
riches of jazz, however precious, cannot for a moment match
the riches of contemporary European music. But it is per-

haps worth while to recall that several centuries of European
music had passed before the mind of a genius, Arnold
Schoenberg, gave birth to the idea of a "melody of timbres"
(*Klangfarbenmelodie*) —that is, a musical sequence in which
each sound is expressed by a different timbre. Isn't that, in
a different way, what jazz musicians accomplished spontaneously by giving to the sonority of one instrument the most
varied possible aspects?

7
A Bouquet of Sonorities

Few records do more than the CONCERTO to make possible
an appreciation of how great a role sonority can play in the
creation of jazz. The trumpet part is a true bouquet of sonorities. The phrases given to it by Ellington, which have a
melodic beauty of their own that should not be overlooked,
are completely taken over by Cootie. He makes them shine
forth in dazzling colors, then plunges them in the shade,
plays around with them, makes them glitter or delicately
tones them down; and each time what he shows us is something new. Even if he had had to put up with a less charming
melody, his art would have been enough to make us forget
its banality. But it mustn't be thought that this gamut of
sonority is merely decorative, artificial, gratuitous. The sonorities he imposes on the melody were conceived in terms
of the melody itself. A different melody would have been
treated differently; but this particular one, under his fingers,
could not have been treated in any other way.

It is interesting to note that there is a different sonority
corresponding to each of the three themes. The reason is
easy to understand. It is appropriate that theme *A*, which we
have already described as static, should be handled in subdued colors; that theme *B*, which is savagely harsh, should

invite free use of the muted wa-wa's stridencies, which here have an extra brutality; and the lyricism of theme *C* can be fully expressed only in the upper register of the trumpet, played open. But there are other, more subtle details. Why is there such a diversity of expression in the different expositions of *A*? (Only *A'* and *A'''* are played in the same spirit.) Why does the trumpet have such a violent vibrato in *A*, whereas *A'* is played with an even sonority that almost prefigures the way modern trumpets sound? Why, in *A''*, is there that sound held like a thread, which is so disconcerting that it is rather hard to believe it is a muted trumpet rather than a violin? To ask such questions, which come naturally to the classically trained listener, would show ignorance of the fact that CONCERTO FOR COOTIE, like many works of jazz, owes its vitality to the contrast of sonorities—a contrast that does not in the least affect its basic unity.

Furthermore, with what taste, with what a sense of proportion Cootie uses his amazing technique for producing different timbres! How admirably he knows how to bring to bear on expressive detail the resources of an art that, used with less discipline, would risk being nothing more than an advanced exercise—far from ordinary, to be sure, but without special significance! Unreserved admiration is the only possible reaction to his discreet and sensitive use of the glissando, which is scarcely noticeable in the various versions of *A*, is more developed in *B*, and becomes in *C* an essential part of his lyricism. This judicious use of sonorities is perfectly paralleled by the intelligence of his phrasing. We have already noted that Cootie deliberately twisted the rhythmic values of theme *A*. It is not easy to bring off that sort of treatment. Even when the melody lends itself to it—and this one does—there is the constant danger of being corny in the worst possible way. Cootie's performance does not for a moment seem in the least bit mannered. From the very first,

the listener cannot doubt that the kind of vibrato he uses is
profoundly felt.

8

How the Piece Stands

Let's try to place the CONCERTO now, first of all among the
great trumpeter's performances. The job is not so simple as
it might seem at first. The CONCERTO seems to represent a
synthesis. Nowhere else has Cootie appeared under more
varying aspects; nowhere else has he succeeded in bringing
into such radical opposition serenity and passion, lyricism
and simple tenderness. Nonetheless, what traces are to be
found here of the magical, incantatory Cootie of ECHOES
OF HARLEM, of the mocking Cootie of MOON GLOW, of the
hell-bent-for-leather Cootie of IT'S A GLORY, and of all the
other Cooties that there isn't room to mention? At the most
there is, from time to time, an intonation or the fragment
of a phrase to serve as a furtive reminder that it is, after
all, the same artist. And yet, who could make any mistake?
What soloist leaves a more indelible imprint on his work
than this disconcerting Cootie? In a way, he is one of those
who constantly show the public a different face. Someone
like Louis Armstrong is always more or less himself. It is
his incomparable inventive gift that saves him from being
repetitious; it doesn't take any time to recognize his tri-
umphal accent, his straightforward phrasing. Cootie covers
a wider range; he seems always to be discovering something.
For all that, he doesn't lose his identity. This man of a thousand sonorities is still one whose particular sonority you
would recognize in a thousand.

In any case, the CONCERTO is certainly one of the most successful records Cootie has made. It can be said that he com-

pletely lives up to the music that Duke Ellington wrote for
him and surrounded him with. He attains real greatness
here, both in feeling and in taste; there is nothing in this
music that is not authentic. I don't know of many soloists
who rate such praise.

Before concluding, it might be appropriate to try to re-
fute two objections that will surely occur to those who,
taking advantage of the similarities we have more than once
indicated, would like to place this work in relation to the
classical concerto. These objections are not unimportant; it
is simply that they don't apply to the scale of values by which
jazz is to be judged.

The first objection would be that CONCERTO FOR COOTIE
is a sample of "easy" music; in other words, a work without
depth, one of those that reveal all their secrets at a single
hearing, and to any kind of listener, without requiring any
effort. That may be. By comparison with the great pages of
contemporary music, the CONCERTO is not a complex work,
and it is even less a revolutionary work. Neither its harmonic system nor its perfectly tonal melody can offer the
slightest problem to a trained person. The classical critic,
accustomed to judging modern music by certain criteria,
will naturally be disappointed at failing to find here, apart
from effects of sonority, anything that can't be grasped immediately.

But, in an age when creators have got so far ahead of the
public that the bridges threaten to be cut off for some time,
is it not fortunate that a composer can resume contact with
a more accessible kind of music and give us a well-balanced
work that is simple in idiom, sound and not bare of nobility in thought, admittedly easy to understand but individual, even original, and savorful in a way that withstands
repeated listening? Isn't there room, alongside Schoenberg's
Suite for Seven Instruments and Webern's *Chamber Sym-*

phony, for an art designed to please without making any concessions to vulgarity or bombast? Doesn't the CONCERTO satisfy this definition just as do certain pieces by Haydn and Mozart that are not scholarly music but have nonetheless withstood the test of almost two centuries of listening?

The other objection is less important. It has to do with the piece's proportions. CONCERTO FOR COOTIE takes only one side of a ten-inch seventy-eight—three minutes. Judged by the standards of European music, by which a symphonic idea of no great significance may well be stretched over more than a quarter of an hour, that is not very much. But what is such a criterion worth? It is to be feared that attaching so much importance to size is one of the prejudices of the European mind, which is under the influence of several grandiose achievements. The *St. Matthew Passion* is not a masterpiece because it lasts almost four hours; it is a masterpiece because it is the *St. Matthew Passion.* For that matter, this prejudice has been gravely breached even in Europe. Didn't Schoenberg, in reaction to the bombast of post-Romanticism, say he would like to see a novel expressed "in a single sigh"? Didn't Webern make some of his compositions incredibly brief? Speaking little makes no difference if a great deal is said. Though it is no miracle of condensation, CONCERTO FOR COOTIE says more in three minutes than such a long and uneven fresco as the *Liberian Suite.*

All that remains is to place CONCERTO FOR COOTIE as jazz. Almost twenty years of experience were required before orchestral jazz produced, within a few days of each other, its two most important works. The first is KO-KO. It has less freshness and serenity, but perhaps more breadth and grandeur. The second is the CONCERTO. In the perfection of its form and the quality of its ideas, the CONCERTO, which combines classicism and innovation, stands head and shoulders above other pieces played by big bands. It has almost all the good features found in the best jazz, and others besides that are not generally found in Negro music. It makes up for the elements it doesn't use by the admirable way in which it exploits those that constitute its real substance. Isn't that exactly what a masterpiece is supposed to do?

Chapter VII

CHARLIE PARKER
AND THE BOP MOVEMENT

1
Minton's and the Development of the Bop Style

Around 1942, after classical jazz had made its conquests, a small group used to get together every night in a Harlem night club called Minton's Playhouse. It was made up of several young colored boys who, unlike their fellow-musicians, no longer felt at home in the atmosphere of "swing music." It was becoming urgent to get a little air in a richly decked-out palace that was soon going to be a prison. That was the aim of trumpeter Dizzy Gillespie, pianist Thelonious Monk, guitarist Charlie Christian (who died before the group's efforts bore fruit), drummer Kenny Clarke, and saxophonist Charlie Parker.[1] Except for Christian, they were poor, unknown, and unprepossessing; but Monk stimulated his partners by the boldness of his harmonies, Clarke created a new style of drum playing, and Gillespie and Parker took choruses that seemed crazy to the people who came to listen to them. The bebop style was in

[1] The presence of Parker in this group has been contested by some observers, notably Milton Hinton (cf. *Hear Me Talkin' to Ya*, p. 337). It seems impossible that Parker did not come to play in this gathering place of New York's avant-garde jazzmen. But he undoubtedly did not take part in the very first group at Minton's.

the process of being born. Later, Gillespie and his group triumphed on Fifty-second Street, but I bet that, deep down, these musicians missed the old jam sessions at Minton's.

When a newspaperman asked, "What is bop?" Dizzy Gillespie answered, "It's just the way my friends and I feel jazz." This reply is worth thinking about. The term *bebop* appeared, we know, when the movement was in the process of formation. The musicians at Minton's had got into the habit of referring to the arrangements they developed in the course of their famous sessions by simple onomatopoetic formulas that imitated the initial rhythmic figure of each, such as *be-bop, re-bop, oo-bop-shbam.* (If Beethoven had used this system, he might have called his Fifth Symphony *Di-di-di-da.*) Later, these nicknames for a new kind of music caught on. It became standard practice, for some unknowable reason, to use the term *bebop* to refer to the whole movement that reinvigorated jazz just after the war. This picturesque name, which was cleverly exploited in advertising, undoubtedly contributed a great deal to the success of modern jazz. But, in a way, it has been the cause of all the misunderstanding created over it by the exclusive partisans of oldtime and classical jazz. From *bop* came the word *bopper,* which invited an easy dialectical distinction between bopper and jazzman. Bop has been pictured as a virus, and the bopper as some degenerate who has been the victim of a shameful disease. The ravages caused by the bop microbe in the ranks of authentic jazzmen have been denounced. Gillespie's statement puts things back in place. Bop is nothing more than the modern expression of jazz as some creators conceived it and as a whole generation, with a few exceptions, practiced it.

Minton's regular customers who, night after night, witnessed the emergence of this new style were really lucky, but their good fortune doesn't concern us. The most wellintentioned and open-minded listener would have been disconcerted; and, as far as critical evaluation goes, his vantage point may not have been better than ours. Modern jazz was a collective creation. Every man in this group was responsible for a certain number of innovations that were synthesized only by a joint effort. There can be no doubt, for instance, that the rhythmic imagination of Kenny Clarke stimulated the melodic genius of his partners. Moreover, the contemporary observer, though he may have had the delight of noting new conceptions as they appeared successively, perhaps would not have been able to make out the over-all character of the group. The passing of time and an examination of each man's work and of the ground he has covered make it possible to get a clearer picture now. It is hard not to recognize in Charlie "Bird" Parker the real leader of the bebop movement. By his personality, the scope and diversity of his gifts, and his influence, he dominated his period just as Louis Armstrong, around 1930, dominated his. Under entirely different circumstances, both got jazz out of a rut, Armstrong by demonstrating its real riches, Parker by creating new masterpieces that gave it a new reason for surviving.

In its effort to renew jazz, the Minton's group decided to do something about one of the most contestable foundation stones of classical jazz (and, for that matter, of all jazz) — the repertory. Tired of having to improvise on themes that were all too often musically threadbare, these musicians had the idea of keeping only the general outline and of making them over by boldly paraphrasing the melodies and revising the harmonies, either in whole or in part. The best-known example of this is HOT HOUSE, inspired by WHAT IS THIS THING CALLED LOVE. Here the paraphrase by Tadd Dameron, always a fertile inventor of melodies, boldly transcends the original tune, even to the point of replacing its traditional *A-A-B-A* structure by a new scheme, *A-B-C-A*. This extension of the arranging process has given modern jazz a specific repertory that boasts a number of pieces which may not match the exceptional beauty of HOT HOUSE but which easily have more musical interest than almost any of the themes in everyday use by jazzmen before bebop. For his part, Charlie Parker has composed a number of paraphrases based on tried-and-true standards: DONNA LEE is his version of INDIANA, SCRAPPLE FROM THE APPLE comes from HONEYSUCKLE ROSE, CONFIRMATION from I GOT RHYTHM, and so forth. In addition to these pieces, his repertory includes many themes based on the blues (BILLIE'S BOUNCE, NOW'S THE TIME, CHERYL, COOL BLUES, and so forth), as well as some slow pieces, though these are rarer and not usually transformed except in the heat of improvisation (DON'T BLAME ME, EMBRACEABLE YOU, LOVER MAN, and so forth).

The renewal conceived by the men at Minton's would have had limited importance if it hadn't got beyond that stage. The great virtue of these musicians is that they faced up to all the great problems presented by the jazz of their time and found solutions in each particular domain. Their enrichment of the repertory goes right along with original conceptions in regard to rhythm, harmony, melody, and the handling of sound. The Minton's group did not fall down on the job. As we have seen, it is difficult to know just what each one contributed toward this new style, but Parker's exceptional importance is confirmed by the fact that no one made a better synthesis than he of the group's acquisitions. The work of this extraordinarily gifted improviser is the most nearly perfect expression of modern jazz. This being so, how can we fail to regard him as a leader? In any case, the fact remains that a study of his work is the starting point for any appreciation of the bebop movement's technical and esthetic contributions.

What Parker has recorded is a mere echo, regrettably sketchy, of an exceptionally rich career. Born in 1920, in

Kansas City, Charlie Parker learned how to play the saxophone when he was still in the grades. Like a lot of jazzmen, he began playing professionally very early. At the age of sixteen, he was playing in the town's best bands. He began as a specialist in the baritone sax, but he gave it up for the alto. He was with Harlan Leonard (1938-1939), and he made his first recordings when he was with Jay McShann (1940-1942). In 1943, he joined the Earl Hines band, which already included Dizzy Gillespie. It was during this period that he took part in the jam sessions at Minton's. The end of the war coincided with the success of bebop. Charlie Parker became famous. First with Dizzy and then in his own name, he made a number of records with some titles— ORNITHOLOGY and YARDBIRD SUITE, for example—that call to mind his picturesque nickname, Bird. However, a nervous disorder got the better of him and he had to spend six months undergoing treatment. One of his least perfect though perhaps most moving records, LOVER MAN, was made in the middle of a nervous depression (July, 1946). Cured and at the head of a remarkable quintet the following year, Parker made a series of records that are without precedent in the history of jazz. The year 1947, which was fertile in such masterpieces as DON'T BLAME ME, SCRAPPLE FROM THE APPLE, PARKER'S MOOD, and the two versions of EMBRACEABLE YOU; was unhappily followed by a break in Parker's production. Did these fine records sell badly? That may be. Charlie Parker remained one of the big stars of jazz, but he recorded very little and, more often than not, under poor conditions, as in 1949 with Machito's Afro-Cuban band and in 1950 with a string ensemble. Here and there, sales-minded suggestions from higher up seem to be at work. It was not until 1952 that Bird was to be heard again at his best in a series of pieces recorded two years earlier with Gillespie—LEAP FROG, MOHAWK, BLOOMDIDO, and so forth. Parker's produc-

tion has thus been limited, but his influence doesn't have to
be proved;[2] moreover, because of his quality, his diversity,
and the collaboration he has attracted, he may be regarded
as a regular anthology of modern jazz.

2
Melodic Conceptions

What Charlie Parker contributed in the melodic domain
is much clearer in his improvisations than in his original
themes. Bird sets himself apart from his predecessors by an
admirable boldness in his invention and by revolutionary
tonal conceptions. His phrase frequently approaches polytonality. By that I mean that the notes he sometimes plays
over certain basses are in a polytonal relation with them.
This is notably the case in MOOSE THE MOOCHE, in which
Parker grafts a major chord based on the sixth degree of
the scale onto a dominant seventh, thus forming an altered
thirteenth that suggests two different keys, even though the
notes played do not violate the laws of natural resonance.
This passage (the bridge) may be profitably compared with
the corresponding point in the following chorus, played by
Lucky Thompson, who is an excellent musician but who
is unable to follow Parker's lead in shaking off the bass's
harmonic tyranny.

To cite another contribution, Parker definitely seems to
have been the first to bring off the feat of introducing into
jazz a certain melodic discontinuity that yet avoids inco-

[2] In spite of this, there would still be quite a bit to say about his personal
influence. It is clear that he created a school. What is more, he has left his
mark even on the current style of some of his famous seniors; you can tell,
upon hearing Hawkins in BAY-U-BAH and Carter in WHAT IS THIS
THING CALLED LOVE (J.A.T.P.), that they have listened to him. But, as we
shall see, the new generation has not completely assimilated his acquisitions,
particularly in the field of rhythm. In this sense, Parker's influence has remained more limited than was Armstrong's in his day.

herence. The conciseness of his phrases is surprising; they sometimes seem to have no connection with one another, and still they fit in together beautifully. HOT HOUSE is an excellent example of this apparent contradiction. Parker's chorus, which at first seems made out of miscellaneous melodic bits and pieces, winds up by giving an impression of perfect balance. Even more astonishing is the beginning of the solo in KLACTOVEEDSEDSTENE, which is made up of snatches of phrases that sound completely disconnected, even though they follow an implacable logic.[3]

Those are personal characteristics, the mark of a creative turn of mind. It would be a mistake to conclude from them that Charlie Parker's melodic style is forced and unnatural. Quite the contrary, Bird's phrase is seen to be perfectly limpid as soon as his procedures are recognized. Most of Parker's choruses may be taken as models of sobriety. Particularly in the blues, Parker's knowledge of how to condense what he has to say, preserving only what is essential, is admirable. His solos in BILLIE'S BOUNCE, PARKER'S MOOD, and MOHAWK rank among jazz's great esthetic achievements. The unstrained elegance of the choruses in SCRAPPLE FROM THE APPLE (78 rpm version) and of GROOVIN' HIGH (with Gillespie) bring to mind the grace of someone like Bennie Carter, whose tradition Bird seems to carry on in his lighter moments. The twofold call at the beginning followed by an ornamented descent and the lovely embellishments on fleeting harmonies in SCRAPPLE are the work of a melodic imagination that is as delicately inventive as the one responsible for the brief but exquisite bits by the alto in Hampton's HOT MALLETS and WHEN LIGHTS ARE LOW. However, Parker's talent is infinitely more vast than Bennie Carter's. In another group of solos—those of SHAW 'NUFF, CHEERS, and KO-KO, for

---

[3] The rhythmic and melodic discontinuity discussed in this chapter must not be confused with the discontinuity resulting from a weakness in musical thought (cf. Chapter X, p. 168).

example—tranquil grace gives way to an angular, tormented phrase that has a restless beauty. Most of his solos fall between these two extremes, ranging from calm to drama but preserving at all times a perfect musical coherence.

Charlie Parker's sense of construction is highly developed. For one thing, he knows how to vary his effects within a single solo, using different contrasts with flexibility; for example, in his solo in BLOOMDIDO, after sticking to a fairly low register, he suddenly moves into the high. But for another thing, on a broader scale, he shows that he can conceive a work in its entirety. The way he connects his solo in AN OSCAR FOR TREADWELL to what goes before shows the concern he has for preserving the continuity of musical thought. Nevertheless, it is in paraphrasing that his intelligence flourishes best. Except for Louis Armstrong, no other jazz musician has been able to paraphrase a theme with so sure a touch. But Parker's manner is decidedly different from Armstrong's. Louis transfigures the original melody by subtly distorting it rhythmically and by adding some extra figures; Bird encloses it and leaves it merely implied in a musical context that is sometimes fairly complex. Occasionally, it is true, as in MY MELANCHOLY BABY, he keeps coming back to the theme; but these repetitions, which are rather exceptional in what he has done, were probably suggested by the men in charge of the recording. In DON'T BLAME ME and EMBRACEABLE YOU, which are much more typical, Parker now and again lets the phrase-pretext put in a brief appearance, but at other times it can only be guessed at behind the garland of notes in which it is embedded and which, far from being useless embroidery, form by themselves a perfectly articulated musical discourse of which the theme, hidden or expressed, is merely one of the constituent elements.

Like all improvisers, Parker depends on certain ways of turning a phrase, and these keep popping up in his choruses.

They are never stereotypes, because they form an integral part of what he happens to be saying; they are, rather, typical figures, just like Armstrong's, Bix's, and Sidney Bechet's. First of all, there is his frequent use of an upper-register diatonic embellishment, in rapid notes or triplets; again, an octave jump to a very high note followed by a somewhat lower one (usually down a third); and again, a rapid chromatic descent followed by a brief mounting arpeggio. TAKIN' OFF, with Sir Charles Thompson, combines all these familiar twists. However, to the best of my knowledge, no other jazz soloist has shown anything like Charlie Parker's ability to find new ways of expressing himself. All you have to do, in order to judge the extent of his melodic inventiveness, is to compare the different versions of such pieces as COOL BLUES, BIRD'S NEST, ORNITHOLOGY, and SCRAPPLE that were recorded in a single session and released either together or separately; and isn't recognition of Bird's melodic genius inescapable in the two paraphrases of EMBRACEABLE YOU, each of which gives new life, in a completely different way, to the Gershwin theme? Sometimes the great saxophonist lets his melodic inventiveness simply be guessed at behind the simple choice of a citation and the way it is presented. But Charlie Parker isn't especially fond of this procedure, which is worn ragged by most of today's soloists; on the contrary, he makes citations rarely and always gives them an unexpected relief. We might mention a version of CHERYL, not made for general distribution, in which the way he parodies the famous introduction of WEST END BLUES is a real masterpiece of humor.

3
Rhythmic Conceptions

Many years have gone by since Charlie Parker's art made its appearance, and still at least one of its aspects—perhaps the most essential—has continued to represent a summit in the evolution of jazz. I refer to his rhythmic conceptions, which have been slowly assimilated by his followers but not yet surpassed.

Charlie Parker's idea of rhythm involves breaking time up. It might be said that it is based on half beats. No other soloist attaches so much importance to short notes (eighth notes in quick tempos, sixteenths in slow). In Parker's art, nevertheless, the accent does not fall invariably on the weak part of the beat. Instead of Hawkins' regular accent on the strong beat and certain pronounced syncopations or of Lester Young's flowing style, Bird's accentuation comes alternately on the beat and between beats. The astonishingly rich rhythm of his music comes from this alternation, from these continual oppositions.

Besides, Parker has developed a technique of accentuation that takes rigorous advantage of the notes' differences in intensity and gives his phrase a very special relief. Far from being distributed haphazardly, these accents follow the melodic line faithfully; for instance, an even-numbered eighth note is accented only if it is higher than the notes around it. Parker makes successive notes show a considerably broader range, measured in decibels, than any of his predecessors. Moreover, he follows this revolutionary technique to its logical conclusion; his phrase frequently includes notes that are not played but merely *suggested*. His phrase is so logical and his power of persuasion so great that the ear hears them anyway. Thus, anyone who writes down a Parker chorus is obliged to include, in parentheses, notes that have hardly been played at all (fig. 6). This conception, by virtue of the rhythmic relief it creates, is distinctly favorable to swing. The subtle use of irregular accents and suggested notes makes an important contribution to the extraordinary swing of BLOOMDIDO and AN OSCAR FOR TREADWELL. (It is hardly necessary to point out that Parker's playing

Fig. 6

shows the kind of rhythmic perfection all the great jazzmen have.)

In Parker's work, the rhythmic construction is based on the same feeling for contrast. He likes to make a stormy period wind up calmly, to follow one phrase by another of a different character. His chorus in A NIGHT IN TUNISIA illustrates this aspect of his idiom. It begins with a break of more than sixty sixteenth notes with embellishments that are hard to place exactly in such a deluge. Parker accents certain off-beat notes violently, in such a way that an inexperienced listener often loses the beat in this rhythmic complexity. However, it is all conceived and played with absolute strictness; at the end of this dizzying break, Parker falls right in on the first beat. The following phrases, consisting of eighth notes, form a striking rhythmic contrast to the volubility of the break.

Furthermore, whether in the form of a break or as part of a chorus, voluble figures are, in themselves, one of the most expressive elements in Parker's rhythmic vocabulary. Before Bird, this element was used as decoration, to underline a melodic phrase. Tatum's arpeggios and some of Hodges' breaks have no other purpose. Parker has taken it upon himself to give them a more purely musical meaning. The final phrases in MOHAWK and MY MELANCHOLY BABY are no longer mere flights of the imagination or displays of virtuosity that are basically gratuitous, however welcome or surprising; they are just as much an expression of musical thought as the other phrases. Similarly, his instrumental technique has

allowed him to undertake certain ultra-rapid tempos, un-
furling notes in long, bounding phrases that create a kind
of tumultuous beauty which apparently few listeners up to
now have fully appreciated. The solos of KO-KO, SALT PEA-
NUTS, and LEAP FROG are something quite different from
commonplace technical acrobatics; they evidence a melodic
and rhythmic imagination capable of finding expression in
the greatest mobility, and illustrate a new facet of the phenomenon called swing.

An examination of rhythmic construction in Charlie
Parker's art shows another extremely fascinating aspect of
his thought—the rhythmic diversity of his phrase. We shall
have occasion to give a brief analysis of one of his solos[6] and
to show the richness of his rhythmic vocabulary, so there is
no need to insist on it here, except to note that the variety
of formulas he uses in a single solo makes it possible for him
to avoid all rhythmic monotony and thus to attain a more
nearly perfect idea of swing than perhaps any of his
predecessors.

The melodic discontinuity that we have observed in some
of Charlie Parker's choruses is occasionally matched by an
equally remarkable rhythmic discontinuity. It sometimes
happens, generally in moderate tempos, that the melody and
the rhythm are disjointed in a way that verges on the absurd.
Snatches of melody then become part of a piecemeal method
of phrasing that is surprisingly intense and expressive. The
chorus of KLACTOVEEDSEDSTENE is an excellent example of
this approach, in which a rest, becoming part of the phrase's
contour, takes on new meaning. In the solo of PASSPORT,
melodic fragments chopped off in this way form a series
of hallucinating contrasts to infrequent held notes.

I have just referred to the new way in which Charlie
Parker sometimes uses rests. In a more general sense, one
can say that rests are an important element in his phrasing.

[6] Cf. pp. 148 ff.

He knows how to let a phrase catch its breath perhaps better than any other saxophonist. Remarks made here and there in this chapter have already implied that his art constantly tends toward a kind of polyrhythmical expression. Since he plays a one-voice instrument, Parker can obviously only suggest this aspect of his thought, and he does so by his accentuation. It is up to his partners to fill in the rest. That explains why Bird needs a certain kind of support, why his phrase is almost always sufficiently open to let this other voice, which is not a mere accompaniment, have all the liberty it needs to develop its rhythmic counterpoint without disturbance. Far from sticking out at the soloist's expense, Max Roach, when he accompanies Parker—in SCRAPPLE, for instance—provides him with just the polyrhythmical element he needs. But that has been beyond the understanding of modern jazz's detracters, who fail to appreciate the broad range and group spirit of men like Roach and Clarke.

4
The Performer and the Band Leader

We have just considered the part of Charlie Parker's style that involves his conceptions. However, since jazz is an art in which conception cannot be divorced from means of expression and the way in which creative thought is given form, we must consider his evolution in terms of elements that a classical musicologist would judge to be extramusical. Such is the case with sonority, which each generation of jazzmen conceives in a different way. Charlie Parker's conception may seem surprising at first, and I know more than one person who judges it severely. My own opinion is quite the opposite. Parker's sound does not have Bennie Carter's fullness or Johnny Hodges' expressive vibrato, and seems to do without them for a special reason. It is taut, smooth, almost without

vibrato except for a slow, very broad one in unhurried
tempos. Now and then, a jabbing point emerges, an accented
note on which Parker seems to concentrate a pent-up excess
of feeling and which has a completely different timbre, particularly in the upper register, all the more because Parker's
tone in the lower register often sounds like a tenor sax's.

It would be hard to imagine Bird's tone used in a more
traditionally balanced, symmetrical kind of phrasing, such
as Hawkins'. Parker's purposely hard, cutting sound fits in
naturally with his angular melodic ideas and rhythmic emphasis on accent. The different elements of his style are very
closely related.

He is scarcely less admirable as a performer than as a
creator. Charlie Parker seems to be one of the rare jazzmen
about whom it is possible to say, in the time-honored expression, that they have their instrument completely under
control. Still, it would be useless to consider the musician
and the instrumentalist separately. They are reciprocally
dependent. Hubert Rostaing sees in Parker "an incredible
improviser, who exploits his virtuosity but does so almost
unconsciously, because he has something to say and not because he has worked up a chorus that is hard to play. His
instrumental technique is extraordinary, but personal; he
plays such and such a figure because he 'feels' it (though
sometimes he plays bits of phrases that 'fall under his fingers')
and the most complicated one always has a typical stamp
that is his alone."[5] It would be difficult not to concur with
this opinion, which comes from a man who knows. Admittedly, every great improviser demonstrates a close union
between the idea and its means of expression, but no one
does so more purely than Parker. It is surprising that such
an ever-changing inspiration should find constantly at its
service such agile fingers, and that the transfer from one to
the other should never entail the slightest accident. Signifi-

[5] H. Rostaing: "Charlie Parker," in *Jazz-Hot*, special edition, 1948.

cantly, the only technical slips in Bird's performances come from the reed. His astonishing instrumental technique is to be explained in part by the supreme ease he shows under almost any circumstances and regardless of the tempo adopted. In places where most improvisers, including the very best, tighten up—even if only mentally—Bird preserves a supreme facility that is one of the basic features of his playing. He is just as much at ease in the incisive and angular phrasing of SHAW 'NUFF as in the aerial tranquillity of STUPENDOUS. Torrential KO-KO and elegant SCRAPPLE FROM THE APPLE are products of the same disdainful absence of strain. There is no apparent effort in even his tautest choruses. The only exceptions are some minor works (I am thinking of BEBOP and GYPSY); and the painful circumstances under which they were recorded are no secret. It should be added that Parker's more recent works show even greater control of both his instrument and his ideas, if such a thing is possible. The solo in BLOOMDIDO may be taken as an example of formal perfection.

Charlie Parker is above all an improviser of genius. He doesn't have Louis Armstrong's or Fats Waller's acting gifts and radiance, Gillespie's stage presence, or Duke Ellington's organizing ability. Nevertheless, when he took over the direction of a little band in 1946, he managed at the very outset to give it a style and to maintain it. He showed a sound intuition in his choice of sidemen. Miles Davis is the only trumpeter who could have given his music the intimate character that is one of its essential charms; and the combination of Max Roach and Tommy Potter brought into being a climate of sound such as the history of jazz had never known (DON'T BLAME ME, EMBRACEABLE YOU). Filled out by pianist Al Haig (whose place Bud Powell, John Lewis, and Duke Jordan occasionally took to good advantage), the small group quickly established its unity; and the masterpieces of 1947 demonstrate how vital this unity was to a full ex-

pression of Bird's personality. At no other time, not even
with Gillespie, has Parker ever been so perfectly himself.
Comparing any side of this series with the recordings he
made for "Jazz at the Philharmonic" is enough to demonstrate the importance that the surrounding atmosphere has,
in modern jazz just as in the oldest kind. Regardless of its
strength, Parker's kind of individuality cannot do without
a climate that is favorable to the manifestation of his message. But I am not inclined to overlook the fact that Bird,
unlike so many other great soloists of whom Louis Armstrong is the foremost example, has always arranged to have
himself ideally surrounded.

Charlie Parker's talent as a band leader can be appreciated in many other ways. Didn't he have the idea of replacing the insipid drum solos that traditionally come at the
end of a concert with lively four-bar exchanges between
the drummer and himself? (An expanded version of this
formula is found in LEAP FROG, in which Gillespie's trumpet
comes to spell Buddy Rich's drums after several choruses.)
Didn't Bird introduce such coda-gags as the one in MY MEL-
ANCHOLY BABY, which shows him in an unexpected light?
(In addition to the humorous element, there is an indication
here that the great artist takes himself less seriously than a
number of his colleagues, but then they don't have as much
talent as he does, either.) Finally, wasn't it Parker who, in
conjunction with Miles Davis, brought to jazz the contrapuntal exposition in two equal voices (CHASIN' THE BIRD,
AH-LEU-CHA) that not merely demonstrates an attempt to
get away from exposition in unison, which represents the
limit of most modern jazzmen, but actually reveals a tendency that is still in an embryonic stage in modern jazz?

Thus, astonishingly coherent in spite of his diversity, one
of the three or four greatest personalities of Negro-American
music has found expression in an output that includes all
but a few of modern jazz's most telling works. It has been

said of Parker that he got away from jazz; it has been claimed that bebop, of which he is the principal representative, turned its back on the Negro tradition. Saying this implies a terribly narrow interpretation of that tradition, as well as a refusal to let it evolve. Parker, as we have seen, has everything a great jazzman needs. Let's admit for a moment, nevertheless, that his art may strike some exaggeratedly orthodox observers as lacking certain winning characteristics of jazz as it was conceived before him. Would it even then be necessary to disown music of such beauty? Wouldn't that be attaching too much importance to labels and playing a childish game? Whether Mozart was "baroque" or "rococo" is a question that lost interest as soon as it became evident that he is a great classic. It won't be long before Charlie Parker, prodigious innovator that he is, will also be recognized, in the perspective provided by the history of jazz, as a great classic. The reason is that Parker's universe, in spite of appearances, is as rigorous and as profoundly human as Armstrong's. His rhythm is complex, his sonority harsh, and his melody sometimes disconcerting, but behind this relative hermeticism Parker hides treasures of the imagination and profound sensitivity. His refusal to parade this sensitivity and his basic scorn for all obliging compliance requires us to make an effort; more than any other jazzman, he compels us to hunt for what is essential in his art. That in itself may well be a guarantee of his durability.

Chapter VIII

MILES DAVIS
AND THE COOL TENDENCY

1
A New Feeling

Once past its great periods of classicism, it is not unusual for an art to lose its unity. What happens then is a division into branches of what was a single trunk. Factional differences, which are no longer the expression of conflicts traditionally opposing one period to its predecessor, begin to spring up among the members of a single generation. Modern jazz seems to be caught in this pattern. The conflicts have not yet assumed an aggressive character, but they exist. The bop movement, which we have just been examining as represented by its foremost creator, is only one part of postwar jazz—the most important, perhaps, but not the only one. While the influence of the Minton's group was emerging triumphantly, another tendency was taking shape among jazzmen who were scarcely younger than Gillespie and Parker. It took root in the art of Lester Young. In this way, a musician whose conceptions were so original that he might have seemed impossible to put in any category turned out to be a precursor. His influence, though it merely touched Charlie Parker and his disciples lightly, is evident

116

today, above and beyond bop, in the work of a whole group of young saxophonists who regard the "President" as their spiritual father. Lester's mark has even extended well beyond the saxophone's domain. For a long while, Young was believed to have given the tenor sax a new style; actually, what he did was to give birth to a new conception of jazz.

This new style has been labeled "cool," undoubtedly in allusion to the "hot" jazz of 1925 to 1935. Chronologically, the cool movement represents the furthest point reached to date in the evolution of jazz. Among its representatives, which include both white and colored musicians, are renegades from the movement headed by Parker, such as trumpeter Miles Davis, trombonist J. J. Johnson, and pianist John Lewis; disciples of Lester Young, such as tenor saxophonists Herbie Steward, Al Cohn, Allen Eager, Gene Ammons, Stan Getz, and Wardell Gray; or declared "progressives," such as Lee Konitz, Lennie Tristano, and Billy Bauer.[1] It is too early to judge the value of the work created by these musicians. Moreover, the European critic, who must rely on recordings, is not always in a position to form a valid judgment on the most recent evolution of jazz; he may lack some essential bit of evidence. It is still permissible to observe that up to now the cool tendency has not produced a body of creations that can compare in quantity and quality with what we were given by bop in its most brilliant period (1945-1947). Personally, I can credit the movement with only two incontestable masterpieces, ISRAEL and BOPLICITY, both by the Miles Davis band. That may seem very little, but it is enough to encourage the greatest hopes for a conception that has given such proof of vitality.

In any case, it is both necessary and exciting to study the

[1] The musicians in this last group remain somewhat in the margin of the movement because of an otherwise praiseworthy concern for musical research that sometimes takes them away from jazz. The recorded work of Lee Konitz, nevertheless, makes him rank among the best alto sax soloists.

cool tendency, inasmuch as it is the most up-to-date expression of jazz. Apart from Lester Young, who was more a precursor than an animator, this movement has not been dominated by one man as bop was dominated by Parker or pre-classical jazz by Armstrong, although it has been more homogeneous than might appear. Nevertheless, Miles Davis seems to be a kind of leader. After collaborating for some time with Charlie Parker, this young colored trumpeter, the most gifted of his generation, took the initiative and produced straight off the most representative of the new school's works. More than any other, his art attests the accomplishments and the promise of today's jazz. It seems reasonable, therefore, to recognize his role as more or less predominant throughout this chapter.

We haven't yet defined the cool style. In a very general way, it represents a striving toward a certain conception of musical purity. This effort, which implies a rejection of the hot way of playing and its most typical procedures, finds its justification in the new element it contributed, a kind of modesty in musical expression that was not to be found in jazz before. Even when the performer seems to be letting himself go most completely (and cool musicians, as we shall see, cultivate relaxation), a sort of reserve, by which we do not mean constraint, marks his creative flight, channeling it within certain limits that constitute its charm. It may be said that the cool musicians have brought a new feeling to jazz. With them, jazz becomes an intimate art, rather like what chamber music is by comparison with symphonies. Analytically speaking, their conception shows three principal characteristics: first, a sonority very different from the one adopted by earlier schools; second, a special type of phrase; and finally, an orchestral conception that, without being essential to the style, is not its least interesting element. We are going to consider each of these aspects in turn.

2
The Cool Sonority

At the very core of classical jazz, a reaction was forming
just when a disciplined but violently colored sonority was
being established by the masters of all kinds of instruments,
from Eldridge to Wells and from Hawkins to Hodges, as
the ideal way to express jazz. Bennie Carter, Teddy Wilson,
and Bennie Goodman were among the first exponents of a
new conception that was more sober, more stripped. Carter
tended to underplay attacks, Wilson's touch was unusually
delicate, and Goodman replaced his predecessors' thick
vibrato with a more discreet timbre. Sharp attacks, rough
timbre, hard touch, and vibrato had for a long time been
regarded as essential characteristics of the Negro's sonority,
whereas they were actually just characteristics of the hot
idiom. Lester Young deserves the credit for showing that it
is possible to avoid almost all these features and still produce
authentic jazz. Young's veiled sonority and his almost imperceptible vibrato, which tends to disappear completely in
quick tempos, brought into being an unprecedented musical
climate, the first fruit of the revolution begun by men like
Carter, Goodman, and Wilson. But the indefinable charm
that is all Lester Young's own comes chiefly from his astonishing muscular relaxation. Good jazzmen have always had
to be supple, but Lester has gone beyond being merely
supple to achieve a kind of relaxation that has become something of a cult among his disciples.

In trying to achieve a maximum of relaxation, the cool
musicians at first were merely taking advantage of Lester
Young's example. However, it seems that the young saxophonists went further than their model. In place of Lester's
cloudy sonority, they substituted a still more wispy sound.
They realized that they could do almost completely without

vibrato and sharp attacks and still manage to create as beautiful a quality of sound, in spite of the apparent indifference shown by it, as that produced by the most violently expressive vibrato. Miles Davis did something similar on the trumpet. Doesn't he seem to reject haughtily all exterior ornaments in order to concentrate on giving his tone a serene, undeniably noble resonance? He achieves this by maintaining a constant breath pressure and by "placing" the sound well (just as a singer may be said to "place" his voice forward).[2] He rarely plays forte, even in the upper register. Moreover, he rarely plays in this register. The logic behind his "introspective" style makes him avoid everything that his predecessors indulged in with abandon. Such effects are, in fact, one of the main things cool musicians have given up.

Modern jazz's opponents won't fail to point out that what we have here is a return to the European conception of "purity of sound," and will cite as an argument in their favor the presence of a large proportion of white players among the cool musicians. Their error is understandable. Miles Davis' playing does have fleeting resemblances to the way trumpets are used in symphonies—imperceptible vibrato, the manner in which notes are strung together, and so forth. But a fair examination of what there is to say on the other side is enough to establish, in our opinion, how little weight these comparisons have when brought into opposition with the outstanding feature of the modern jazzman—his relaxed manner, which very few symphonic soloists have. Thanks to this characteristic, one conception differs very markedly from the other in tone production, in legato, and in the way passages are played in the upper register. By the same token, Lee Konitz has obtained from the alto saxophone a diaph-

---

[2] It will be profitable to read, in this connection, Jean Ledru's interesting study, "Le problème du saxophone-ténor," in *Jazz-Hot*, October and December, 1949, and July, 1950.

anous sound that no soloist in the European tradition
has. It is not unthinkable that some use might be made of
this sonority in a symphony orchestra. Pierre Boulez, for
whom I played some of Konitz's recordings, would like to
see European saxophonists get around to adopting it; and I
subscribe to this opinion all the more willingly because the
conception imposed by Marcel Mule and his disciples has
led me personally to avoid using the saxophone except in
my jazz pieces. To date, though, the cool sonority exists only
in jazz, so there is every reason to conclude that it really is a
jazz sonority.

3
The Phrase: Melody and Rhythm

Whereas the evolution of the cool sonority is of considerable interest, it is in certain respects somewhat disappointing
to study the cool phrase. Ignoring what bebop had achieved,
the cool musicians generally adopted outmoded melodic and
rhythmic conceptions. With a few exceptions, they preferred
Lester Young's example to Charlie Parker's; and, though
Young was a prodigious innovator for the classical period,
Bird obviously went much further. This choice has resulted
in a kind of backtracking that may be only temporary but is
nonetheless one of the most disquieting signs in the history
of jazz.

In the field of melody, the cool soloists seem to stick more
closely to the theme, which is often taken from the most
commonplace part of the repertory. They are not always
concerned, as the better bop musicians were, about creating
a common stockpile by means of boldly paraphrasing the
old standards. Is it because they like to or is it for extramusical reasons that Stan Getz records PENNIES FROM HEAVEN
or that Herbie Steward sticks scrupulously close to the

melody in MY LAST AFFAIR? It wouldn't be so bad if, following the example of Lester Young in THESE FOOLISH THINGS, they had sense enough to abandon these weak themes after stating them; but, far from showing any conviction that their raw material needs to be renewed, they sometimes delight in this melodic indigence and become guilty of the most regrettable error their seniors ever committed.[3] Similarly, their variations are less rich and bold than those of their immediate predecessors. They have a definite melodic charm, but all too rarely do they have that spark which brightens the choruses of Parker or even those of Gillespie on his better days. Without question, the best improvisers in the cool movement are those who have been influenced by the bebop spirit of research. Miles Davis, who strikes me as being by far the most interesting cool soloist, played with Charlie Parker for a long time. Still, Lee Konitz on the alto sax and Gerry Mulligan on the tenor show undeniable originality. The fact that Davis had these two sensitive musicians as the principal soloists with him in the band he organized in 1948-1949 accounts in part for the exceptionally successful recordings he made then.

The cool idea of rhythm differs from the bop idea as much by the way in which phrases are shaped as by the role of the accompaniment. Bop's polyrhythmic aspect is scarcely to be heard in the cool musicians' work, and they seem also to have cut out of their vocabulary the Afro-Cuban elements that Dizzy Gillespie introduced into the language of jazz (but they are hardly to be blamed for doing this). Their idiom is purer, perhaps, but also poorer. No cool soloist seems to have made good use of the prodigious enrichment that Charlie Parker brought to jazz rhythm. Miles Davis is the only one this criticism doesn't apply to. His phrasing, which

[3] It must be acknowledged that, melodically, certain themes of Raney, Wallington, Gryce, etc. come off very well. Nonetheless, the spirit behind them does not seem to be so revivifying as the one that animated theme composers of the bop period.

was formerly based on accenting the weak part of the beat
(A NIGHT IN TUNISIA, BILLIE'S BOUNCE, with Parker), has
infinitely greater relief than most cool musicians'. Is his work
with Bird responsible, in this area also, for his being the
most advanced creator of his group? It may very well be.

In the intelligent and allusive style of many of his solos,
the young trumpeter shows a concern for alternation and
contrast that augurs well for what he may create in the
future. It would be well if more of the musicians we consider,
rightly or wrongly, as represented by him were to follow
his lead. Davis' phrasing has a variety that must be called
rare. It is made up of two complementary kinds of phrase.
The first is characterized by mobility and abundance. In
moderate tempos, Davis uses short notes—eighths and even
sixteenths. Not infrequently there occurs in such phrases a
note that might be called a *resting note*. Coming at the end
of a period, it serves as a sort of calm zone between two agi-
tated phrases. Curiously—even paradoxically—the less vibrato
the resting note has, the more it stands out. The second
kind of phrase, which contrasts with the first, is based on a
rhythmic and melodic discontinuity of the kind we observed
in Parker's work. Like Bird, Miles Davis likes to put together
a lot of little melodic fragments separated by rests. The beginning of his chorus in MOVE (fig. 7) constitutes a remark-

FIG. 7

able example of this conception, which is reflected in most
of his quick-tempo solos in the 1949 period. A reasonably
attentive study of this brief fragment shows how well Davis
knows, consciously or unconsciously, how to vary rhythmic

figures within a single phrase. The three-note motif that fills the first four measures of this chorus, repeated in a symmetrical, scale-wise descent, has a central accented note. This note, which is longer than the ones around it, appears three times, like the motif itself, and each time it has a different time value—first it is a quarter note, then a half, finally a dotted quarter. Similarly, first it falls on the second beat, then on the third, and finally on the second half of the third. This asymmetry produces great rhythmic freedom. In that respect, Miles Davis seems more like a bopper than a cool musician.

In both kinds of phrase, the soloist occasionally introduces one or more detached, stressed notes that stick out in their context as an antithesis. They would undoubtedly hurt the music's swing if they weren't played with perfect rhythmic precision. Don't they come directly from Lester Young's vocabulary? In his more recent works, Davis tends to make a more general use of detached notes (s'IL VOUS PLAIT).

At the same time, Davis' essential contribution consists in a variant of the second kind of phrase. This variant is based on a new conception of the long note, the *dancing note,* of which there are abundant examples in the chorus of GODCHILD, between the ninth and twenty-fourth bars. Usually begun on the weak part of a beat, the dancing note —almost always the next to the last one of a motif—finds its resolution in a single note played on either a strong or a weak beat. But what gives it all its value is not so much its syncopated character as the vibrato that enlivens it—a discreet vibrato, though a very perceptible one, which pulsates in a strictly measured way (four oscillations per beat) that has the effect of making the rhythm of the phrase rebound. Besides, this treatment is reinforced by a variation of intensity that puts the note "off center." This rhythmic manipulation of a note taken in its structural unity seems to me a completely new swing phenomenon. Thus Miles Davis, who so willingly does without vibrato, takes it up again and gives it a rhythmic—and accordingly very important—function[4] just when its chances for survival in jazz were becoming doubtful. In the diversity of rhythmic values that make it up and by virtue of the resting and dancing notes it has contributed, Miles Davis' phrase goes further, in some cases, even than Parker's. The only regrettable thing is that these tendencies should be, as they seem to be at present, strictly personal.

The perfectly relaxed playing of cool musicians would call for an equally supple phrasing, a construction of phrases following some precise but rigid idea of rhythm. The truth is that most of the new school's adherents lack rhythmic imagination. Lester Young's phrase represented definite progress, fifteen years ago, because it tended to get away from the bar line. In this direction, his disciples do not seem to have bettered their master's accomplishments. Their phrase always fits into the contour of strong and weak beats. It is true that they got away from a minor tyranny—that of the dotted eighth plus sixteenth, which gives Armstrong's and Hawkins' phrase its characteristic aspect. But they weren't responsible for this liberation, which dates from before the war and was already demonstrated by Lester Young in the first Basie records. Such highly gifted soloists as Stan Getz, Al Cohn, and Zoot Sims have not renewed either the rhythmic or the melodic language of jazz. Herbie Steward is the one who seems to have understood Parker's lesson best; his phrase shows a use of rests and suggested notes that gives it a more intense life. Gerry Mulligan, an artist of exquisite sensitivity, has to his credit above all the emotional impact of his solos, which are sometimes particularly successful melodically. As for Lee Konitz, who also has brilliant gifts, he is more an explorer than an inspired artist; though he

[4] True, many other soloists use a measured vibrato; but its rhythmic function is not so evident anywhere else as in Davis' dancing note.

occasionally tries to use a technique of accentuation rather like Bird's, he falls back at the first opportunity into a regular pattern in which the strong beats are like immovable posts. There is a hundred times more rhythmic richness in Parker's solo based on WHAT IS THIS THING CALLED LOVE (HOT HOUSE) than in the version that Tristano's partner has given of the same theme (SUBCONSCIOUS-LEE).

Just what has the cool style brought to rhythmic infrastructure?[5] Here again there seems to be a kind of backtracking. An ardent defender of the cool musicians, Henri Renaud, after noting that "the same accompanists are found in both styles" (bop and cool), recognizes that "drummers have a general tendency [in the cool style] toward a greater rhythmic continuity," because, he adds, "the cool soloists' phrases, which are more legato than Parker's, call for a more sustained support."[6] This implied disavowal of Kenny Clarke's contributions, supplementing a general disavowal of Parker's rhythmic ideas, would in most cases bring us back to Count Basie's rhythm if the modern accompanists didn't strive for a kind of complete relaxation that makes actual performance cast a different light on the basic meaning behind what they do. Whereas the classical rhythm section joined punch to flexibility, played somewhat nervously, and made the hearer feel, just when everything was swinging along most smoothly, that the tempo was being accelerated, the cool rhythm section performs similar figures in a completely different spirit. The tempo may be equally strict in both cases, but the drummer's perfectly relaxed manner of playing in today's jazz is enough to modify the whole rhythmic perspective; in this case, the listener will have a vague feeling that the band is slowing down, though not swinging any the less for that. This new manner, which was

[5] What the author means by *infrastructure* is explained in Chapter XII, pp. 197. ff.—D. N.

[6] Henri Renaud: "Qu'est-ce que le jazz cool?" in *Jazz-Hot*, April, 1952.

already perceptible in certain bop works of 1947, is one of modern jazz's principal contributions.

4
The Miles Davis Band

Is the cool style appropriate for bands of the size reached by those at the end of the classical period? Probably not. The ten brasses and five saxes in Hampton's 1946 band had one object—to create maximum shock power. The sound aimed at by the band that Miles Davis organized in 1948, on the contrary, was a kind of unified half-tint. It was essentially a "chamber orchestra" by virtue of both its composition and the style imposed on it. Its melodic section consisted of six instruments: trumpet, trombone, French horn, tuba, and alto and baritone saxes. It was a rejection of the hot idiom that permitted use of the French horn, which had for a long time been excluded from jazz bands. Similarly, Davis reintroduced the tuba, which had been highly rated by the oldtimers but eliminated during the pre-classical period. It wasn't brought back, be it noticed, simply to turn out rudimentary basses, but rather to be included among the melodic instruments. This plebeian was becoming an aristocrat. To the usual distribution of ranges, with two middle voices balanced by two high and two low ones, was added a distribution of timbres, with each instrument supplying a special color that still blended harmoniously into the whole. The rhythm section was limited to three basic elements—piano, bass, and drums. Davis didn't keep either the guitar, which would be difficult to manipulate in the harmonic and rhythmic climate he had in mind, or the bongo drums, which provided an element of exterior coloration that would be out of place in this intimate music. Accordingly, the band

had no more than nine men, just one more than King
Oliver's.

What remained to be done was to give the group a basic
homogeneity. Did Miles Davis manage to do this by a careful
choice of collaborators—arrangers and instrumentalists—or
did the initiative come from Gerry Mulligan and Gil Evans,
as Barry Ulanov[7] leads us to understand? Was it these two
musicians who foresaw Davis as the leader of a band that was
really their idea and for which they had composed scores
even before it was actually organized? In any case, the problem for these arranger-composers was to write music that
the performers could play in the same spirit as they would
have improvised solos. Evans and Mulligan were joined by
John Carisi and John Lewis. All of them had participated,
as improvisers, in the cool movement, so there was every
reason to hope that the music they conceived would be profoundly impregnated with that spirit. The instrumentalists
themselves were chosen among the young school's most remarkable improvisers. It was vitally important that they
should express themselves naturally in a common language.
The presence of an outside element, even a valuable one,
would have weakened the band by destroying its unity. As
it happened, only Bill Barber, on tuba, was not one of the
movement's leaders, and he showed great flexibility, fitting
into his new surroundings very well.

Although the Miles Davis band played in public on several
occasions, it owes its fame to records. Nevertheless, it recorded very few sides. Its reputation was made by eight
pieces recorded during two sessions in New York in 1949.[8]
In the first, the band included seven white musicians (Kai
Winding, Junior Collins, Lee Konitz, Gerry Mulligan, Al
Haig, Joe Shulman, and Bill Barber) and two colored ones

---

[7] Barry Ulanov: "Gerry," in *Metronome*, April, 1951.

[8] A third session took place the following year. ROCKER, DECEPTION, and
MOON DREAMS were recorded then but not released until much later.

(Miles Davis and Max Roach). In the second, this proportion was almost reversed, since Winding, Collins, Haig, and Shulman were replaced, respectively, by J. J. Johnson, Sanford Siegelstein, John Lewis, and Nelson Boyd. Furthermore, Max Roach was replaced by Kenny Clarke, so only Davis, Konitz, Barber, and Mulligan remained. It is hard to compare the work of the two groups. One thing is certain: the second plays in a more relaxed way than the first. The two most successful sides, ISRAEL and BOPLICITY, both come from the second session. It should be noted, however, that the first group, which perhaps had less practice, had to handle arrangements that were trickier to perform.

Since some of the pieces (BUDO, MOVE, VENUS DE MILO) are interesting almost exclusively for the playing of the soloists and the rhythm section, we shall consider only four sides in this brief study of the cool orchestral language. Two of them, JERU and GODCHILD, arranged by Gerry Mulligan, were recorded during the first session; BOPLICITY, arranged by Gil Evans, and ISRAEL, John Carisi's work, come from the second.

What do these two records bring us? They seem to offer, not merely the promise, but the first fruits of a renewal that has a twofold significance, first for what the music represents in itself and second for the conclusions it permits us to draw about certain conceptions demonstrated in it. To begin with, let us limit ourselves to a consideration of melody, harmony, and orchestration. The convergence of a fairly special orchestral combination and the cool style of playing created an absolutely new sonority, which is what was meant by calling it a *fresh sound.* The term is a good one. It gives a fairly accurate definition of this music's special climate and obviates certain misunderstandings on the part of listeners whom its small quota of the hot element might have led to speak in terms of "straight" jazz or even of "sweet" music. There is no justification for making such comparisons. Both "straight" jazz and "sweet" music, which are commercial products, make use of a sonority and a melodic and harmonic language that are exaggeratedly sugar-coated. The work of the Miles Davis band, on the contrary, boasts excellent melody and expresses it, as we have observed, by means of a sonority that is to be admired precisely because it forgoes all ornament; and if the firmness of its harmonic language is sometimes veiled by an apparent indistinctness of timbres, analysis shows it to be there nonetheless. Davis uses some of the same clusters as Gillespie, although the latter made them seem more aggressive because of their violently expression-istic context. Elevenths, thirteenths, and polytonal chords alternate with more consonant combinations; the successions are generally more supple, less mechanical than in Gillespie's work. Frequently—and this is one respect in which the new works fit into the jazz tradition—the harmony develops in the form of chord clusters garnished with acid dissonances. Judging by ear (naturally, I haven't had a chance to look at the scores), I'd say that the rather special character of these dissonances comes less from the actual notes than from the orchestration. Since the most dissonant note is more often than not assigned to the French horn, which has a less pene-trating timbre than the other instruments, the result is an equilibrium in the superposition of timbres and intervals that is not the smallest charm of GODCHILD and BOPLICITY. This sort of interpenetration of instrumentation and har-mony would repay closer study, with the scores in hand.

Generally speaking, the arrangements played by the Miles Davis band treat each section as a unit. Nevertheless, as we have just observed, the diversity of timbres among the winds adds a great deal of freshness. Moreover, the arrangers have shown a certain amount of flexibility, occasionally dividing this section. The voices are not yet really independent, but they are clearly moving in that direction. The writing of the middle voices in GODCHILD and the attempted polyphony of ISRAEL are evidences of an effort to achieve some still vague goal, which I would define as a worked-out counterpoint in which each voice is conceived as if it were improvised. Such music would require its creators to study a lot and to make a great effort of adaptation; but what possibilities a kind of jazz based on this principle would have! Miles Davis' beautiful passage in the second part of the central bridge in BOPLICITY, which imitates so delicately the ascending melodic figure stated a few bars earlier by the clear voices of the band, gives a cautious glimpse of what an orchestral language based on this conception might be.

Other details of orchestration and melody are worth noting. Octave doubling, a holdover from bop's unisons, is fairly frequent, notably in the central bridge of BOPLICITY and in the exposition of ISRAEL and GODCHILD. On this last side, the exposition, which is assigned to the tuba and baritone sax, begins in a very low register; the color of the sound becomes brighter as the melody rises; then, in a second phase, the theme is taken up by the whole wind section. The gradation is skillful, and George Wallington's nimble theme lends itself nicely to such treatment. In terms of melodic analysis, the piece contains in the fifth measure a figure in triplets that is typical of the classical period; on the other hand, the central bridge of BOPLICITY begins with a phrase obviously inspired by bop. Except for these two relatively minor reminiscences, the melodic language expressed by the themes and the arrangements would seem to account in large part for the originality of these works. On this score, the most remarkable side is probably ISRAEL, which offers a rather astonishing renewal of the blues.

ISRAEL is an example of blues in a minor key, like Ellington's KO-KO. Combining the minor scale and the scale used in the blues results in a scale like the mode of D With true musical intelligence, John Carisi has played around with this ambiguity, extending the modal color of his composition by making fleeting references to other modes and by using

defective scales. The most significant passage in this respect
is the end of the trumpet solo (fourth chorus), in which a
countermelody in parallel fifths accompanies Davis' improvisation. Since the soloist, too, has caught the modal atmosphere of the piece perfectly, the combination of his melody
and the underlying harmony is an exceptionally happy one.
It should be added that the blue notes, which figure naturally
in each of the modes employed, help to make the piece sound
like the blues but do not have the kind of expressive singu-
larity that makes them stand out from the other degrees in
the regular blues scale. Finally, ISRAEL suggests two other
observations, one concerning the melody, which moves chiefly
by scale steps at some times and largely by leaps at others,
and the other concerning the orchestral language, which
curiously heightens the effect of the lower voices by making
them very mobile (particularly in the second and seventh
choruses, which are the most polyphonic of all)

5
Is Modern Jazz Opposed to the Four-Bar Unit?

Broadening our horizon, let us now consider the second
part of what has to be said about the Miles Davis band. The
problems posed here touch upon the very essence of jazz. A
double challenge seems to be hurled at the jazz tradition by
these works, a challenge that has scarcely been formulated so
far, but that will undoubtedly become acute sooner or later
and that throws into question the two aspects of jazz that
have up to now been regarded as unshakable—its four-bar
unit of construction and its 4/4 time. Actually, the challenge
to the four-bar unit is not the first of its kind. Duke Ellington, in CONCERTO FOR COOTIE, had made a bold break with
this tradition. We know that Ellington, however, even when
he conceived a seven-bar phrase,* didn't completely follow

* Cf. Chatper VI, pp. 82-83.

through with it and used a kind of transitional figure to re-establish a certain equilibrium, winding up with an even number of bars. Gerry Mulligan, as we shall see, goes much further.

In BOPLICITY, Gil Evans begins an attack on the tradition by making the last phrase of his theme run into the following chorus; however, here as in CONCERTO FOR COOTIE, there is a compensation. Mulligan doesn't begin his solo before the end of the first bar, so that there are still thirty-two bars in the exposition and sixteen in the baritone sax chorus. Nonetheless, the melody's final rebound, which has an exquisite musical effect, seems to show its resistance to being tied down to a rigid framework. This resistance shows up again during the second chorus, where the first part of the bridge extends over six bars (instead of four), giving the two voices, which play in octaves at first, time enough to split up in an attractive counterpoint before coming back together. The last part of the phrase, in which the trumpet evokes the figure just played, covers only four bars. It introduces a particularly successful paraphrase of the theme, which remains in suspense and blends very smoothly into the following chorus, in which each eight-bar period is treated in a different way, like a series of variations. We should call attention here, even at the price of being taken away from our subject, to the astonishing musical quality of the first eight bars of this final chorus, in which the dialogue between the soloist (Miles Davis) and the band is worthy of Ellington at his best. Mention should also be made of the gradual leveling off of sound that begins with the paraphrase at the end of the second chorus. First there is the whole band, then Davis accompanied by the winds, then the rhythm section alone, then just the piano; and finally the initial theme is taken up again by the band in a decrescendo that one might wish more pronounced. BOPLICITY is enough to make Gil Evans qualify as one of jazz's greatest arranger-composers.

The admittedly rather weak challenge to traditional structure that an analysis of BOPLICITY reveals is strengthened, in GODCHILD and JERU, by a much more sensational challenge to the unity of the bar. If my recollection is accurate, it is the first time in the history of jazz that the permanence of the 4/4 bar becomes doubtful. Will this revolutionary attempt bear fruit? It is much too early to tell. All the analyst can do is record facts. The exposition of GODCHILD drastically "reconsiders" the traditional structure of this classical thirty-two-bar theme with bridge. The addition of first two beats and then four to the initial phrase makes the first period cover seventeen and a half bars instead of sixteen. The bridge, on the other hand, is half a bar shorter than customary. Only the final phrase keeps its original structure in the exposition. JERU is still more revolutionary. It includes four choruses in all. The exposition begins in the traditional way with a double eight-bar phrase. The fact that the bridge has twelve bars would not be surprising in itself if five of them—from the fourth to the eighth—were not in 3/4 time.[10] The reprise covers nine bars. Here, then, is an exposition with an uneven number of bars and of beats. The same is true of the final re-exposition. Only the second chorus, which is set aside for Davis' improvisation, is brought back to the customary proportions. The third has thirty-two bars also, but two of them, the fourth and the twelfth, are in 2/4.

It is apparent that the traditional four-bar unit of construction meets a definite check in this composition. The most interesting innovation is undeniably the 3/4 bars in the first and last choruses. They do not, in reality, seem so much a change of measure as a suspension of meter. The question that inevitably arises is, Does the music continue to swing? A decisive answer is hard to give. Certainly, listen-

---

[10] Gerry Mulligan, who wrote the arrangement, will surely excuse me if my description does not correspond exactly to his manuscript. I have no way of being absolutely sure just how to divide the forty-three beats in this bridge.

ing to this passage creates an incontestable annoyance, a feeling of floating around; but neither effect is enough to destroy the impression of swing established by the preceding phrases. There is a kind of momentum that could be modified only by brake pressure, and what the listener feels is that there is not more control but less. Moreover, even if the attempt were a total failure, that would not rule out certain possibilities. Who could be surprised if a jazz musician, accustomed to playing 4/4 rhythms, were to be thrown for a loss by the sudden appearance of 3/4? But Davis and Mulligan's attempt, precisely because it is neither an unqualified failure nor an unqualified success, authorizes us to wonder whether it hasn't actually become possible to express swing using other bars beside 4/4 and 2/4. The experiment had never been given a fair trial. Before the war, Bennie Carter had recorded—if I remember correctly—a WALTZIN' THE BLUES that was entirely in 3/4, but he did so under poor conditions and without the help of a band made up of real jazzmen. As far as I am aware, no one since then had tried to follow up his attempt, so it could not have much effect. We must hope that good jazz musicians will pursue the experiment begun in JERU with enough perseverance to make possible some definite conclusion, favorable or not. But Davis and Mulligan deserve credit for having made it possible to ask the question. JERU and GODCHILD show a determination to get away from the four-bar unit that may soon spread from arrangers to improvisers.

As we said, it is too early to draw up a balance sheet on what the cool musicians have done. All we can do is modestly give our impressions, which are contradictory. Cool jazz presents a mixture of reassuring and disquieting elements. The very artists who repudiate Parker and go back to Young are looking, sometimes timidly but with a certain persistence, for a way to renew jazz. They make music for music's sake, scorning even the most remunerative of spectacular effects.

Many of them who are as good as any professional musicians would rather hold another job on the side than have to make commercial concessions. This attitude speaks well for their conscientiousness and their sincerity, both of which are attractive qualities, but valuable works are not necessarily the result of either one or the other. To date, the cool musicians have brought us more promises than results. But isn't the existence of these promises the essential thing, however uncertain the path in which they seem to involve jazz may be? Quite apart from their value as pure jazz, sides like BOPLICITY and GODCHILD direct jazz toward a language that seems to hold great potential riches; ISRAEL shows a fertile determination to investigate polyphonic writing; JERU boldly calls for a re-examination of form, construction, and meter. Men like Evans and Mulligan seem to have understood that the principal objective of the arranger should be to respect the personality of each performer while at the same time giving the group a feeling of unity. There may well result from all this, sooner or later, a completely renewed jazz that, without renouncing its tradition, would find its justification in a new classicism, which bop no longer seems capable of bringing about. True, it is also possible to believe that music so essentially intimate and excessively polished may lose some of jazz's essential characteristics and cease to be anything but a devitalized successor. Only time will tell which of these two hypotheses corresponds to what the future actually holds.

III

THE PROBLEM OF IMPROVISATION

Chapter IX

MELODY
IN
JAZZ

Rhythm and the sound itself, by which jazz is usually distinguished from European music, are not the only elements of which music is made up. What jazz has contributed in these two areas is revolutionary, in a sense; but has it not made a contribution in other domains? And, if it has, what can be the nature of this contribution?

Looking for the answer to just such questions is the purpose of studying jazz, which, like any other new discipline, has important blank spaces to be filled in. There are three fields to explore—melody, harmony, and architectonics. The last may be put aside right away, for it seems certain that jazz's contribution in this domain is virtually nil. Jazz is not constructed music. To date, it has avoided structures of even the slightest complexity. What is there to be surprised about in that? For one thing, the improviser needs a simple structure, without which he would risk either getting lost or at least being hampered in his movements. For another, the jazz arranger has not yet even turned his attention to the problems of architectonics that have constantly preoccupied European composers since the Middle Ages. The only structure used in jazz is the theme and variations, which is the simplest of all and the one best adapted to improvisation. Generally, the succession of choruses that make up the body of a piece are supplemented merely by an introduction, occasionally by a coda, and still more infrequently by one or more interludes. Since, in addition, dance music requires a systematic squareness of construction, there is clearly no reason to look in that quarter for jazz's originality. All these processes are employed with greater flexibility in seventeenth-century dance suites and even in the Viennese waltzes our great-grandparents were so fond of. Let us, therefore, turn to another aspect of the musical universe, noting merely that architectonics is the only domain in which the jazz musician has taken almost no interest and in which no evolution worthy of the name has taken place so far.

1
Does Jazz Have a Special Harmonic Language?

In the field of harmony, on the other hand, its evolution has been considerable. From the almost exclusively consonant harmony of ragtime to the polytonal clusters of bebop, jazz has never stopped enriching its language. Does that mean that this language is peculiar to it, that it created it, or at least revived it, as it did the 4/4 bar in the field of rhythm? I'm afraid not.

We know that the harmony of the first ragtime pieces came from the polka, the quadrille, and the military march. In all these forms is found the same rudimentary language, centered entirely around the use of two main chords, the tonic and the dominant ("C major — G seventh"). Little by little, this language became richer and more refined. Other degrees of the scale were called into play. The added sixth was inserted to sweeten the major triad, the ninth to go the seventh one better. It wasn't only pure jazz that followed this

evolution, but all kinds of popular music in America, from
Paul Whiteman to Hollywood film scores. Did the impetus
come from the jazzmen, or did they merely follow the example set by "commercial" musicians? The second hypothesis
is the more persuasive. It would definitely seem to be the
harmony of Tin Pan Alley songs that influenced jazz pianists
and arrangers; except for Duke Ellington and, later on, certain boppers, jazz musicians merely strung along with a
movement that was much larger in scope than Negro music.

Jazz's harmonic language, therefore, seems largely borrowed, both directly, from popular American music, and
indirectly, from the influence of European art on this music.
Nevertheless, there can be no question of confusing King
Cole's harmonies with those of Debussy, from which they
are indirectly derived. The reason is that jazz musicians' ears
are better than their education, and that they often have
more feeling than taste. If a new combination of notes falls
pleasantly enough on the ear, it has every chance of being
adopted by them and of outliving several generations of
harmonic "innovators." Such has been the case with the
added sixth, which has persisted in jazz for more than thirty
years despite its deplorable tameness. In other words, jazz
musicians, with a few rare exceptions, do not have strict
enough standards of harmonic beauty to know how to avoid
certain chords or progressions.

On the contrary, the really good European composer will
not write a harmony that "caresses" the ear. He will reject
such shoddy wares just as the good painter will voluntarily
do without certain easy effects. It is partly for this reason
that the greatness of jazz is still contested by many musicians
of classical training who, though attentive and open-minded,
cannot help being annoyed and irritated by these harmonic
weaknesses. On the other hand, jazz musicians—or fans—who
don't have the proper background for an appreciation of the
harmonic density and weight of so-called "serious" music's

masterpieces may well find in the harmony of men like King Cole or Tatum a pleasant and not at all negligible substitute. There is no harm done except when such music becomes pretentious. Some of Gillespie's semi-symphonic works come to mind, but charity dictates silence.

Naturally, these reservations must not be taken too literally. There are, fortunately, some exceptions. Certain arrangements of Gillespie's band—the one of 1946-1949—trampled on conventions. Ellington sometimes had admirable strength harmonically (ko-ko). Occasionally Teddy Wilson's countermelodies touch up a commonplace background with real musical intelligence. But such summits are all too rare. The rest of the time, jazz musicians spoil their gifts by a systematic harmonic sugar-coating that, precisely because it makes possible some pretty effects from time to time, shows how far they are from realizing that prettiness is the enemy of beauty.

That leaves the blues, which are the exception that proves the rule. The modal color of the blues engenders an harmonic climate that avoids banality. Here again the language is made up of rudimentary chords, but, unlike ragtime's "tonic-dominants," the original blues' subdominant sevenths and the modal undercurrents resulting from the blue notes have a real beauty of their own. Unfortunately, the blues could evolve only at the expense of an almost total renunciation of their origins. Their harmonic language was padded out with much of the trash used in popular songs. Thus emasculated, some of King Cole's blues, for example, are as weak harmonically as a slow piece used in Hollywood.

True, the blues have been handled in various ways. The boppers filled them with passing chromatics and polytonal chords, obtaining results that were sometimes interesting but often not appropriate to their original climate, which Erroll Garner has stuck to more closely by not going so far toward modernization. In moving from the street to the

night club and from the night club to the concert hall, the
blues have lost their simplicity. It is not certain that what
they have gained in exchange has been a sufficient compensation. But if they had remained faithful to their origins, they
undoubtedly would not have evolved at all; and music that
fails to evolve is dead.

To sum up, jazz musicians have no special reason for
taking pride in an harmonic language that, besides being
easily acquired, does not really belong to them but rather
to a "light harmony" that North America borrowed from
decadent Debussyism.

These observations do not work in jazz's favor. It was only
honest to make them, and I have done so without worrying
about the arguments that opponents of this music may draw
from them. Jazz is well enough established by this time to
be able to stand the truth, even when it is unfavorable.
Moreover, it would be a mistake to exaggerate the importance of these restrictions. Harmony is not the only thing in
music. In jazz, precisely, its importance remains secondary.

2
The Melodic Phrase in Jazz

I took up the subject of harmony only by way of introduction. What I have said about it was necessary for an
understanding of what follows. However, the main object
of this study is to throw light on certain problems that more
particularly concern *melody*.

Melody may be defined as "a succession of sounds that
describe, by their varying pitches, a musical curve."[1] This
definition, however, takes into account only what is absolutely essential, and for this reason is necessarily summary.[2]

[1] Evelyne Reuter.
[2] That is exactly why I have chosen it. The problems considered in this
chapter would become still more complex if they had to be examined in

The two principal elements of melody are the *interval*, by virtue of which it generally has some connection with a modal series of tones such as the major or minor scale, and its *rhythmic articulation*, which establishes a hierarchy among the sounds by making some longer or more accented than others. In this way is formed the *phrase*, which is usually accepted as the basic unit of musical discourse.

Two types of phrase exist side by side in jazz, just as in European music; one might be called *theme phrase* and the other *variation phrase*. They can hardly be confused, for their rhythmic equilibrium is not the same. The theme phrase is more stripped, less diffuse, because it has less ornament than the variation phrase. The latter may be subdivided into two principal types, the *paraphrase* and the *chorus phrase*. The first retains definite melodic affinities with the theme phrase from which it springs; the second, which is a kind of free variation, gets away from it completely. Thus, it may be said that the first eight bars of Hawkins' BODY AND SOUL are of the first type, the paraphrase; the main notes of the melody clearly correspond to those of the theme. On the other hand, in the second chorus of the famous improvisation may be found good examples of the chorus phrase, in which the only thing the theme and the variation have in common is the harmonic foundation (fig. 8)

Whereas the paraphrase may very well be the work of an arranger—Duke Ellington has turned out a number of written examples—the chorus phrase is by definition part of the soloist's improvised language. It is conceived, for understandable reasons, in complete liberty. Freed from all melodic and structural obligation, the chorus phrase is a simple emanation inspired by a given harmonic sequence. In the case of certain themes, especially riff themes, that do not

terms of modern conceptions that recognize the basic identity of harmony and melody.

FIG. 8

First line: BODY AND SOUL—Green's original theme (published by Chappell).
Second line: Hawkins' paraphrase (beginning of the exposition).
Third line: Measures 9 to 12 of Hawkins' second chorus.

have enough melodic relief to support paraphrase, the chorus
phrase seems to be the only possible way of making a solo
variation. Take Hawkins' CRAZY RHYTHM, for example. From
a strictly melodic point of view, there is no relation whatsoever between one of the four saxophonists' choruses and the
theme; it might even be said of such a variation that it is a
variation on no theme at all. It is well known, for that
matter, that some improvisations on the blues are not based
on any melodic theme, as in the case of many BLUES IN B FLAT
and other BLUES IN F recorded in jam sessions.

3
The Melodic-Harmonic Relationship: The Do-Mi-Sol-Do Technique

That brings us to one of the most important aspects of

the problem of improvisation in jazz—the melodic-harmonic
relationship. What form does this problem assume at the moment when the soloist gets ready to take a chorus? All he
has to go on, if his improvisation is to be the kind of free
variation we are now considering, is the harmonic foundation, made up of a certain number of interrelated tonal
sequences. According to the shape of these sequences and
their number, the foundation may be said to belong to the
"usual" type (CHRISTOPHER COLUMBUS, I GOT RHYTHM, and
so forth), the blues type, or some other more complex type.[3]
There is only one rule: the improvised melody must fit
in with the basic harmonies, either by using only notes that
belong to these chords or, if other notes are introduced, by
having enough key notes to permit the melodic-harmonic
relationship to be clearly established around them.

It is perfectly clear that each improviser reacts in his own
way to an harmonic progression, according to his own musical ideas and his creative ability. A musician with only a
mediocre gift of melodic invention will naturally choose the
first procedure, which consists of breaking each chord up
and stringing out the notes in a more or less freely chosen
order (for the melodic line is sometimes determined, not by
real creative invention, but by habit-guided fingers). It may
not be completely impossible to invent an admirable melodic
line using only notes of the major triad, but such an exception would be a real work of genius; usually an exclusive
use of this procedure results in uninspiring monotony.
Vivaldi was able to write, in the solo parts of his concertos,
fairly beautiful melodic lines largely based on breaking up
chords; but jazz has a different perspective. Apart from the
rich accompaniment he joined to them, Vivaldi's periods,
which evolved harmonically rather than melodically, were

[3] Harmonically, the "usual" type is based on a succession of the first,
sixth, second, and fifth degrees, the blues on one of the first, fourth, and
fifth degrees.

brightened by important modulations. Jazz themes—and particularly the blues—have a static structure that does not permit such developments.

Milton Mezzrow's solo in ROYAL GARDEN BLUES provides a good illustration of what has just been said. A quick glance at these two choruses (fig. 9) makes one thing clear at the outset: most of the solo is based on a continual use of chords

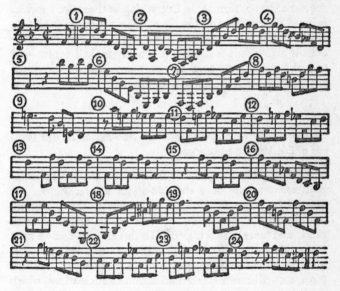

FIG. 9

ROYAL GARDEN BLUES—Milton Mezzrow's solo.

played in arpeggio. Measures 1, 2, 6, 7, 8, 13, 14, 15, 17, 18, 19, 21, and 22 proceed directly from what might be called the "do-mi-sol-do" technique.[4] The rest of the solo is con-

---

[4] The last D in measure 12 seems to be simply an involuntary note, a slip in performance, like the F in measure 17. The effect of both is too unpleasant to be attributed to Mezzrow's taste as a musician; it is surely his awkwardness as a performer that is responsible for them.

structed in the same spirit, the exceptions to the rule of breaking up the chord being too superficial to give the melodic line even a minimum of character. Some of these exceptions are clearly mechanical. Thus, the E♭ of measures 11 and 12 might be considered a melodic find if it weren't visibly part of a formula, a kind of stereotype that the soloist "has in his fingers"; measure 23, where it shows up in exactly the same way, confirms this. Everything in these two choruses is based on breaking up the chord. Their melodic indigence would make this technique deserve formal condemnation even if a rhythmic weakness—to which we shall return—did not also contribute here to the poor effect of continual arpeggios (that is, of broken-up chords).

4
The Melodic-Harmonic Relationship: The Problems of Foreign Notes and of Enriching the Foundation

If the mediocre improviser is in a way obliged by unin-ventiveness to use only the "do-mi-sol-do" technique, the great artist knows how to free himself from this yoke and, starting with the same harmonic base, to create a much richer and more varied melody. To this end, he uses—almost always without going out of his way to do so—a large number of such devices as appoggiaturas (or grace notes), passing tones, embellishments, retardations, and anticipations, which add flexibility to his musical discourse and free him from the harmony's tyranny. A comparison of how Charlie Parker handles the blues (fig. 10) with the example by Mezzrow already discussed is enough to show the gulf that separates the improviser of genius from the musician of limited gifts. True, Bird's choruses do not at all appear as a systematic negation of the principle of breaking up the chord. Such an attitude would be arbitrary and would lead to even more stiffness than Mezzrow's oversimplified technique. There are

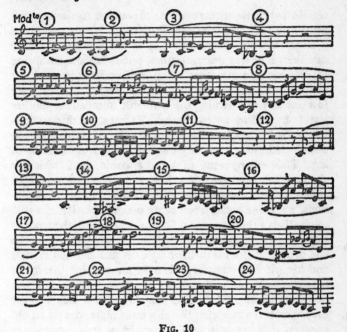

FIG. 10

COOL BLUES—Charlie Parker's solo.

fairly frequent borrowings from this technique in the example cited (notably at the end of measures 3 and 7). However, the chord played in arpeggio shows up here only as one element of the phrase, blending harmoniously into a whole that is homogeneous and varied at the same time. It is a far cry from the monotonous, unrelieved procedure followed in ROYAL GARDEN BLUES.

To be fair, we should note that Parker is helped out in what he does by the use the rhythm section makes of passing chords. But this kind of chord is one of the elements of Parker's language; the way Parker treats the blues involves certain harmonic sequences that are added to the original progression at the soloist's instigation.

Such an observation does not at all detract from the significance of this demonstration, but it has the advantage of drawing our attention to an interesting aspect of the melodic-harmonic relationship. The passing chord is actually just one way of enriching the harmonic foundation; another way is by adding notes—ninths, elevenths, or thirteenths— to the basic chord, and still another is by grafting to the principal chord a secondary one borrowed from a different key. This enlargement of the harmonic field, which is characteristic of modern jazz, is matched by a corresponding enlargement of the melodic field. To say nothing of successions, a six-note chord offers more melodic possibilities to a soloist than a three-note one. On the other hand, the modern improviser, accustomed to branch out on complex harmonies and dependent for his melodic style on such harmonies, may find himself in a quandary when he has nothing but major triads to work with (for it is not always true that if you can do what is difficult, you can do what is easy). What happens when a musician like this must improvise on an old standard that has only such harmonies as it was customary to use in dance music twenty years ago? The soloist asks the accompanying pianist to remodel the old theme's harmony, using the procedures we have just enumerated. This harmonic rejuvenation—which is just like the treatment undergone by the blues, to which we have already referred— is generally enough to place the piece within the modern improviser's range. Some pieces that prove especially resistant to this kind of rejuvenation are abandoned once and for all. Often, this treatment becomes traditional in turn, so that the original harmonies are forgotten. Since Hawkins, BODY AND SOUL is no longer played with the harmonies indicated by Green, its composer.

Inversely, a musician of the old school, getting hold of a

relatively recent theme, may feel hampered by the nature
of the harmonies wanted by the composer. Such a musician
will accordingly ask his pianist to remodel the harmonic
line to correspond to the principles on which his own
melodic style is based. It is rarer for things to happen this
way, admittedly; the oldtimers usually stick to the repertory
of their epoch. But Sidney Bechet's attitude when he asked
Peiffer to play LAURA without ninths and passing chords was
basically just as legitimate as Parker's when he made KO-KO
out of CHEROKEE.

For that matter, it would be stupid to consider a broadening of the basic harmony as necessarily leading to the
invention of more valuable melodic lines. It has been amply
shown that very beautiful melodies can be created out of a
small number of very simple chords. By enlarging their
harmonic range—and, consequently, their melodic range—
musicians of the last generation have simply been obeying
the inexorable law of evolution.

The chorus phrase, then, seems closely tied to the harmonic foundation that engenders it—all the more closely,
it may be said, as its melodic connections with the theme
become more and more tenuous. Even the example of records
made without rhythm section—notably by Hawkins—does
not invalidate this observation: Playing alone, Hawkins
makes a mental reconstruction of the harmonic foundation
and improvises over that. The harmonic foundation is not
only a springboard that the improviser needs but also a
framework without which his invention could not flourish,
at least under present-day conditions of jazz, with that minimum of form which music of any value needs.

5
The Rhythmic Articulation of the Phrase

Thus far we have considered the chorus phrase only in
terms of the melodic-harmonic relationship. The melodic-

rhythmic relationship, which now comes up for discussion, is not the least important. What is involved is, more precisely, that rhythmic articulation which, as we have already said, determines the hierarchy of the different notes that make up a melody.

In any given melody, no two notes have the same importance. Though they may have the same metrical value, two quarter notes, two half notes, or two whole notes are never absolutely *equal*. One of them will inevitably be more accented than the other.[5] However, it goes without saying that a solo made up of even-length notes will have less rhythmic relief than a solo with notes of varying length. Considering the example of choruses by Mezzrow and Parker that we have already cited, it is clear that the melodic monotony of the first is doubled by an equally unfortunate rhythmic monotony. Nine of the first chorus's twelve bars are made up of a uniform group of eight eighth notes, and the same kind of group occurs six times in the second chorus. On the contrary, the diversity of Parker's solos is as apparent to the eye as to the ear. Even without considering the syncopated accents that emphasize the high points of the melody so opportunely, a simple comparison of each of these twenty-four bars with the other twenty-three shows that no two make use of the same rhythmic figure. Remembering that this fragment, far from being the result of patient research, was spontaneously improvised, it is impossible not to bow in admiration.

This perfection of rhythmic construction is found also in Parker's phrasing. I am thinking not so much of the ad-

[5] The accentuation referred to here is *virtual* and proceeds from the very structure of jazz themes. Just as the uneven-numbered beats of the measure are harmonically stronger than the even-numbered ones, so the uneven-numbered measures are stronger than the even-numbered ones. And there is even a definite hierarchy among them. In a 32-bar theme (16+16), measure 1 is the strongest, measure 5 is less strong than measure 9 but stronger than its neighbors 3 and 7, and so forth.

mittedly remarkable way he "airs out" his phrases by a
generous and judicious use of rests as of the supremely
intelligent way he makes long and short phrases alternate.
True, Parker respects the four-bar unit of construction
characteristic of jazz themes, but instead of conforming to it
mechanically, like Mezzrow, he *interprets* it and preserves
his flexibility in spite of the framework's rigidity, which he
is not afraid to modify from time to time (notably, and with
particular elegance, in the ninth measure).

6
The Instrument's Effect on the Phrase

A free interpretation of the four-bar unit of construction
and rhythmic contrasts are essential elements if the phrase
is to have good rhythmic equilibrium. However, this equilibrium is affected by factors that are in a sense more concrete, notably by the nature of the instrument used. The
subject touched upon here is one of the basic differences
between European music and jazz. Composers in the European tradition conceive a phrase by itself and then make it
fit the requirements of a given instrument.[6] The jazz improviser creates only in terms of the instrument he plays. In
extreme instances of assimilation, the instrument becomes
in some way a part of him; under less favorable conditions,
his ideas are channeled, if not completely guided, by it. Thus
it is appropriate to consider the relationship between the
phrase and the instrument, the latter's "heaviness" determining the former's abundance. Putting aside the piano, which
naturally has broader rhythmic possibilities than any of the
wind instruments, the hierarchy may be said to go from the
saxophone, which is the most mobile, to the trombone, the

[6] The reader undoubtedly knows how infinitely more complex the problem
is than this gross but, we trust, excusable simplification would indicate.

most static, with the clarinet and the trumpet in between. Of course, considerations of instrumental technique affect this summary classification. Modern trumpets have a mobility that puts them in the same category as clarinets. Nevertheless, a typical clarinet phrase is more abundant and fluid than a typical trumpet phrase.

Broad, general types of the chorus phrase may be defined according to the instrument used. Innumerable subdivisions appear as soon as individual cases, rather than general categories, are considered. An interesting study might be written about the various types of trumpet phrase. What differences there are between King Oliver's phrase and Armstrong's, between Gillespie's and Davis'; and, at the same time, what affinities! Even on the general level, an effort to find a common denominator between extremes may present excitingly knotty problems. For example, what can the phrase of trombonist Kid Ory have in common with that of saxophonist Charlie Parker? The first is heavy, static, melodically shapeless, scarcely divorced from the bass line, which it seems to depend on more than on the general harmonic foundation, whereas the second is as flexible as a vine, following unanticipated ways and byways. These are subjects that await study by future jazz analysts.

7
The Essence of Melody: The Blues Scale

We seem to have left to one side the most fundamental aspect of the problem of melody—the musical curve resulting from the intervals, the very essence of melody. The reason is that the melodic richness and originality of jazz depend less on this than on the internal organization of the phrase. Jazz, which owes most of its harmonic language to European music, is equally indebted to it for its melodic.

vocabulary. The tonal system and the major and minor
modes exist in jazz only because they were borrowed from
European art. Melodically and harmonically, jazz offers only
one innovation, the blues scale. The only melodic lines that
can be recognized as belonging peculiarly to jazz come from
it. The theoretician might claim that the blues scale is none
other than that of the mode of D, designated by some historians as the Dorian. Actually, the blues scale, as we have
seen,[7] has quite a different nature. Moreover, it is to be
distinguished from the Greek mode by the variability of its
blue notes. The third and seventh degrees are lowered or
not depending on how open or how disguised an allusion
to the major scale is desired. Frequently, blue notes and
unaltered examples of the same degrees occur within a
single phrase (fig. 11). Sometimes the two are superimposed,
and in such cases the blue note's being a kind of suspended
appoggiatura is emphasized (fig. 11a). It is to be noted that
the real resolution of these appoggiaturas would be—and
actually is, more often than not, in actual performance—

FIG. 11 and 11a.

not on the degrees just below them, but on the dominant
and the tonic, which are the actual magnetic poles of the
blue notes.

Is the blues scale part of the essence of jazz? Superficially,
it would seem to be. When the narrowness of their repertory
has obliged jazzmen to borrow or to hold onto other kinds
of themes than the blues, they have often transformed them
by introducing, under cover of improvisation, melodic lines

[7] Cf. Chapter III.

coming directly from the blues scale. However, this transfer
of blue notes from their natural setting is not always possible.
Certain melodic lines are the only ones that can possibly be
created under the conditions imposed by certain harmonic
climates. The modern American slow piece, with its harmony that is characterized by alterations, added notes, and
passing chords, lends itself very poorly to the kind of treatment just referred to. Alterations, particularly, are often
implacable enemies of blue notes. Hawkins realized this
very well when he made a radical choice in favor of alterations in his famous improvisation on BODY AND SOUL. There
is not the slightest allusion to the characteristic melodic
lines of the blues in this solo.[8] The alternative is this: Either
Hawkins' work is not really jazz, or else the melodic language
of the blues is not an essential part of such music. Common
sense indicates which of these choices is the one to make.

8

A Contribution in the Field of Melody

It is time to try to draw a conclusion from the points
made in this brief examination, but first let us review them.

There would seem to be little question that the most original melodic expression in jazz is the chorus phrase, or
even that it is by means of this phrase that jazz has contrib-

---

[8] Not only the melodic lines but also the inflections that characterized the
original blues style are missing from this work. It cannot be repeated too
often that the blues are one of the sources of jazz, but they are not jazz. The
Negro-American minstrels' art is divorced in a number of ways from the
jazzmen's. It is true that the blues are a constant element of the jazz
repertory, but they are not the only one. The influence of the popular song
has grown at the blues' expense, although the influence of the blues has
not been eliminated. Record lists contain many more titles of popular
songs than of blues. Some jazzmen, such as Fats Waller, Hawkins, and Byas,
play the blues only by accident, as it were. On the other hand, some very
fine players of the blues, like Johnny Dodds, may be merely mediocre jazzmen, as we have seen.

uted something in the field of melody. This contribution is not at all negligible, even though jazz's great richness lies in its handling of rhythm and of sound itself. Unless we are greatly mistaken, the chorus phrase does not have an exact equivalent in European music. It behaves and looks like a variation, but it does not arise directly from any melodic theme. Its rhythmic equilibrium depends on the instrument by which it is expressed. Usually abundant, it can be ornamented to the same degree as a melodic phrase. It exploits no given figure. It includes no repeats. The only things it sticks to are the basic construction and the harmonic foundation from which it springs. This freedom is what makes us prefer it to jazz's other forms of melodic expression—the theme phrase, which is too often stilted or unimaginative, and the paraphrase, which, by obliging the melody to follow the theme, nine times out of ten makes it remain unattractive.[9] Admittedly, jazz harmony, or rather what might be called the "harmony of light American music," is not always of a very high quality. What can be expected of a melody based on such harmony? This is where the jazzman's genius comes into play, for by a bold effort he has succeeded in extracting from excessively sugar-coated harmonies a surprisingly high-quality melodic quintessence. It is assuredly one of the great miracles of jazz that the same harmonic humus in which Gershwin, for all his gifts, had raised only the vapid EMBRACEABLE YOU could produce, in the hands of Charlie Parker (to name once more the greatest inventor of melody in the history of jazz), such a marvelous melodic flower as his famous solo.

---

[9] Armstrong's or Parker's ability to transfigure a theme is too rare to enter into a general consideration of the question. It is not the principle of paraphrase that is under attack here, but the melodic indigence of an all too large proportion of jazz themes.

Chapter X

MUSICAL
THOUGHT

1
How the Improviser's Thought Works

Any kind of music in which the act of creation plays a role is, for this very reason, music of which thought is a determining ingredient. Such is the case with jazz, even though, as we have seen, any attempt at construction appears in it only incidentally and in a rudimentary form. In jazz, the act of creation can be performed almost as freely in the simple exposition of a theme as in the invention of a chorus. By the way he handles sound itself and by a kind of rhythmic remodeling of the theme being interpreted, the musician is able to renew it in its very essence without actually getting very far away from it. When the instrumentalist is improvising freely, this important role of *creative performance* is seconded by the resources of melodic invention in the traditional sense. However, in both cases, it is thought that is behind creation. Unless it is claimed that a pianist's hands move haphazardly up and down the keyboard—and no one would be willing to claim this seriously—it must be admitted that there exists a guiding thought, conscious or subconscious, behind the succession of organized sound patterns. Even in the case of an instrument that, to the hasty glance of a superficial observer, may seem a more direct extension of the musician's body than the piano—the trumpet, for instance—it is still true that the slightest inflection is directed, if not rigorously controlled, by the performer's thought. Of course, it does happen, and not too infrequently, that an instrumentalist's fingers "recite" a lesson they have learned; but in such cases there is no reason to talk about creation.

Musical thought has two roads to follow, then, in jazz— the interpretation of a pre-existing melody or the invention of a new melody that replaces the theme from which it springs. The first of these two techniques may result, under the most favorable conditions, in a kind of inner transfiguration of raw material that often does not have any intrinsic melodic interest. The best examples are to be found in the work of Louis Armstrong (and particularly in what he did from 1936 to 1939). Without changing a note or even a time value, Armstrong sometimes succeeds in making the dullest musical line positively glitter. Thus, the only liberty he takes with the theme in the first six bars of his solo in JEEPERS CREEPERS (fig. 12) is the lengthening of certain notes in

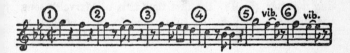

Fig. 12

measures 1 and 2. This is a skillful but trifling variant. The real metamorphosis of the theme under Armstrong's hands depends much more on his attacks, on the precision of his syncopations, and on the vibrato he uses on certain sounds, giving them an expressive density that makes each completely different from the others. In this way, the rhythmic variant of measures 5 and 6 takes on its full significance only in terms of the vibrato that heightens the effect of the second note each time. It is in this sense that such a strict interpretation may still be called an act of creation. Just like an original melody, it reflects a conception and a style.

The second technique consists in substituting for the given theme a melody that resembles it in structure and is based on a similar harmonic progression. This was the principle of the chorus phrase discussed in the last chapter. But sometimes the phrase doesn't resemble a variation at all and insists on becoming a theme in its own right, just like the one it is supposed to replace. Lester Young's version of THESE FOOLISH THINGS, for example, brings the listener into a completely new melodic universe from the first measure. Except for the harmonic foundation, the fact that the second melody comes from the first is indicated by nothing whatever, unless we consider a vague similarity in measure 3, arising from the occurrence of F, E♭, and C in both. Emotion has here given rise to something new melodically that is enough of a personal creation to justify publication under a different title. In this initial phrase, the theme of THESE FOOLISH THINGS is neglected, even forgotten, in favor of a melody whose beauty we need hardly call attention to. Simply putting together (fig. 13) the first four bars of Marvell's song and of the melody Young substituted for it is enough to demonstrate what this technique has to offer when used by

FIG. 13

an authentic creator. By comparison with the slightly commonplace insipidity of the original theme, the marvelous simplicity of Lester's phrase represents a thorough, essential renewal of the melodic raw material and its emotional content.

Lester Young's creation in THESE FOOLISH THINGS is comparable to Armstrong's in JEEPERS CREEPERS only to the extent that it uses the same means of expression. It is true that vibrato, tone production, and phrasing contribute to the success of each, but not in the same proportions. In JEEPERS CREEPERS, Armstrong imposes a shift of interest. The listener's attention is focused on what he does with the actual quality of sound. In THESE FOOLISH THINGS, on the contrary, the ear is first of all attracted by the purity of the melody. It is clear, then, that the two procedures analyzed here may be simultaneously complementary and opposed to each other. The idea of style does not take the same form of expression in both cases. In order to appreciate Lester's inventive richness fully, it would be necessary to make a melodic analysis (just as we shall do in studying Armstrong's use of the paraphrase), to show how motif *A* is based on melodic sevenths and ninths, to compare the step-wise character of this motif with the arpeggio style of motif *B*, to appreciate the melodic advantage taken by the soloist of the passing dominant (measure 4), and finally to point out the very free rhythmic texture of the phrase (which our necessarily sketchy outline cannot cover in all its nuances[1]—note, for example, the way the notes are held back in measure 3).

Between the extreme attitudes represented by the strict rendition of a given melody and its total disappearance, a number of compromises are possible. Among the jazz musi-

---

[1] A musical example or summary can never, for that matter, convey everything about a work. All it can be expected to do is make some points more perceptible. The reader may try it at the piano, and then listen to the record.

cian's means of expression, the paraphrase is one of the richest and most frequently used. The exposition of the theme with which a jazz piece traditionally begins is usually a paraphrase. Only a few of the greatest jazzmen are capable of bringing off a note-for-note exposition. Even Armstrong, who knows better than anyone else how to give a melody life without distorting its shape in the least, rarely fences himself in by conforming strictly to the suggestions of artistic directors whose concern is more with not upsetting the public than with making possible the creation of a real work of art. His conception of the paraphrase is conveyed by this perhaps unpolished but nonetheless accurate observation (in *Swing That Music*) : "It takes a swing player, and a real good one, to be able to leave that score and to know, or 'feel,' just when to leave it and when to get back on it "

A comparison of Armstrong's two versions of I CAN'T GIVE YOU ANYTHING BUT LOVE will show us the two most frequently used types of paraphrase. Both these works begin with the same melodic-harmonic material, which is of an extreme indigence that need hardly be pointed out, but they belong to very different periods of Armstrong's career, so a comparison of them can throw light on certain aspects of his evolution. In the 1929 version, the exposition covers half a chorus (the other half of the first chorus being devoted to a trombone improvisation) and demonstrates the simplest paraphrasing technique. At first, Armstrong takes certain rhythmic liberties with the theme, thus giving it a more syncopated, jazz-like character. If we divide the initial phrase of the theme into three parts, *A*, *B*, and *C* (cf. fig. 14) , it appears that *A* undergoes a slight rhythmic contraction in its exposition by the trumpet. The same is true of *B*, which, sharply separated here from *A* (which it follows without break in the original theme) , thus catches up, you might say, for the delay caused by this separation. The result is a flexibility of articulation and a rhythmic relief that the

theme did not at all have. Secondly, though Armstrong may
follow the original melody note for note at times—as in *A*
and *B*—he doesn't hesitate at other times to add, to suppress,
or to replace certain sounds and sometimes even certain
motifs. In our example, *C* is interesting not only for its
rhythmic structure, which is very free for that epoch, but
also for its melodic independence; it constitutes a kind of
variation on the theme within an exposition that is essentially just a paraphrase.

Let's skip several measures and get to the vocal chorus,
which comes in the middle of the piece. Like the trumpet's
initial exposition, of which we have just looked at a fragment, this vocal is accompanied by the saxophones giving,
in unison, a textual reproduction of the original melody. Is
the singer going to add his voice to theirs, weigh this statement down, commit a pleonasm? Not at all. Here is a new
proof of musical intelligence. Armstrong treats the vocal as
a kind of countermelody to the principal one (fig. 14). He

FIG. 14

does not so much make up a new statement of his own as
reply to the one made in the background by the saxes. It
would seem that the great jazzman has here rediscovered one
of the favorite techniques used by the sixteenth-century
masters of French vocal writing. Like them, he establishes
a kind of reciprocal relationship between the theme and its

simultaneously expressed variation. This variation would not be of much interest out of context; its value depends on the theme's being explicitly stated with it. Its rhythm is condensed, like that of the trumpet's exposition, and it can thus be inserted in the form of what amounts to a commentary on the piece. It may well be regretted that the rest of the vocal fails to live up to this standard. Armstrong doesn't take as much advantage as might have been expected of the way he starts off, and at times even strays from the road he seems to have laid out for himself. Regardless of its high emotional content, is it to be deplored that this vocal is not, when all is said and done, the perfect work it might have been? That would be listening to jazz with too demanding an ear. It would be useless to try to find in it the formal rigor of European art, even in the work of Louis Armstrong.

Thus far, we have considered only some of the simpler forms of paraphrase. The time has come to look at more complex forms. The final solo of the 1929 version, which begins with a free variation in which the theme is evoked only at the eleventh measure, returns for a moment to the original melody after the break of measures 15 and 16. Under cover of a convention (the band momentarily stops playing the theme in the background in order to sound a series of chords on the weak beats), Armstrong once again paraphrases the principal motif of I CAN'T GIVE YOU. Instead of bunching up the various parts as he did before, he spreads them out with long rests, the addition of some extra notes, and a lengthening of the second G (fig. 15). This short paraphrase occurring in a variation that is itself based on the principle of the chorus phrase has a beautiful effect. It is curious to note that, in the 1938 version, Armstrong proceeds in exactly the opposite way, treating the solo in general as one long paraphrase except for this reprise of the principal motif (measures 17 to 19), which is skipped over.

The trumpet chorus of the second I CAN'T GIVE YOU would

Fig. 15

merit an extremely detailed analysis, because it is not only the most beautiful solo Armstrong ever recorded but also one of the most successful feats in the history of jazz. Between the vehement improvisation of the first version and the admirable line of this one, there is as much difference as between the early organ works of Bach, which show a somewhat unbridled imagination in the manner of Buxtehude, and the perfectly balanced Leipzig chorales. It is a similar evolution that can be seen, in spite of the differences between the two musicians, in a comparison of these two choruses of Armstrong. In less than ten years, the great trumpeter not only moved toward a purity of expression that is the most certain sign of an artist's maturity, but actually reached it.

We must limit ourselves to considering only the purely melodic aspect of this solo, and even more specifically the relationship between the paraphrase and the theme. From the first bar on (fig. 16), the rhythmic transformation is an

Fig. 16

absolute work of genius. The beginning of motif *A*, slightly embellished, is shortened in favor of its last note, which takes on an extraordinary relief by lasting more than four beats. Motif *B* is expressed in a balanced rhythm, note for note, except for the final B♭, which Armstrong replaces with a ninth (C), a melodic find that is startlingly effective and completely transfigures the theme. To the statement of this motif, Armstrong adds a brief commentary—six notes of the chord based on the second degree, played in arpeggio. This decorative commentary is typical of his style in that period; sober enough to have no ill effect on the purity of what he is doing, it prevents it from seeming at all dry. For motif *C*, the soloist modifies slightly the contours of the theme, introducing a melodic dominant (E♭) that he makes especially expressive. The following motif gives rise to an astonishing melodic-rhythmic variation. Scarcely changing the theme (to the five notes of the original motif *D*, he adds only two), Armstrong transforms it by displacing the rhythm and substituting a melodically very beautiful third (C) for the second passing note (G). This unexpected drop lets him get right back to the original melody. Motifs *E* and *F* are modified only rhythmically. The triplet of quarter notes in measure 7 serves to render still more flexible a language whose richness of syntax is already evident.

The paraphrase continues throughout the following measures; it includes, among other finds, an amazing alteration which, overhanging the chromatic slide of the harmony in measure 12, takes on prodigious expressive intensity by virtue of its unusualness (it has no vibrato). However, the crowning point of the piece comes at the re-entry following the break of measures 15 and 16 (fig. 17). Taking advantage of the momentum built up during this break, which is constructed on seldom used contrary rhythms, Armstrong deliberately ignores the theme here and goes into the rhythmic repetition of a melodic dominant, which is followed by an eighth-note motif that is one of the most beautiful descending figures ever conceived by a jazzman. The juxtaposition

Fig. 17

of rhythms, the musically sensitive use of the passing diminished seventh (measure 18), the resulting contrast between D♮ and D♭ (the latter of which takes on an unforgettable accent), and finally the phrasing with its displaced connections—everything contributes to the exceptional successfulness of this phrase, which Armstrong places very intelligently in its context by the transition of measure 20, in which occurs the beginning of a return to the theme.

Taken as a whole, this solo may be regarded as an example of what might be called the *paraphrase-chorus* as opposed to the *exposition-paraphrase* demonstrated by the initial half-chorus of the first I CAN'T GIVE YOU. The paraphrase-chorus amplifies the theme rather than stating it; it is related to the development-without-repeat idea and therefore is better suited to a two-part piece (16 + 16) than to a theme with bridge (*A-A-B-A*). On the other hand, the exposition-paraphrase follows the general contour of the theme closely, faithfully taking all the repeats, and does its best to introduce variety. This technique may be applied without difficulty whatever the structure of the given theme. This simple kind of paraphrase serves a necessary function because, as we have seen, the literal statement of a theme is rarely satisfying on a musical level. But obviously the richest melodic developments are to be expected from the paraphrase-chorus and the free variation. However beautiful some of Armstrong's or Hodges' note-for-note expositions may be, there is always something more in their improvised choruses.

2
Continuity of Thought

The problem we take up now is one that is too important to be put off any longer. Whatever kind of work may be under consideration, continuity of musical thought is vital to its success. Admittedly, this observation applies less strictly to jazz than to classical music. A succession of improvised choruses cannot be expected to have as perfect a degree of continuity as a composition that has been long labored over and constructed in a spirit that we have seen to be foreign to jazz. Nevertheless, it remains evident that a coherently developed chorus has a much better chance of being musically satisfying than one whose phrases are haphazardly thrown together, without any thought of musical continuity. Jazz musicians have perfectly well taken into account this necessity; when they compliment an improvisation by saying "It tells a story," don't they show that they recognize the value of good development?

It must be admitted that many recorded improvisations suffer from a lack of continuity that becomes overwhelmingly apparent upon careful and repeated listening. One of the most obvious causes of this non-continuity is the heterogeneity of style with which many musicians are afflicted. However, a number of soloists who have a homogeneous style show an incapacity for thinking through a thirty-two-bar chorus without falling back on disconnected bits of nonsense two or three times (I am not referring to the occasions when they do this on purpose, as a pretext for gags that frequently come off very well, for I recognize the Shakespearean aspect of this music, which admits the grotesque right

alongside the sublime). This inconstancy of thought leads
to the music's being inconsistent.

The great improvisers are rarely guilty of this fault. They
know how to stick to a general line, although this does not
exclude diversions suggested by creative imagination. Sometimes a high-class improviser adopts the principle of contrast, which is dangerous for continuity. There again, only
the existence of a focus will avoid chaos. Such is the case with
KEEPIN' OUT OF MISCHIEF NOW, Fats Waller's famous piano
solo. KEEPIN' OUT is an excellent example of clear, well-
directed thought serving a marvelously felicitous melodic
simplicity. It has been said that the melodic continuity of
this solo comes from the fact that Fats doesn't get very
far away from the theme. This opinion won't stand up under
analysis. Fats may make frequent allusions to the original
melody of KEEPIN' OUT, but most of the time he remains
completely independent of it, treating what he is doing as,
successively, an exposition-paraphrase, a paraphrase-chorus,
and a free variation. On the other hand, the endless contrasts
he uses are not merely an easy way to avoid monotony. They
are not arbitrary; they not only are joined to the creative
musical thought, but are part of it. It would scarcely be
paradoxical to write that continuity here springs from
contrast.

Analysis of KEEPIN' OUT

Exposition. The theme, which has a fairly unusual structure (*A-B-A-C-A*), covers twenty bars. The tempo adopted
is a slow moderato, and the piece includes four choruses
(including the exposition); a coda lengthens the last, and
there is a four-bar introduction. This introduction is made
up of a rapid motif (fig. 18) that forms in its repetitions a
descending scale, which is repeated an octave lower. The
exposition of the theme, which follows without transition,
begins in an extremely original way. The beats are suddenly

interrupted in the second and fourth measures and do not become regularly established before the fifth. The result is an impression of willful ambiguity. The listener wonders whether this is still the introduction or if the exposition has really begun. Such an interruption might spoil the continuity, but this is not at all the case, for the theme has enough unity to permit the necessary joining to be effected from the fifth measure on. The method Fats uses, therefore, appears as a remarkable find which adds interest to a theme that is charming but a trifle banal by itself. Another effect of a similar kind occurs at the ninth measure, where Fats avoids repeating the principal motif, substituting for it a cadential formula that seems to underline what has just been played but actually belongs to the current phrase. This ambiguity does no more damage to the logic of what he is doing than the preceding one, for the listener continues to perceive the continuity of the theme.

FIG. 18   FIG. 19

Second chorus. The following choruses are made up of four-bar sequences that contrast with one another by emphasizing different formulas or procedures. We are going to try to determine to just what extent and by what means these contrasts, far from ruining the work's continuity, contribute to reinforcing it. To make the analysis clearer, we shall designate the sequences by the letters *A, B, C, D,* and *E.*

Sequence *A* of the second chorus is made up of a series of triplets that form a kind of scale in which each degree is embellished from above at the distance of a third. This descending scale, which covers three whole bars, brings to mind the double scale in the introduction. Then, in the fourth measure, appears a motif (fig. 19) that obviously resembles the one in the introduction; and this isolated motif, similarly used in the form of descending scales, appears in sequence B. This may be regarded as a simple coincidence; but it is not impossible that Fats, who undoubtedly had some knowledge of European piano music, had a good idea of what could be done with a piano solo built around elements decided on before actual performance. In any case, these four bars in which a motif already heard in the introduction is used over the harmonies of the theme constitute one of the rare examples jazz has to offer of a variation that is not gratuitous.

The contrast between sequences A and B of this second chorus are rhythmic; the triplets of A are followed by more complex groups in B. The contrast between B and C is principally melodic; the theme reappears here, paraphrased in the first two bars and then simply stated in the next two. There is a new contrast between C and D, both rhythmic and melodic; an evocation of the theme is followed, without transition, by a succession of syncopated chords in the middle register. Fats seems to have realized the danger of a longer citation of the original melody—realized that he had to get away from it, and in no uncertain terms. The brutality of the contrast affects the continuity of the piece less adversely than a more indecisively accented sequence would have.

Moreover, it must be noted that sequence D comes between two references to the theme. Without actually quoting the theme, E has several points in common with the corresponding passage in the first chorus. Thus, sequence D constitutes a kind of diversion, which the melodic continuity of the work takes in stride. There is no gap, in any case; in fact, sequence D gives Fats a chance to introduce a type of phrase that he makes use of again at the beginning of the last chorus.

Third chorus. Up to this point, the musician's thought

has been guided by a spirit of paraphrase or variation that is far from being uncommon in jazz. An infinitely rarer procedure appears in the third chorus. What it amounts to is a new, modified presentation of the theme, or you might say the creation of a new theme by simplifying the initial one. The original theme (fig. 20) was based on a seven-note

FIG. 20

figure. In its new form (fig. 21), the last three notes are

FIG. 21

eliminated. The fourth note, G, which hadn't much importance at all originally, becomes essential; it is repeated and held; it is what gives the new theme such a different physiognomy.

The phrase is condensed in time as well as in space. The seven notes of the initial figure took a full measure, whereas in its modified, five-note form it takes only half a measure. That in itself completely renews the melodic sense of the phrase.

It is too bad that Fats didn't follow his idea through to the end; it is interesting enough to rate a whole chorus. What he does is to branch off, in sequence *B*, to a new citation of the original theme, this time quoted exactly, but this citation is broken off, with fortunate results, at the end of two bars to make way for an intelligent harmonic variation. Sequence *C* begins with a modified reminder of the theme and, without any noticeable transition, continues with another textual citation of the initial melody. Such as it is, this sequence resembles the corresponding part of the preceding chorus too closely not to seem repetitious; it is perhaps the weakest passage in the piece. The allusions to the initial melody play the role of a guideline; they are what makes possible, by way of contrast, passages as willfully neutral, both rhythmically and melodically, as sequence *D*, in which voluble arpeggios on the upper part of the keyboard emphasize only the harmonic texture. After this letup—which corresponds, logically, to the most static part of the theme—a whiplash is called for; and that is the function served, in sequence *E*, by the violently syncopated chords in the right hand, under which the bass has a restrained melody with a boogie-woogie-like rhythm. It is apparent from this analysis that the same method is being followed here as in the preceding chorus; the continuity is accordingly on the same order.

Fourth chorus. In the last chorus, Fats Waller takes serious liberties with the theme. Sequence *E* is extended by a coda with an organ point played in arpeggio, and—this is even more remarkable—sequence *B* disappears completely! Undoubtedly Fats decided that an unaccompanied soloist didn't have to worry too much about sticking to the outlines of a theme, especially when it happened to be one of his own invention. The continuity doesn't suffer a bit. *C* follows *A* all the more smoothly since both phrases, which are identical in the theme, are treated in the same spirit. Chords of the kind introduced in sequence *D* of the second chorus are here used felicitously to form riffed figures that show great restraint.

The voluntary dryness of these eight bars is followed by a new contrast, which a clever change of register emphasizes. The first two measures of sequence *D* bring back the theme in the form of a paraphrase; the second part of the sequence

is a rhythmic and melodic variation that uses a series of
syncopated accents to underline the importance of this next
to the last return of the theme, which it interrupts, and to
announce the last return. We have already observed that
sequence *E*, where the theme puts in its last appearance,
breaks off short and leaves the way clear for a coda, whose
principal feature, after a series of rhythmically free arpeggios,
is a return to strict tempo, with strongly syncopated chords
in the right hand—one last contrast, and not the least
expressive.

The last two bars of *D* constitute a kind of parenthetic
commentary that parallels sequence *D* in the second and
third choruses. The similarity of these passages is significant;
the way Fats proceeds is so precise that he isn't afraid to let
what he is saying lose its sense of direction and to enrich
it with skillful diversions, re-establishing continuity by a
reference to the original theme.

To what extent was KEEPIN' OUT improvised? Was it not
worked out at all? It is impossible to judge at this distance
in time and without knowing all the details. Certain indica-
tions lead me to believe that Fats, as a result of playing this
piece often, had succeeded in polishing up a concert version
that he revised freely, according to the dictates of his fancy,
but that always kept the same general lines. This would
account for the concern about construction that is apparent
in at least two places—sequence *B* of the second chorus (use
of the introduction motif in the development) and the beginning of the following chorus (new theme).

The piece may have been worked out, but we must make
clear what we mean by this. It is not an organized composition, nor even the product of creative meditation, but the
result of a crystallization of thought in the course of successive improvisations. Even such a limited kind of working
out makes it possible to eliminate weaknesses in continuity
that pure improvisation lets by. This sort of working out

therefore favors continuity, but it certainly would not be enough to guarantee it. What is required is a certain rigor of thought that not everyone has. A significant example in this respect is that of such a brilliant soloist as Art Tatum, whose concert "improvisations" pretty clearly show that they have been worked out. Lucien Malson used to compare Art Tatum to a professor who would no sooner finish writing one set of brilliant demonstrations on the blackboard than he would erase it to begin another on a completely different subject. That observation strikes me as being justified, at least to judge by the great pianist's recordings. Tatum, who has every other gift, does not have the gift of continuity.

We have just said that working out favors continuity. Does this mean that a worked-out style is necessarily to be preferred? I don't think so. Working out has at least two considerable disadvantages. As concerns creation, if it takes the place of pure improvisation, it may lead to a routine manner and, consequently, to sterility. It brings about a deplorable change in the attitude of the creator, who begins to favor a certain security and stops playing for his own satisfaction. The listener also loses by the change. Isn't it one of the essential attractions of jazz to listen to a great improviser with the exciting hope of hearing something completely new, some real find? Even more serious is the effect on the relationship between creation and execution that results from too elaborate a crystallization of musical thought. Willy-nilly, boredom sets in. How can you "believe" in a chorus that someone is playing in the selfsame way for the hundredth time? For one Fats Waller who has kept his freshness, how many Barney Bigards, in the course of too many concerts, have let themselves become the victims of sclerosis?

A choice, for that matter, is not necessary. One form of expression does not exclude another. A good chorus, even though learned by heart, is better than a bad chorus. Nevertheless, it is hard not to cherish a preference, at least secretly, for the miracle of perfect continuity in a burst of pure improvisation.

3
Collective Creation

A third aspect of musical thought in jazz remains to be examined—collective creation. This takes place in various ways, depending on whether one artist, while creating, has in mind some other artist whose own inventiveness will be superimposed on his, or whether several musicians work together, simultaneously and in equal proportions, to bring a piece into being. The composer works in a kind of absolute; but he works, in a sense, on the same level as the arranger, whose creative effort is very specifically destined for a given band or soloist. Duke Ellington or Sy Oliver thus prepare tailor-made arrangements that they know will be interpreted principally by Cootie or the Lunceford band. Sometimes this kind of semi-individual creation develops into a fairly elementary but nonetheless interesting form of collective effort. Frequently, one or more members of Ellington's band make suggestions to the principal arranger in rehearsals. All this must be taken into account; but it is time to come back to the forms of improvised creation, which is our real subject.

Some contributions may seem fairly modest—that of a pianist who modifies the harmony of a theme, or of a drummer who puts his skill and his rhythmic sense at the service of the soloist he accompanies. However, any musician who has played in a jazz band knows the stimulation that can be expected from a harmony that falls just right or a way of playing the cymbals that really swings. It is certain, for example, that if Carter, Hampton, and Hawkins never played better than in WHEN LIGHTS ARE LOW, it is largely because they were carried along by an impeccable rhythm section. No one will doubt that there is a particularly subtle form of collective creation at work in such cases; but there seems to be no way of analyzing it with the means currently at our disposal. We must therefore look at an aspect of this problem that can be grasped more directly—the phenomenon usually called collective improvisation, which Charles Delaunay has very sensibly designated by a more precise term, spontaneous polyphony.

There is a manifestation of spontaneous polyphony when several instruments improvise simultaneously and in equal parts on a theme. This definition has the merit of eliminating, as not being essentially polyphonic, accompaniments in the form of a countermelody that some pianists favor and that have been used by clarinetists and trombonists in a number of works in the New Orleans style (for example, by Ladnier and Bechet for their solos in WEARY BLUES). We shall accordingly limit our study of collective creation to improvised ensembles of two or more voices of equal importance—ensembles, that is, in which no voice is subordinated to its neighbor but in which, on the contrary, all voices contribute with the same amount of power toward a single end, the joint work.

It is well for the different members of a group to speak the same language, but it is to be hoped that this language will not be absolutely identical with any other group's. Considering an improvising band as a whole, one must try to appreciate its homogeneity without neglecting its creative originality. These two elements do not always go together. It may even be claimed, in fact, that they are contradictory. Thus, Armstrong's first Hot Five shows greater originality than King Oliver's Creole Band, but it is incontestably less homogeneous. The reason is that the originality of a group depends on the personality of the elements that make it up. Two things can happen: The band may be dominated by a creative genius whom his sidemen don't always understand (the case of the first Hot Five), or several personalities of more or less the same stature may get together in a group without achieving the necessary fusion (the case of the Clarence Williams band with Armstrong and Bechet). That explains in part why spontaneous polyphony, the most usual means of expression in old jazz, never produced a truly great work and was abandoned beginning with the pre-classical period and revived only because of the renewal of interest in the New Orleans school. On the other hand, some groups that include no really top-grade musicians have brought off valuable and even remarkable works, thanks to a homogeneity that was not disturbed by any excessively strong personality (I am thinking of the Mezzrow-Ladnier COMIN' ON WITH THE COME ON, of Jelly Roll Morton's KANSAS CITY STOMPS, and so forth).

A closer look at the problem of collective creation reveals another contradiction that must be considered. In this kind of expression, where it is the group and not the individual who creates, is it not logical for the creation to be contrapuntal in spirit? At first glance, this would seem to be true, and such is the opinion of most commentators, who are only too willing to oppose the "counterpoint of the New Orleans style" to the melodic-harmonic language of classical jazz. Does this mean that jazz offers examples of purely contrapuntal thought, in the sense referred to when speaking of Machaut or Dufay? Certainly not. The chorus phrase, as we have seen, is essentially harmonic; the melody is not only supported by the harmony, but actually comes from it. The "counterpoint" of jazz might be defined as the superposition of several types of chorus phrase, each conceived in terms of an ensemble in which it plays a well-defined role.

Accordingly, the clarinet, because of its build, its timbre, and its range, cannot change parts with the trombone; and both must bow to the requirements of the part played by the trumpet, their encroaching neighbor, whom they cannot afford to ignore. This technique is derived less from a contrapuntal spirit than from an expanded notion of the countermelody. Equality of voices, as in the fugues of Bach, appears only incidentally in jazz. The different parts undeniably preserve a certain independence as they move along, but that is not enough to qualify musical thought as being essentially contrapuntal. One requirement of such thought is that it should not be determined by any harmonic precedent. In other words, the fact that the chorus phrase must conform to a given bass is incompatible with the freedom required for the flourishing of true counterpoint. That is why the spontaneous polyphony of the New Orleans school, which is completely subjected to the tyranny of chords—and predetermined chords, at that—must be regarded as offering, at best, only incidental examples of counterpoint. It would be possible for real contrapuntal thought to take root and flourish in jazz only as the result of intelligent working out, the only method, as I see it, by which flexibility might be introduced into the system of variation that is the basis of creative techniques used currently by jazzmen of all kinds.

Before concluding, one extremely delicate question must be brought up. Does "collective thought" exist in jazz? Aren't the successes of spontaneous polyphony to be attributed, instead, to equal parts of chance and routine? Personally, I believed for a long time in the "genius" of the musicians who were heard improvising together on the best records of oldtime jazz. I thought these works testified not only to a solid tradition but also to a superior level of talent, a kind of almost miraculous prescience. Experience has shown, since then, that a number of students who couldn't even be called especially gifted musically are able to equal the glorious Louisiana veterans in this domain when they put their hand to it as a pastime. Miracles lose their aura when they occur too frequently; these days, it would be hard to substantiate any hypothesis concerning a "collective genius" that pervaded the principal bands in the twenties. There is no alternative to concluding that our conception of the difficulties of group improvisation was infinitely exaggerated. Carefully considered, the New Orleans masters' famous "feel for playing together" can be seen to have depended less on divination than on prudence.

This rapid and admittedly incomplete study cannot claim to exhaust such a vast subject as improvisation. We have nonetheless identified the principal ways in which the improviser expresses his musical thought. In doing so, we have observed the different forms of exposition and paraphrase, acknowledged the necessity of continuity of thought, and defined certain aspects of collective creation. Perhaps it is possible for us now to pass some judgment on the very existence of improvisation, considered as a means of expressing musical thought. After half a century, improvisation remains one of the keys to the creation of jazz. But it is still not essential. We have seen that many originally improvised choruses have been worked over afterwards and sometimes improved; in many cases, the initial burst has been followed by regularization and crystallization. But whatever the shortcomings of improvisation—imperfection of form, uncertainty of success, and above all weakness of construction—it is a favorable factor in the creation of jazz, which depends on the here and now for its fullest realization. It would seem that jazz can expect to speak a perfect collective language only if it is worked out by individuals (this paradox is more apparent than real). And if this is what were required for jazz to attain a higher level of expression and be truly contrapuntal—if, in other words, jazz had to become more and more like music that is composed "purely," by being written out—then it would be up to the creators to let their thought take the place of the performers', and the performers, as Don Byas has observed, would have to make the listener think he was hearing improvised music even when he wouldn't be doing so at all.

Chapter XI

NOTES
ON THE
PROBLEM OF CREATION

> The newer a song sounds to the ears
> of man, the more it is appreciated.
> —HOMER

In connection with the Graeme Bell orchestra, Boris Vian wrote: "The only means in this domain [literature], as in music, of doing something *different* and truly personal is ... to know *everything else that has been done;* for want of doing this, it happens that, as in the case of Graeme Bell, this 1951 Australian jazz (purely by chance, no doubt) is indistinguishable from the revitalized Dixieland that countless young people with good intentions but a refractory ear are turning out in both hemispheres."[1]

A completely different opinion is expressed by Ernest Borneman, who, in his novel *Tremolo,* thus describes the feelings of his hero, Mike, as he takes a solo in a public jam session: "Mike knew, while playing, that he was doing exactly what he wanted to avoid at all costs, trying to make an effect. He began a new chorus solely to 'give them an earful,' and

[1] Boris Vian: "Revue de Presse," in *Jazz-Hot,* No. 52.

in order to do this, he felt obliged to remember all the blues
choruses he had ever heard so that he could try to avoid
repeating them and to make his chorus something new,
'different' and advanced'; and naturally all he succeeded in
producing was a cold outpouring of notes and a frantic
demonstration of his breath control in the upper register."⁹

In these few lines, Borneman and Vian pose the problem
of creation in jazz and, beyond it, the vaster problem of the
nature of jazz. Vian insists implicitly on the necessity of
doing something *different;* Borneman denounces this idea
as, in his opinion, an error; and both of them, curiously
enough, call special attention to the word. Which is right,
to invent or to copy? The reply made to this question touches
on the very substance of an art.

There are two kinds of artists. The one who sees or hears
with the eyes or ears of others is by far the happier. Quite
apart from the force and assurance to be found in numbers,
he has on his side an overwhelming majority of the public
and even of the critics, whom he doesn't risk alienating by
what may be thought unseemly audacities. The man who
expresses himself in a language of his own invention is a
dangerous creature, fortunately rare, and he is generally
avoided, at least during his first appearances. But it is he,
nonetheless, who wins out in the end. One such artist may
be responsible for the existence of thousands of artists of
the first kind, but the opposite has never happened. One of
the greatest musicians of our time, Béla Bartók, died in
poverty; but today sub-Bartóks flourish by the dozen.

It must be admitted, furthermore, that there are two
categories of artists of the first kind, two sorts of everyday

⁹ Ernest Borneman: *Tremolo,* pp. 121-122.

artists—imitators, that is. There is, in the first place, the
simple plagiarist, who is incapable of inventing anything
and uses the ideas of others more or less skillfully. On a
higher level is the very common and perfectly respectable
kind of artist who borrows his style from an original creator
in order to express with it ideas of his own that are sometimes perfectly valid. Whereas the plagiarist, except for some
understandable lapses of memory, is rarely unaware of what
he is doing, the stylistic imitator almost never seems to be
aware of his spiritual filiation, especially if his imitation is
based on two or three different models.

Who doesn't recognize the pure plagiarist? What record
collector cannot pick out, in the course of a concert, the
thousand-and-one borrowings that make up the grab-bag of
choruses? The connection a solo may have with a given
generative style is much more subtle. When the imitation
is pure, of course, it is easy to notice that such and such a
saxophonist plays like Lester Young or Coleman Hawkins;
but if several influences are combined, it is often difficult
to distinguish between the main color and the color produced by the mixture.

To be a creator oneself requires more than doing something as well as the creator being imitated. Consider the
case of the Dutch painter, Van Meegeren, who produced fake
Vermeers with an exceptional talent. Disdaining plagiarism,
he was not at all satisfied with merely copying originals; he
produced new canvases in the Vermeer manner, just as the
famous Flemish master would have done. Because he had
managed to find the chemical secrets (glazes, colors, and so
forth) of the period and because his execution was perfect,
all the experts were ready to attribute these paintings to
Vermeer—until Van Meegeren, in prison, painted one last
fake Vermeer that seemed even more astonishingly authentic

than the others. This was the cue for some critics to compare Van Meegeren to Vermeer and to herald the genius of the man "who had made seventeenth-century Flemish painting live again in all its purity." Their error was a fundamental one, and other specialists with better judgment had good reason to denounce it. The fact is that Van Meegeren, despite his great sureness of touch, was only a second-rate painter. He was an exceptional follower—since it is extremely rare for the imitator not to remain far below his model—but he was never able to leave the beaten track, to give to the world a single painting of his own. Without Vermeer, Van Meegeren would have been a mere robot without a memory; and it is impossible to avoid the word *memory* when speaking of him, since in the final analysis it is this faculty that he had to substitute for the creative impulse. He may have chosen the subject and the motifs, but the only thing that is important in the end is the non-originality of his style. What this amounts to saying is that the only truly valid works are those that draw their inspiration from an authentically new style.

Is the same thing true in jazz? In other words, is it valid to go on playing, year after year, the same phrases of the blues, and in the same way?[3] Reference must be made here to modern conceptions of the history of man, distinguishing two types of civilization: a static group, in which man is satisfied with copying his ancestors' way of life without any changes (this is the .type of civilization that characterizes any people called "primitive"), and an evolving type, in which the mass follows the influence of a few initiators whose action tends to transform this way of life. The same thing is true in music. Certain kinds of music, which might

[3] These last words should, perhaps, be underlined; for, where jazz is concerned, execution—the *way of playing*—is obviously a part of creation just as melodic invention is.

be called "pure folklore," don't have to be renewed; they remain what they were a thousand years ago. Others, on the contrary, undergo the influence of a small number of personalities—the creators—who keep them in constant motion, at some times faster than at others.

Which of these types does jazz belong to? In my opinion, the question is hardly worth raising. Those who classify jazz as a kind of pure folklore deny the obvious; or perhaps, more simply, they demonstrate their uncomplicated wish to preserve unchanged a way of expression that has given them their greatest artistic pleasure in the past; but this refusal to face reality is not very constructive, and is still less efficacious. If they do not see the artificiality of such throwbacks as Graeme Bell's—whether or not it is called "1951 Australian jazz"—they must get ready for a rude awakening.

The most ridiculous part of it is that most of the "immobilizers" are convinced that jazz belongs to the Negro. In that case, jazz could remain what it was in King Oliver's time only if colored people had remained the same. A static kind of music would correspond to a static society. Can anyone seriously claim that this has been the case? Isn't it evident, on the contrary, that the vertiginous evolution of jazz can be explained only in terms of the no less vertiginous evolution of the Negro in America? Is there any point in once more observing that the "New Orleans Revival" was the doing of a few very old Negroes and a majority of very young whites?

Let's make an hypothesis. If, all things considered, these people are correct and if jazz, being a kind of folk music, rightfully consists of the same things played always in the same way, why do they talk about geniuses? How can they go into ecstasies over Armstrong's inventive gifts, since there is nothing wrong with copying Armstrong? Who can fail to see that, viewed in this way, Buck Washington is as great as Earl Hines, and Sonny White as great as Teddy Wilson? Because, judged by such criteria, an imitation is as good as the original, Van Meegeren as good as Vermeer. We might even go further and say that whoever introduces something new is a traitor, guilty of upsetting the unchangeable order of things. In that case, it is logical to banish Gillespie, Parker, and Davis from the unchangeable society of jazz. It is even less logical to hold onto Armstrong, who gleefully kicked over plenty of this society's standards as he went along. But logic doesn't happen to be one of our immobilizers' strong points.

Indeed, Parker, Davis, and Gillespie have been banished. It has been claimed that their music is no longer jazz. That is easy to say. Where does jazz begin, and where does it end? Sticking to certain fundamental criteria that may seem subjective but have proved their workability, I won't be convinced that bop is not jazz until I hear a sonata that has the same kind of rhythm as a Miles Davis recording, or a symphony orchestra musician who plays with the same kind of sonority and inflections as Charlie Parker. Somehow, I think I'll have to wait quite a while for such surprises.

The creators of bop have been reproached for showing certain European influences. This attitude fails to give the Negro's receptivity its due. Without such an ability to assimilate, bop may not have existed; but jazz would not have existed either, and North American Negroes would still be playing the music of their African ancestors.

Either Negro-American music is essentially static, in which case a kind of inbreeding is the natural thing for it, or it is essentially evolving, in which case it must undergo all kinds of exterior influences and assimilate them as best it can. Up to the present, it has preserved enough vitality to be able to do so. If in the future it were to become incapable of this and were to be annexed by the music of the whites, the explanation would be that the Negro-American people had adopted the whites' way of living and their feeling. A number of arts, representing a number of civilizations, have been absorbed in this way during the course of man's history. It does not seem that such a destiny can be predicted at the present time for the Negro in America.

As an evolving kind of music, jazz depends on invention for its very life. That brings us back to Mike, Borneman's hero. In the midst of a world in motion, he reasons as if jazz were the product of an immobile society. He would like to be a plagiarist, reproducing exactly the phrases of blues that he had learned by heart from the recordings of Dodds or Rappolo. Only a foolish regard for what people would think prevents him from playing them; they burn his lips. In reality, Mike is all wrong not to play them. What difference would it make? He will never be anything but a follower, made to repeat—and to repeat less well—what has already been done. (There are, spread over the world, thousands if not millions of Mikes—painters, musicians, sculptors, writers.) But what makes the scene ridiculous is that Mike wants to *invent*. This boy who has never created anything, who has never even tried to create, wants to become a creator on the spot, right there in public, in the middle of a jam session!

Poor Mike! He is like a boxer entering the ring for a world's championship bout without ever having fought before or even been in training. Such a fighter's chances of success would be just about as good as the chances of Mike's inventing a worth-while chorus that would be neither a more or less literal repetition of stereotyped phrases heard a thousand times nor the "cold outpouring" he winds up with. How could Mike, a clarinetist of the New Orleans tradition, invent a truly original chorus? Ravel said that harmony could not go on being enriched perpetually; similarly, there is a limit to the melodic and rhythmic combinations possible within any one style. If Louis Armstrong has often repeated himself during the last few years, it is because he had already invented almost everything there was to invent in the field of his style. The attempt of a modest imitator of Dodds and Rappolo like Mike is childish. He knows himself that it is doomed to failure before he even puts the clarinet to his mouth. The way to create is not by following narrow paths already trampled by generations of creators and imitators. In order to create, Mike would have had to get away from the New Orleans style he loved so much. But getting away from one style implies getting into another; and this other style must not be one that has also been trampled in advance.

When all is said and done, the only real creation is one that springs from an original style. But a style, even in jazz, is something that develops slowly. Armstrong was not the Armstrong we know from the first moment he ever blew into a cornet; we can be sure that he began by imitating his elders, Bunk Johnson or King Oliver or someone else. Every creator is an imitator for a while. It is only little by little that he succeeds in disengaging his personal conceptions from the ideas he has picked up and the influences he has undergone. It remains to be determined what role the will plays in this frequently difficult process of giving birth. René Leibowitz, theoretician of dodecaphonic music, believes its role is all-important. According to him, it is the "compositional conscience" of the creator that makes him turn to what is new. But how can we speak of "compositional conscience" when we have to do, as in jazz, principally with improvisers? It is more tempting to think that there takes place in the creator of jazz, without his being fully aware of it, a secret process of growth that does not become fully effective until the musician finds himself placed in certain conditions that are especially favorable for the blossoming of his personality. There is no reason to expect an artistic conscience that is looking for its way to be fully aware of what it is doing. Something new cannot be obtained without a definite effort; this effort may very well be something that the reflective consciousness does not register, that is not "known" distinctly. It is nonetheless real.

A jazzman, therefore, has to make an effort to produce his music, and before making this creative effort he must first make the effort necessary to master his instrument. The jazz musician passionately wants to express himself. His style is not worked out, like the European composer's, in solitary meditation. It is born as a result of actual experience, individual or collective (the nights at Minton's come to mind), but may be brushed up at leisure. It is easy to imagine someone like Garner working at home to perfect, not particular phrases themselves, but a type of phrase that he will use in his improvisations, just as a tennis player works out special strokes in preparation for coming matches. As a music that evolves, jazz requires and demonstrates the musician's concern about being free in relation to the art of his predecessors.

What conclusion can we make? We have done no more

than state the problem. Only an improviser of genius who is also a consummate esthetician would be able to reconstruct, by careful reflection, the different phases in the creation of his style. Even he might not be able to do so. And if he succeeded, we would still have just one man's answer, which might not apply generally. In these few notes, I have tried above all to convey the scope of the problem, to define its aspects. Perhaps, all the same, certain points may be regarded as established. It seems that Vian is on the right side when he insists that anyone who wants to do something new must be thoroughly acquainted with what has been done; that Borneman is correct in showing how incapable of creation someone like his hero would be; that an imitator can never be really as good as the creator from whom he gets his inspiration; that jazz is the reflection of a civilization in motion rather than of a static world; that, because this is true, it is governed by an evolutionary dialectic; and that, finally, the jazzman, like any creator worthy of the name, is physically and intellectually bound by the uncompromising, salutary law of effort. But we must not be under any delusions. Only a complete analysis of these problems would show the absurdity of failing to keep up with the times esthetically in jazz.

IV

THE PROBLEM OF THE ESSENCE OF JAZZ

> All attempts at definition give rise to
> difficulties; let us therefore not hope
> to escape them in our present effort.
> —FREUD

Chapter XII

THE PHENOMENON
OF SWING

The problem of the essence of jazz has never been seriously posed. Confronted with a particular work, everyone knows—or thinks he knows—whether or not the word jazz may be properly used to describe it. We have seen that disagreements sometimes have arisen, principally when modern works were under discussion. It is not surprising that this capital problem has been avoided or only partially faced for such a long time; is it not quite as vast as it is thorny? We might also add, anticipating the conclusions ahead, that it promises to bristle with paradoxes. Before undertaking a survey of this important question (we can hardly hope to treat it exhaustively), we must consider two central problems, rhythm and the handling of sound.

The analysis of a good work of jazz in the classical style reveals the coexistence of two characteristics that seem opposed to each other—an element of tension and an element of relaxation. This is not a case of the traditional alternation between tension and relaxation to be observed in classical European music, which results from the succession of dissonances and consonances, of periods of movement and periods of repose. In jazz, the feeling of relaxation does not follow a feeling of tension but is present at the same moment. For a long time, it was believed, on the strength of poorly established definitions, that "tension" was a product of the phenomenon called swing, or even that it *was* swing.[1] This was clearly an error. Only the element of "relaxation" results from swing,[2] the tension being an effect of the way the jazz musician handles sound (in other words, an effect of "hot" playing). Could it be that swing and hot playing are therefore the two essentials that make up jazz? Only a detailed study of both can authorize us to say so.

It is almost impossible to analyze such an impalpable element as swing. No effort at rationalization seems capable of catching this notion that defies valid explanation and that cannot be put down on paper, this phenomenon that has no existence before it is manifested in a specific work but that frequently constitutes the work's chief merit. We know that "to swing" is an act; but this act is not fully grasped except by the sensitivity of someone who perceives its effect. All the analyst can do is define what the phenomenon is made up of, or even, more modestly, the circumstances under which it comes into being.

In an earlier work, I suggested this definition of swing: " . . . a certain way of making the rhythm come to life." This truism did not, of course, throw any light on the phenomenon itself, but at least it had the merit of calling attention to its purely rhythmic character, which is too often neglected. It would really be impossible to overemphasize the fact that swing is an essentially *rhythmic* phenomenon.[3]

---

[1] Cf. Joost Van Praag: "Etude sur la musique de jazz," in *Jazz-Hot*, No. 6, January, 1936: "Swing is the psychic tension that comes from the rhythm's being attracted by the meter."

[2] More recently, Lucien Malson (cf. "Le jazz ne meurt pas," in *Les Temps Modernes*, No. 99, p. 1, 476) suggested that it is possible to find, in connection with swing, "one of the Freudian paradoxes: an unpleasant tension which is associated with pleasure—that is, with a partial satisfaction, with a partial relaxation." The thesis is a tempting one, admitting as it does a tension-relaxation duality at the very core of the rhythmic element.

[3] The rhythmic phenomenon is not simply a question of *time values*; the succession of *attacks* and *intensities* is also an important part of it.

There would seem to be five optimal conditions for the production of swing. (I couldn't deny the theoretical possibility of swing's resulting from others, though I have never seen this happen.) They·are:

1. the right infrastructure;
2. the right superstructure;
3. getting the notes and accents in the right place;
4. relaxation;
5. vital drive.

The first three are technical in nature and can be understood rationally; the last two, which are psycho-physical, must be grasped intuitively. Only the second (and, to a lesser degree, the first) has to do with what·is properly referred to as musical conception; the others belong to the domain of performance. At the same time, poor rhythmic construction of a phrase may be enough to destroy the equilibrium of forces that is required for the production of swing. It will be seen that a combination of all five conditions is indispensable if the phenomenon is to be satisfactorily manifested.

1
The Infrastructure: Tempo and Accentuation

What I call the infrastructure is the regularly produced two- or four-beat meter (2/2 or 4/4 measure) that characterizes any jazz performance. Supplying it is the role assigned to the part of the band called the rhythm section. It constitutes the necessary metrical foundation without which, except for breaks, codas, or stop choruses, swing is impossible for the soloist. The infrastructure requires, in jazz, a tempo or movement of a carefully regulated speed and kind. It must not·be either too fast or too slow. Tempos at which swing is possible range from about 54 quarter notes a minute to about 360. Below 54, the tempo loses all "centrifugal" force and the rhythm section acts like a dying roulette ball. Above 360, it becomes very difficult for the performer to preserve the minimum of flexibility and accuracy that swing requires. However, these limits should be regarded as records that may still be broken, not as unsurpassable bounds. Certainly before Charlie Parker no one supposed it possible to swing at 360. In addition, these limits have a personal character that should be underlined. For an only moderately gifted soloist with a weak technical command of his instrument, a tempo of 240 may be too fast. The infrastructures that have proved most favorable to swing are those with tempos that represent a happy medium. The "medium tempo" or "moderato"—around 168 quarter notes a minute—has been called "swing tempo."

Once the speed of a tempo has been decided on, its quality is up to the musicians in the rhythm section. I mean by this that the tempo should not vary enough for the ear to notice. A noticeable acceleration or a slackening, however brief, is usually enough to destroy the swing. Swing is possible, in classical jazz, only when the beat, though it seems perfectly regular, gives the impression of moving inexorably ahead (like a train that keeps moving at the same speed but is still being *drawn ahead* by its locomotive). For that matter, I have observed that one work in which the tempo is particularly good—Hampton's WHEN LIGHTS ARE LOW—has a steady acceleration, though the ear does not recognize it so well as the metronome. The difference between 198 quarter notes a minute in the exposition and 204 in the last measures is notable. This observation merely corroborates the empirical judgment of jazz musicians, who say that "you can't beat swing by a metronome."[4]

───────────

[4] There must also be a balance between the tempo and the melodic theme. A little further on we shall look into this problem, which is part of the

The notion of metrical accentuation, which is regarded by a number of specialists as one of the essential elements of swing, does not strike me as playing so constant and necessary a role as the conditions already mentioned. True, a survey of many works belonging to various periods confirms the existence of some general characteristics. Thus, the grave accent, falling on the uneven-numbered beat (or strong beat), contrasts with the acute accent, which comes on the even-numbered beat (the weak beat). The former calls into play the big-sounding instruments—the bass drum or the open high hat cymbal, depending on the style—whereas the latter is entrusted to drier-sounding instruments—the closed high hat cymbal or the snare drum. Bernard Heuvelmans correctly points out that the strong beats are "accented by length (horizontally) and the weak beats by force (vertically)."[6] Nevertheless, the exceptions are so numerous that it is better not to make an absolute rule out of this observation, though it is valid in a very general way. At least four types of metrical accentuation may be found in jazz. Depending on the school and the instruments involved, the principal accent may fall on the strong beat, on the weak beat, on all four beats equally, or on the weak part of the beat. Each type of accentuation results in a different type of swing, which is perfectly valid if it suits the soloist it is meant for; otherwise, however good the beat itself may be, it stands a good chance of being completely ineffective.

2
The Superstructure: Rhythmic Equilibrium of the Phrase

The beat of the rhythm section represents the foundation on which the solos and ensembles are constructed. The most problem of the relationship between the infrastructure and the superstructure.

6 B. Heuvelmans: *De la bamboula au be-bop,* p. 29.

melodic solo is never purely melodic. We have seen* that the
rhythmic articulation of the phrase is just as important as
the melodic line in itself. What I call the superstructure is
this rhythmic construction of the phrase conceived in terms
of the infrastructure.

Empirically, certain rhythmic figures can be identified as
being more favorable to swing than others. Among the most
favorable comes the syncopation, which may be defined as
the anticipatory emission of a note, shifting it from the
strong part of one beat to the weak part of the preceding
beat. This procedure is not peculiar to jazz. It appears constantly in European music, notably in Bach. However, the
ternary division of each beat, which is usual in classical
jazz for all moderate tempos, has introduced a kind of unequal syncopation—the note is played a third of a beat ahead
of time and lasts through two thirds of the next beat (fig.
22)—that is seldom found in European music. The "swing

FIG. 22

syncopation," which as we shall observe becomes binary in
rapid tempos, is further characterized by the kind of attraction it exercises on the meter just when it is creating a
rhythmic dislocation between the superstructure and the
infrastructure.

The ideal "swing phrase" includes at least one syncopated
note. It seems that the American Negro has found in an
alternation of syncopations and notes played on the beat the
best expression of his rhythmic genius. By turns the melodic
phrase seems to depend rhythmically on what is being played

* Cf. Chapter IX, pp. 151 ff.

underneath and to be completely independent of it, and this
unending alternation gives rise to a kind of expectation that
is one of jazz's subtlest effects. Modern jazzmen frequently
pave the way for a strong beat by a series of displaced accents
(coming, for example, on four dotted quarter notes) that
nurse and tease this expectation with the promise of an
imminent explosion. On the other hand, Louis Armstrong
likes to build a phrase with a series of quarter notes played
on the beat, followed, by way of conclusion, by some syncopated notes (usually two) that emphasize the feeling of
swing. Sometimes a single syncopation is enough for him;
and he is not averse to reducing it to its simplest form by
playing the note on the weak part of one beat but not pro-
longing it into the next (fig. 23). Taking advantage of the

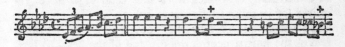

FIG. 23

saxophone's greater mobility, Johnny Hodges scatters his
phrases, which are more abundant than Armstrong's, with
syncopated accents on short notes (eighths) that fall on the
weak part of the beat. His famous break in WHOA BABE (with
Hampton) is a perfect illustration of this approach, on
which Charlie Parker has based his rhythmic ideas. It is
to be noticed, nonetheless, that this break ends with two
long syncopations that have a striking effect rhythmically
(fig. 24). This is an excellent demonstration of what synco-

FIG. 24

pation contributes to jazz. It is easy to imagine how much less swing these two notes would have had if played on the beat.

But it would be wrong to suppose from this that the feeling of swing rises in proportion to the number of syncopations used. Certain combinations of syncopations are felicitous, and others are not. An extreme abundance of syncopations is usually not desirable. Some of Pete Brown's solos that are made up almost exclusively of syncopated notes produce a rhythmic monotony that ultimately destroys the feeling of swing in spite of the excellent saxophonist's flexibility and precision. Moreover, a very syncopated language is impossible either in extremely fast tempos, when it becomes very difficult to place the syncopation accurately, or in extremely slow ones, when the "centrifugal force" required for its full effectiveness is lacking.

This observation brings us to another aspect of the problem of the superstructure, the division of the beat. In jazz, the internal equilibrium of the phrase depends essentially on the tempo adopted. We have just seen that in moderate tempos this division is ternary. A classically trained musician would be surprised to hear this after looking at a score written by a jazz arranger. He would have found no 6/8 or 12/8 bars, and though he may have noticed numerous triplets, he would have noticed still more beats divided into four units (a dotted eighth note plus a sixteenth). This misunderstanding arises from the inaccurate system of notation imposed by custom, according to which a triplet made up of a quarter and an eighth is written as a dotted eighth and a sixteenth, which may be easier to read but would be anti-swing if played exactly. As the tempo becomes faster, this ternary division of the beat tends more and more to become binary. The syncopated note then has the same value as the unsyncopated notes around it (cf. the last measure of fig. 23). On the other hand, in slow tempos, which modern jazzmen

and the most advanced segment of classical jazzmen handle
by mentally breaking the movement up in two, the beat may
be divided into four or even six parts. This rewarding procedure consists in imagining two beats for every one that
the rhythm section actually plays. The soloist may then
fashion his phrase in terms of this moderate tempo, which
is bound to be better for swing. The procedure was invented
by Louis Armstrong, who used it as early as 1927 for his solo·
in ALLIGATOR CRAWL. However, its use did not become general until ten or twelve years later. The most brilliant
examples of it are in Count Basie's BLUE AND SENTIMENTAL,
Hawkins' BODY AND SOUL, and Charlie Parker's EMBRACEABLE
YOU. The arranger of BLUE AND SENTIMENTAL enriched the
procedure by introducing the half-beat syncopation; but
Charlie Parker seems to us to be the one responsible for
making this important acquisition become part of the soloist's language.

Generally, then, as the tempo becomes faster, the divisions
into which each beat is divided become fewer and farther
between, as if compensating in this way for the fact that the
beats themselves are closer together. It is as if there were a
metronomical unit (involving the speed at which notes and
phrases are played) that is favorable to swing, regardless of
the tempo adopted. This unit, which is the eighth note in
fast tempos, frequently becomes the eighth note of a triplet
in medium tempos and the sixteenth in slow tempos. In slow
movements, Parker occasionally raises this mental subdivi-
sion to the second power, in which case the thirty-second
note becomes the "unit of swing" (LP version of EMBRACE-
ABLE YOU). The relationship between this notion and that
of syncopation is evident, since both are based on a division
of the beat.

Very long notes are not favorable to swing, nor are very
short ones used in great abundance. The latter are rarely
employed by good jazz musicians except to prepare a contrast

that will make the swing of what follows all the more remarkable for having been preceded by a passage in which this quality has been purposely slighted (note, for example, the entrance of Hawkins in HONEYSUCKLE ROSE; a prolongation of this passage would have run counter to the effect desired). Long notes are much more frequent. Armstrong, in particular, uses them freely; and when he does, even though his vibrato continues to be rhythmical, he seems to throw onto his sidemen the responsibility for keeping up the swing. Here again it is a concern for contrast—expressive contrast, in this case—that makes the soloist get away from the customary characteristics of the "swing phrase."

Generally speaking, the jazz soloist constructs his phrase by choosing time values and figures that are best suited to producing swing, depending on the tempo adopted, the inherent possibilities of his instrument, and his personal conception of what the instrument can be made to do. However, the type of phrase is also affected by the logic of musical thought, which does not permit just any rhythmic figure to be used with a given melody. Nor does it permit certain themes to be taken at unsuitable tempos. Furthermore, the phrase and the tempo must be strictly co-ordinated. To the extent that the phrase is subordinate to the theme, it may be said that the theme—or, more precisely, the band leader's conception of the theme—is what determines the choice of tempo.

3
Getting the Notes in the Right Place

An ideal tempo and an accurate conception of the phrase's rhythmic structure are important elements in the production of swing, but they will remain ineffective if the notes are not placed exactly where they should be. All musicians know

how important this factor is, but it has been curiously neglected by most jazz specialists. Faults of this kind (call them,
if you prefer, failures to play in time) are numerous in the
work of many well-known musicians. We have pointed out
some examples in recordings by Johnny Dodds and Kid
Ory.[7] One of the oldtimers' most common weaknesses results
from their playing syncopated notes prematurely, in moderate tempos, on the second third of the beat. This "corny"
syncopation is a carry-over from the polka style. Rhythmically, the effect is deplorable, as is easily shown by the musicians who, following Louis Armstrong's example, have
acquired the habit of attacking the syncopation on the last
third of the beat, thereby giving their phrasing much more
flexibility.

Nonetheless, some styles permit rhythmic liberties in the
relationship between the notes and the rhythm section's
beat. Hawkins' "rhapsodic" style in slow tempos and some of
Lester Young's improvisations have notes that are rhythmically irrational. However, these phrases that apparently follow no measure always have some central notes that fall
squarely on the beat, and these serve to bring the phrases
back from time to time into a regular metrical framework.
Similarly, when Erroll Garner plays series of eighths or
triplets a fraction behind the rhythm section's beat in moderate tempos, his phrase is still strictly dependent on the
infrastructure. The phrase that follows no measure is exceptional in jazz. It can appear only under certain circumstances, when the tempo is extremely slow (Don Byas'
LAURA); it cannot be said to favor swing.

If getting the notes in the right place is indispensable to
the expression of swing in solos, it naturally is not any less
indispensable when several musicians play together in a section, notably when performing an arrangement. The problems of articulation and accentuation that arise in such

[7] Cf. Chapter IV. pp. 52-53.

cases only make it harder to get everything in place. Every
musician has his own way of articulating and accenting notes.
He must give it up in order to adopt the way of the man who
is playing first alto, first trumpet, or whatever his instrument
may be. It is necessary to work at forming a blend just as
a football team must work at making out of its eleven men a
single team. It is hardly surprising that big bands are much
more rarely satisfying than small ones in swing. Playing in
a section, very good musicians occasionally get the notes in
the wrong place, either because they have misinterpreted
what the arranger wanted or because they have misunder-
stood what their section leader wanted. Errors of this kind
can be partially redeemed by the other musicians if their
part is more prominent. Still, the swing invariably suffers.
The example of the final ensemble in WHEN LIGHTS ARE LOW
is significant in this respect; every rhythmic weakness, however small, results in a proportional weakness in the swing.
Finally, it should be noted that the problem of getting everything in place concerns the members of the rhythm section,
too, not only in their basic function as accompanists (pro-
viding a steady pulsation), but also every time they stop
doing this—in a break, for example—and express a rhythmic
figure, however uncomplicated.

4
Relaxation

That brings us to the non-technical conditions of swing.
Here, musical analysis will not do us much good. It is possible to determine mathematically how many notes a musician fails to play in time; it is not possible to determine in
the same way how relaxed he is. Relaxation plays an essential role in the production of swing. It is what gives to the
rhythm section's pulsation the bounce that characterizes

swing; it is what makes it possible for the soloist to get every-thing in the right place without seeming to try, which is the ideal way. Many musicians, both accompanists and soloists, have a perfectly correct idea of tempo and phrase structure and just where the notes should go, but still cannot get across the swing because their bodies betray them. It is the American Negroes who created jazz; and the number of them who are capable of complete neuro-muscular relaxa-tion is very remarkable. This characteristic has been demon-strated in track and field events, where colored sprinters' and jumpers' ability to relax is regarded as the principal reason for their speed and agility. Some white sprinters, by dint of much work, have managed to equal them. Similarly, if a gifted white musician works assiduously at it, he may be able to play in as relaxed a way as the great colored jazzmen. The possibility exists, but examples do not abound.

5
Vital Drive

There is another element in swing that resists analysis and that I would hesitate to mention if my personal impressions had not been echoed by many jazz musicians. What is in-volved is a combination of undefined forces that creates a kind of "rhythmic fluidity" without which the music's swing is markedly attenuated. Some excellent bands that play well-conceived phrases with the notes just where they should be, in an ideal tempo and in a relaxed way, still fail to convey much of an impression of swing to the listener. It seems that the musicians are beating time, that they are playing intel-lectually, that they are carrying out a plan rather than play-ing jazz. This observation is frequently true of white bands, even some of the best. The explanation is that their vital drive is weak. If I weren't afraid of straying too far afield,

I would suggest that this drive is a manifestation of personal magnetism, which is somehow expressed—I couldn't say exactly how—in the domain of rhythm. That is just an hypothesis. Nevertheless, it seems impossible to understand the

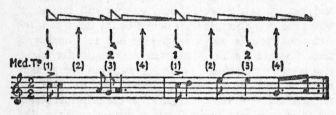

FIG. 25

The superstructure of this riff shows poor rhythmic construction. There is an inflexibility about the way syncopations and notes played on the beat alternate. All accents coincide with the beat. The execution (top diagram) is as faulty as the conception. The way the notes are played shows extension of the long ones at the expense of the short ones ("corny" syncopation). The infrastructure betrays a slackening of pace (the beats get further apart) and a heavy, very irregular accentuation of the off-beats (2 and 4). Moreover, the pulsation is dry and stiff.

FIG. 25a

The riff has been modified to good advantage. The superstructure is now favorable to swing. The accents fall alternately on the beat and on the weak part of the beat. The execution shows similar improvement. The notes are placed exactly where they should be (the beat is divided into three parts). The infrastructure has a steady beat, with a light acute accent on the even-numbered beats, counterbalanced by a discreet grave accent on the uneven-numbered ones. The relaxed manner of the execution is symbolized by the bounce from one beat to the next.

phenomenon of swing without taking into consideration the idea of vital drive. I shall not bar it from my description, therefore, until someone suggests a more satisfactory explanation.

The purpose of Figure 25 is to make it easier for the reader to understand the conditions required for the expression of swing. Each of its two parts represents the conception and execution of a two-bar riff. In the first, the essential characteristics of the phenomenon are purposely distorted. We shall suppose, moreover, that the ideal tempo has not been found and that the vital drive—which I can't see how to indicate graphically—is not what it should be. On the other hand, we shall suppose that both these elements supplement the ones indicated in the second illustration. The staff and the notes represent the rhythmic construction (superstructure). It seemed to me right to follow the notation that jazzmen regularly use, in spite of its being, as we have seen, inexact. The triangles represent the sounds with their more or less accented attacks. The infrastructure is represented by the odd- and even-numbered beats of the rhythm section (vertical arrows), over which the notes of the riff are placed just where the ear hears them. Grave and acute accents are indicated by arrows pointing, respectively, down and up.

These two charts will repay very careful study. The eye can sometimes help the ear to grasp phenomena that are too many-sided for even the most attentive listener to catch. But it is evident, of course, that they must not be taken too literally. The phenomenon of swing cannot be reduced to such a simple demonstration. This impossibility is sufficiently shown by the fact that some of the elements we have talked about have had to be omitted from the figure.

Chapter XIII

THE EVOLUTION
OF
RHYTHMIC CONCEPTIONS

By borrowing the principle of a two- and four-beat bar
first from hymns and then from polkas and military marches,
the American Negro made a sharp break with his African
ancestors. However, his sense of rhythm was not completely
at home in this rigid framework. An opposition arose between the container and the thing contained. Half a century
after the birth of jazz, this opposition has not been smoothed
away, and it probably never will be. The Negro has accepted
2/4 and 4/4 bars only as a framework into which he could
slip the successive designs of his own conceptions. Just like
someone trying to find the most comfortable position in a
new bed, he has experimented with different ways of accom-
modating himself to the space between measure bars. The
phenomenon of swing should not be regarded as the immediate and inevitable result of a confrontation between the
African rhythmic genius and the 2/2 bar. What we know
about primitive jazz excludes the hypothesis that swing
sprang into being like a spark at the collision of two stones.
Pre-Armstrong recordings reveal, on the contrary, that swing
was merely latent at first and took shape progressively over
a long period; moreover, later works show that it has never
assumed a definitive aspect. We are going to follow its trans-

formations from one period to another, trying to keep the
account clear by considering only moderate tempos. It happens to be in these tempos, actually, that the differences
are sharpest.

1
The New Orleans Two-Beat?

The first jazzmen's conception of rhythm resulted from a
combination of elements of the military march and the
polka, and of the Negro's sense of rhythm. By introducing
the polka's off-beats into marches and by syncopating the
accents that traditionally marked the first three half beats
in the polka, the Negroes made a timid but nonetheless
decisive step toward rhythmic emancipation. The measure's
two beats were divided into two equal parts, the first getting
a grave accent and the second an acute one, which was more
pronounced in the Negroes' playing than in the polka. This
favoring of the off-beat shows the pioneers' fondness for
syncopation, which appears later on in all sorts of guises.
We have observed that syncopation is a constant element
of the Negro-American genius. However, neither the superstructure nor the infrastructure had yet reached a stage where
any mention of swing would not be premature. What we
know of rhythmic conceptions and executions during this
primitive period (in addition to what we can logically de-
duce) would seem much closer to the first diagram presented
at the end of the last chapter than to the second.

Twenty years of trial and effort—almost unconscious, perhaps, but nonetheless real—produced, at the beginning of
the second period of jazz, an embryo of swing that contained
all the characteristics needed for an expression of this
phenomenon. Vital drive and relaxation, which are "natural"

qualities, probably existed before swing; they merely began
to serve a more effective rhythmic conception. The accompanists seem to have learned how to keep the beat better,
the soloists how to phrase with more flexibility. Perfection
was no doubt still a long way off. As late as 1927, as good
a man as John St. Cyr shows himself incapable of keeping
up the tempo for eight bars at a stretch when left on his
own.[1] During that period. a number of pieces begin in one
tempo and finish in another.[2] The superstructure often had
to do without syncopations, which the musicians wouldn't
know how to do justice to. The series of three quarter notes
played on the beat in King Oliver's DIPPER MOUTH BLUES
avoid any such risk; but the rhythmic figures that result are
too much like the polka to be compatible with real swing.
They would be unthinkable, several years later, in the classical jazz framework of men like Basie and Hampton.

However, along with a better conception of the phrase,
the capital element of *getting the notes in place* was added
around the middle of this period by the advent of Louis
Armstrong, in whom the rhythmic genius of the Negro-
American people flowered in full perfection. There can be
no doubt that Armstrong's presence is what places the work
of the King Oliver Creole Band (1923) so far ahead of other
jazz of that time, in spite of the band's shortcomings; its
rhythm already shows considerable evolution. Nevertheless,
as we have had occasion to note before, the great jazzman's
immediate associates were not able to assimilate what he had
to teach. Except for a few first-rate musicians who, after Armstrong, seem like precursors, the rhythmic conception of the
"advanced New Orleans" style resulted in a fairly crude kind
of swing. Holdovers from the military march and polka are
absent only in the best works of this school, the ones in
which Armstrong's influence is most noticeable.

[1] Cf. ALLIGATOR CRAWL, by Louis Armstrong's Hot Seven.
[2] Cf. INDIGO STOMP and BLUE PIANO STOMP, by the Johnny Dodds Trio.

Like primitive jazz, oldtime jazz rests on the two-beat bar, including in the infrastructure a prominently emphasized off-beat. The superstructure, in which syncopations and notes played on the beat alternate according to relatively unchanging rhythmic formulas, is nevertheless less rigid than it had been. Aided by the notes' being accurately placed and resting on an infrastructure influenced by the classical conception, it produced, in certain works of the Revival (those of Armstrong's new Hot Five, for example), swing of an incontestable quality that is found only exceptionally in recordings of the second period, when these two elements were lacking. Still, one thing seems certain: The two-beat bar, in itself, is inimical to a full expression of swing.

2
The Four-Beat of Classical Jazz

Beginning with the third period of jazz, a profound revolution took place in both the infrastructure and the superstructure. Little by little, the drummers and then the bass players got into the habit of beating four to the bar, and at the same time pianists stopped playing exclusively Boston. While the number of bass notes increased, acute accents were handled more discreetly. This led to a suppression of the notion of off-beats—that is, the 2/2 measure was replaced by the 4/4. Since the off-beat had become an even-numbered beat (also called weak beat, although it answers this description only harmonically, being still accented), there were now two distinct beats where before there had been one beat divided into two parts. The four-beat bar had replaced the two-beat. The effect of this new conception of accents on swing was radical. The new pulsation, by modifying the waddling character of the New Orleans rhythm, encouraged a completely different kind of swing, one that was at the same time lighter and more concentrated. Similarly, performers got better at turning out the beats; they became more relaxed and made technical progress that permitted the pianist as well as the drummer not only to express new rhythmic combinations, but also—and this is more important —to execute the simplest figures better and therefore more effectively.[3]

The superstructure was modified in the same way. Except for the clarinet—which, perhaps for this reason, became less important—phrasing grew more flexible and richer, and called into play syncopated figures of greater variety. In conception as well as execution, Armstrong's influence, which had been superficial, became widespread. Beginning with the end of the pre-classical period, the notion of getting the notes in the right place may be regarded as assimilated by most good jazz musicians. From then on, it was possible for groups to play together with sufficient rhythmic excellence. After 1933-1934, arrangements accordingly tended to exploit the phenomenon of swing, sometimes at the expense of melodic diversity. Riffs became extremely important. Made more supple by syncopations, which were put to better use than in the past and produced a more pronounced sway,

[3] This is the way one must understand Lucien Malson's statement (cf. *Les Maîtres du Jazz,* p. 28) that swing depends on the musician's technical skill just as it depends on rhythmic perfection and on the construction of the phrase. The objection has been made that swing is a special gift. There can be no doubt about that; it is only too clear that many musicians will never be able to swing. But any gift can be developed and improved, whether it be a high-jumper's ability to leap without strain or a band leader's discriminating ear. If a musician's conception of swing did not depend to a certain extent on his musical education, an African Negro would be capable of picking up the whole rhythmic basis of jazz in a few minutes. If one's ability to put this conception into practice did not depend on muscular training, such and such a famous bass player could sit down at the drums and do better than most regular drummers from the very first. The truth is that the process of getting the right idea and then putting it into practice has required a considerable amount of groping around.

the riff became the ideal vehicle for jazz's new conceptions. Most orchestrations included long series of repeated riffs that were interesting only for the amount of swing that the performers were able to get out of them. This idea is sound for big bands, when different riffs can be heard simultaneously (Count Basie's SENT FOR YOU YESTERDAY), but is less so for small groups. However, the perfect execution of some of Hampton's works gives rise to such a high quality of swing that any criticism of the musical thought they stem from loses some of its value.

While the most varied kinds of phrasing flourished according to individual styles, in the domain of the infrastructure the classical period was notable for bringing to its logical conclusion an evolution that had begun even before the two-beat bar was abandoned. For years, the infrastructure had been moving toward the establishment of an ideal tempo, in which strong and weak beats would rebound with the same elasticity. This notion of four equal beats; which was heralded by Count Basie's earliest works, found its first realization, undoubtedly, in Lionel Hampton's masterpiece, WHEN LIGHTS ARE LOW.

The rhythmic basis of WHEN LIGHTS ARE LOW deserves a moment's attention. First of all, there is the incomparable homogeneity of the accompaniment—Clyde Hart (piano), Charlie Christian (guitar), Milton Hinton (bass), and Cozy Cole (drums). It doesn't seem that there are four instruments played by four musicians; the impression of unity is so strong that the plurality of voices becomes questionable. Even the dry slap of the high hat cymbal on the even-numbered beats—a holdover—is not really *heard*. By fitting in together so perfectly, the timbres become fuller and richer by mutual contact. Such a blending would not have been possible ten years or even five years earlier, when the training of accompanists still had ground to cover. It was not for nothing that two generations of specialists in rhythm had worn down their fingers looking, whether they fully realized it or not, for a way to express the swing they felt in themselves. The young men benefited from the effort of their seniors. Isn't that just what every real tradition makes possible?

The homogeneity of this foundation is so effective rhythmically that it becomes almost unnecessary to heighten it with any special stresses. Actually, the only elements of variety that the rhythm section uses in WHEN LIGHTS ARE LOW come from the drummer. First of all, there is the classical rhythm that all disciples of Chick Webb beat out on the high hat cymbal—a three-note unit (dotted eighth, sixteenth, quarter) of which the first two notes constitute the anacrusis and the last is the accent. This differs from pure 4/4 because of the emphasis given to the accented note by the open cymbal and also because of the sixteenth, which plays the role of up-beat and therefore calls attention to the quarter note it precedes. It should be noted that the impression of rhythmic perfection is less strong when Cozy Cole uses this rhythm than when he confines himself to playing the snare drum legato. The second element of variety is the break. Cozy Cole underlines the last two bars of the middle interlude by an expressive rhythmic figure that forms a magnificent preparation for the section's re-entry together. But the breaks that he plays in the margin of the initial exposition, during the first sixteen bars of the piece, seem even more effective. What is original about these breaks is that they are made up of only one sound. This single percussion is enough to launch the band in an astonishing way, because it is placed with incomparable rhythmic precision. It furnishes striking proof that a single right accent does more for swing than a more brilliant and fuller break in which so much as one note happens to be out of place. The extreme sobriety of the drummer's flights of fancy and their small number show that what was important for the classics was an infrastructure that could support the soloist under any circumstances. The classical drummer rarely took the trouble to create amusing rhythmic counterpoints, as the New Orleans drummer used to do so freely on the woodblock or the big cymbal and as the bop drummer was to do later on in a different spirit and with different means. He kept himself in the background of the jazz band, supplying it with a constant pulsation.

WHEN LIGHTS ARE LOW may be regarded as the apex of the ascending curve that symbolizes the evolution of swing. We have observed that this element, which was latent in primitive jazz and not yet licked into shape in oldtime jazz, did not really come into its own until the pre-classical period. By giving the name *swing era* to the period I call classic, American musicians and critics have expressed an historical fact that there is no getting around. Admittedly, they understand it in a very broad sense, lumping together under this term all characteristics of the classical style; but isn't it true that, to a large extent, the classical style is incomparably more favorable to swing than the styles that preceded it? Of course, the word had existed for a long time. In his solicitude over the pioneers' claims, hasn't Jelly Roll Morton reminded us that one of his 1906 compositions was called GEORGIA SWING? That does not at all prove that the word had the meaning it has today. On the contrary, I don't believe it was merely by chance that the word *swing* began to be used in its current rhythmic sense only around 1930, when jazz musicians were becoming aware of the relatively new element that was enriching their language in such an extraordinary way.

3
The Modern Conceptions (Bop and Cool)

The conception of "four even beats" has proved so effective in the production of swing that there is cause to wonder

whether it will ever be surpassed. The chances are small.
Once it has reached the kind of classical maturity shown
by the work we have just been talking about, an art can
hardly go on progressing, it can only evolve. After the joy
of discovery comes the boredom of repetition. Knowing
that they would never do better than this perfect 4/4, the
musicians in the next generation began to break up each
beat. Cozy Cole's ideas of rhythm are based on the quarter
note, Kenny Clarke's on the eighth. Naturally, the resulting
swing under these conditions was as different from four-beat
swing as that swing could possibly have been different from
the two-beat. One thing to notice here is that, by multiplying
rhythmic possibilities, modern jazzmen have also multiplied
the difficulty of swinging. Although some of their works are
undeniably successful rhythmically and although they have
undoubtedly found as perfect a beat as that of WHEN LIGHTS
ARE LOW, perhaps this extra complication explains why it
is still true that only a fairly limited elite among them bring
things off with complete success.

Compared with the classical conception, bebop's infrastructure is characterized by three notions: decomposition
of the beat, disintegration of the rhythm section, and non-
continuity. The first is the ultimate consequence of the
tendency toward syncopation that appeared from the beginning as one of the constant elements of Negro-American
music. In place of the oldtimers' accentuation of the off-beat,
which became an accentuation of the weak beat in classical
jazz, the bebop drummers substituted a new syncopation of
the divided half beat. Of course, there could be no question
of doing this constantly and winding up with a measure of
eight occasionally uneven beats, so the new syncopation was
expressed by means of scattered accents. Between the even
cymbal strokes by which the regular beat is maintained, the

4 This may also explain why young drummers have returned to a language
that is rhythmically more simple,

snare and bass drums give out either muffled or clear percussions, sometimes singly and sometimes in series, on subdivisions of the beat. Thus the accentuation, in modern jazz, falls between beats.

Disintegration of the rhythm section represents for the orchestra the result of the same kind of evolution as the one that resulted metrically in decomposition of the beat. The historical development is easy to follow. Just as the perfection of the classical musicians' continuous and even beat made it necessary to break up the beat, the unsurpassable unity obtained by the best rhythm sections of the Hampton variety couldn't help causing later sections to break up. What characterizes the classical rhythm section is unity; what characterizes the modern section is diversity, which cannot be better expressed than in polyrhythms. The group, which operates in a dissociated way, is a projected image of the drummer's style. Metrical continuity is provided by the bass, sometimes helped out by the guitar; against this are heard the contrary rhythms of the drums, the piano, and occasionally a newcomer of African origin, the bongo or congo drum. The result may be simple anarchy when things don't go well, but it may also be an admirable rhythmic richness when the section is made up of first-rate musicians who understand one another. Far from being gratuitous, this richness is very often a vital element of the new style. Many modern soloists, on the model of Charlie Parker, can express themselves freely only when they feel themselves supported by a polyrhythmic foundation.

Non-continuity is the result of this twofold disintegration. The introduction of syncopated percussions between beats broke up the regular succession that was characteristic of classical jazz; the specialization of each instrument in the section led at least one of them, the piano, to break the continuity of steady beats in favor of little syncopated and spaced-out figures (the distant origins of this conception are apparent in the work of Earl Hines, and it was developed by the great pianists of the classical period—Teddy Wilson, Billy Kyle, King Cole). Taken by itself, an accompaniment by Bud Powell or Al Haig would require close listening to be recognized as being based on a steady tempo. But it would be a serious error to consider by itself a part that has meaning only in terms of the whole for which it was conceived. Would anyone think of looking for an independent meaning in the second violin part of Debussy's *Quartet?* Behind the ultra-syncopated percussions of Max Roach or the rhythmically disjointed chords of Hank Jones, don't the bass, the guitar, and the cymbal take care of expressing the four beats? Besides, one thing to be said in favor of non-continuity is that it arrived at a time when both the musician's and the listener's idea of the beat's permanence was sufficiently developed to make it possible to *suggest* where the oldtimers and the classics had been obliged to *express.*[5] The example of Armstrong's stop choruses in POTATO HEAD BLUES and SKIP THE GUTTER shows, moreover, that the suggestion of metrical continuity which is characteristic of the modern style is not contrary to the spirit of the most traditional jazz.

Far from being a heresy, then, the modern conception of the infrastructure can be seen in historical perspective to be the logical and necessary consequence of the classical conception. There is no more of a break between Cozy Cole and Kenny Clarke than between Zutty Singleton and Chick Webb. The two-beat broke up into four; it was only logical for the four-beat, in its turn, to break up. Steadiness of the tempo, which is a fundamental law of jazz, persists. It has been said that bop ideas of rhythm were anarchic. That opinion neglects the extraordinary coherence demonstrated

[5] In other words, acquiring a feeling of the beat's permanence involves renouncing this very permanence.

by good modern rhythm sections, in which the most diverse elements, contributed by three or four different musicians, blend in an astonishingly homogeneous synthesis. It has also been said that modern accompanists were less concerned about supporting the soloist than about standing out at his expense. If it were true that Max Roach gets in the way of a soloist, wouldn't band leaders choose some less exceptional but more discreet drummer instead of him? Anyone who has seen someone like Kenny Clarke from close up and in the heat of action must have realized how carefully the great modern drummers listen to the soloist in order to create for him a rhythmic counterpoint. Certainly, their conception would not suit musicians of older periods, but it must be judged within the framework of a given style. If Johann Sebastian Bach had been a jazzman, he undoubtedly would have had a hard time getting along with Schoenberg at the piano and Bartók on drums!

Charlie Parker, for his part, gets along very well with Max Roach's collaboration. As we have seen, the great drummer puts into practice certain tendencies, certain polyrhythmic "desires" that are latent in Parker's phrase. This aspect of modern jazz cannot be neglected. However, a study of the principal bop soloists shows that the polyrhythmic spirit is always expressed in a framework of metrical continuity. Jazz is still controlled by the measure bar. The rhythmic construction of Gillespie's and Parker's most astonishing solos reveals that these musicians "understood" the four beats even when the accompanying section seems to be disregarding them in the background. And such moments are exceptional. Jacques Henry[6] has very wisely pointed out that most bop drummers, Max Roach above all, used the high hat cymbal to mark the even-numbered beats regularly.

[6] J. Henry: "Jazz moderne, musique à deux temps," in *Jazz-Hot*, September, 1952.

This is part of a tradition that jazzmen have always felt very deeply. As we know, accentuation of the even-numbered beats, which was first expressed by the hand cymbal, was later assigned to the high hat cymbal, but this tended to get swallowed up in the rhythm section. In most cases, the drummer's left foot nevertheless continued to make the cymbal sound twice every bar. The disintegration of the modern rhythm section necessarily brought out this secondary but fundamental percussion, which the extreme unity of the classical rhythm section had, as it were, absorbed. It would undoubtedly be overbold to identify this as a return to the oldtime two-beat, which depended essentially on the regular distribution of grave accents. But how would it be possible not to conclude that the modern drummer is considerably more concerned than he is generally thought to be about marking the beat's steadiness in a precise way?

Finally, we have seen[7] that, following Lester Young, both white and colored musicians took pains to develop their ability to relax. Relaxation seems to have become as essential a part of the jazzman's training as of the sprinter's. There is no other way to explain the amazingly relaxed manner of young white musicians in the cool movement; up to then, colored musicians seemed to have an almost complete monopoly in this respect. It is too bad that this step forward, which brought into being a new kind of beat, was accompanied by a certain regression in the domain of rhythmic construction.

Thus, from one period to another, swing has been manifested in very different forms, by means of extremely varied conceptions, assuming occasionally contradictory aspects even though remaining essentially the same. Hawkins in HELLO LOLA, Lester Young in SOMETIMES I'M HAPPY, Parker in COOL BLUES, and Konitz in ISRAEL are all expressing the same fundamental reality, each in his own way. Conceptions of

[7] Cf. Chapter VIII, p. 119.

the infrastructure, of the superstructure, of getting the accents in place, and of relaxation have changed with the times; vital drive has remained essentially the same. Of the curious subjects uncovered by a study of jazz, this multiform aspect of its most mysterious but also, perhaps, its most necessary element is certainly not one of the least interesting.

Chapter XIV

THE HANDLING
OF SOUND

Unlike European composers and interpreters in the classical tradition, the jazz musician treats sound itself as something real that can be shaped and modified. He gives it a
form at the same time that he fits it into a melodic sequence.
His creative personality can find its expression in the color
of his sonority just as completely as in the style of his phrases.
Jean Ledru goes even further when he says that, "more than
an element of creation, sonority is the very foundation of
style," and "A musician who plays naturally has the style
of his sonority."[1] It may be impossible to prove this idea,
but it is nonetheless an extremely attractive one to the extent
that it accounts for the homogeneity of some styles and the
heterogeneity of others in cases where melodic analysis fails
to provide a complete explanation.[2] It would be out of the
question for us to compare here the different types of sonority
that can be produced on each instrument. We shall limit
ourselves to a brief examination of the procedures followed
by jazz soloists in their handling of sound.

[1] J. Ledru: "Le problème du saxophone-ténor," in *Jazz-Hot*, October,
1949, p. 10.

[2] The reader will have understood that it was for the sake of simplicity
and clearness that we considered (cf. Chapter X, p. 161) the melodic
element separately in Lester Young's solo based on THESE FOOLISH THINGS.
The fact that this solo is exceptionally successful can be accounted for to a
large extent by the perfect correspondence between melodic sensitivity and
"sound sensitivity."

1
Vibrato

Generally speaking, vibrato is put to a much wider use by jazz musicians than in the European tradition. Often a phrase can be recognized as being jazz only by virtue of the vibrato with which the performer animates the sounds of which it is made up. Sometimes, even, vibrato is the only thing that gives an apparently insignificant phrase its esthetic sense.

The types of vibrato used in jazz are almost as numerous as the leading soloists. One differs from another sometimes as much as Renoir's lighting differs from Rembrandt's. There is a world of difference between the panting, high-frequency vibrato of Sidney Bechet and that of Lester Young, which is fairly slow and restrained. Nevertheless, certain standards were observed during the classical period as a result of Armstrong's and Hawkins' influence on their juniors. In their search for a rich and expressive sonority, most of the soloists of that time adopted types of vibrato that were similar to those used by the two great leaders.

Armstrong's vibrato is vocal by nature. In other words, even on the trumpet it sounds like an instrumental adaptation of a vibrato conceived for the voice. The relationship in Armstrong's art between his vibrato as a singer and his vibrato as a trumpeter is demonstrated in many of his recordings. The phrase endings in BACK O' TOWN BLUES, for example, show the importance in both of the "terminal vibrato" that we ran across in our study of Dickie Wells.[3] Except for short notes, which have no vibrato, and very long ones, which require a certain evenness, Armstrong sets up his note before beginning to work on it. He starts out with no vibrato and finishes with a very strong one, like Wells; but, as might

[3] Cf. Chapter V, p. 67.

be expected from the difference in their instruments, Armstrong's vibrato has less breadth.

Hawkins' vibrato is more distinctly instrumental. There is no reason for not believing it may come from Armstrong's, but a new synthesis of its components was made unavoidable by the fact that the tenor sax and the trumpet have so few points in common. Even the range of the instrument must be taken into consideration. Doesn't an instrumentalist tend to use a broader vibrato as he plays lower notes? Hawkins' vibrato is more regular than Armstrong's, and he accentuates it at the end of a note much more rarely than Armstrong does. If a connection between voice and instrument exists, it is pretty well hidden.

The esthetic importance of vibrato is evident; its rhythmic value seems less well known. Nevertheless, it appears certain that vibrato can frequently reinforce the feeling of the tempo. One of our best drummers used to claim that a single note, played by a good musician, was enough to get him started. This would be possible only if the note had a movement of its own; and how could it have one except by virtue of its vibrato? We have seen that Miles Davis elevated this fact to the status of a technique, and we have observed the use to which he put it in the production of swing.[4]

2
Inflections

The jazz soloist has found in portamentos (or glides) another means of extending the range of his expressive language. Like vibrato, inflection is vocal in origin. It comes from the blue notes, whose genesis has been so well explained by Ernest Borneman.[5] These blue notes passed from the vocal to the instrumental style, carrying with them the emo-

[4] Cf. our discussion of the *dancing note*, p. 124.
[5] Cf. Chapter III, p. 42.

tional potential that the blues singers had given them. Still today, when an expressive intention shows up in the blues, whether instrumental or vocal, nine times out of ten it is concentrated on a blue note. The same thing is true of many other pieces that have only passing resemblances to the blues. Thus, in spite of the theme, which has neither the form nor the spirit of the blues, Johnny Hodges' solo in WHOA BABE (with Hampton) is a typical example of the close relationship that exists between inflection and the blue note. Take the third phrase of this improvisation, for example. A series of descending portamentos emphasizes a certain number of sounds (fig. 26). In three cases out of four, blue notes are

FIG. 26

involved (Eb and Bb). The fourth case, in which the inflection begins on a G (dominant of the key), can be explained only by the symmetrical arrangement that fits this note into an expressive ensemble built out of rhythmic imitations.

Of course, jazz musicians have not failed to enlarge their horizon by applying inflection to the other degrees of the scale. Louis Armstrong very quickly put into practice a system of ascending and descending glissandos that produced effects which have become classic. Before him, New Orleans trombones had been in the habit of introducing their principal re-entries by a big dominant-tonic glissando (which was in rather questionable taste, to tell the truth). Some clarinetists, like Bigard, and some saxophonists, like Hodges, have managed to draw very diversified figures from this same portamento principle. The fact remains, nonetheless, that jazzmen associate inflection with the blue note.

It sometimes happens that vibrato and inflection join

forces to produce a paroxysm of tension. Occasionally, even, whether or not it is associated with a portamento, a smooth sonority in a vibrato context leads, by contrast, to the same result. Barney Bigard, in his chorus of SOLID OLD MAN, uses these alternating effects with sobriety. This solo, for that matter, deserves attention for more than one reason. In it, the tension that is characteristic of the hot manner of playing is superimposed on harmonic tension in the European sense of the term. The maximum voltage coincides with the parts that are harmonically the most tense—that is, those where the blue notes culminate. Similarly, the final resolution on the tonic chord is accompanied by a parallel drop in volume.

3

Other Elements

Vibrato and inflection may be regarded as the most important elements of the hot manner of playing, but they are not the only ones. Also to be cited are attack, use of the top register, distorted timbres, and harmonics. They are used less frequently than vibrato and even than inflection. Except on the clarinet, it was customary, during the first periods of jazz, to attack each sound (or each series of sounds) cleanly and sharply. No doubt this is another vestige of the influence military marches had on the newborn jazz, but it must be granted that jazz was all the better for this discipline. The physical shock caused by a trumpet attack completed the sensation that an inflected or vibrated note gave rise to. Still, as the phrasing of soloists became legato rather than detached, it was evident that the attack was losing its reason for being. This was clear to a precursor, the saxophonist Bennie Carter, who was undoubtedly the first to try to limit its effect. Right up to Miles Davis, this conception has not stopped gaining ground.

On the other hand, the top register of wind instruments—and especially of the trumpet—was used more and more, until very recently, by instrumentalists whose technical skill was getting better from year to year. Louis Armstrong and particularly Roy Eldridge have demonstrated the expressive potential that can be expected from an intensive exploitation of the trumpet's upper register. Men like Cat Anderson and Al Killian have gone much further in this direction, but without getting as much profit as might have been hoped from such an extension of the instrument's supposed possibilities. Their dizzying ascents resemble a sporting event more than a search for some new musical climate. Not being integrated in a coherent style—like those of Eldridge or Gillespie—these high notes cannot help striking the listener as gratuitous. Illinois Jacquet has pushed these effects to the limit of absurdity; his ultra-high saxophone harmonics would be hard to fit into any musical context whatever. On the contrary, those of men like Byas and Hawkins, though they also fall outside the usual register of the instrument, always translate an exasperation of the senses, the logical consequence of a musical discourse that tends toward the most violent expressionism. It is the same kind of exasperation of the senses that made Bechet adopt astonishing distorted sonorities in WEARY BLUES (with Tommy Ladnier), even though he did not leave the clarinet's normal range. Finally, the art of Cootie in the CONCERTO or of Tricky Sam in KO-KO is more subtle. Just by itself, their use of the mute shows to what extent their craftsmanship, which can turn out grating and tortured notes, is the fruit of careful working out.

These are the principal elements of the hot language. They translate with force certain musical emotions that are not found in European art, and taken together they constitute an undeniable expressive richness. The extremely low notes that Leo Parker plays as gags, the strange sounds Rex Stewart gets by playing with the valves halfway down, and

Bubber Miley's comic or tragic wa-was are different aspects
of this unusual universe. The jazzman resorts to them, as
the painter resorts to his colors, in order to create. When
Harry Edison works around with one note during half a
chorus in SWINGIN' THE BLUES (with Basie), he deserves to
be called a creator just as much as Benny Carter when he
carves out phrases so delicately in HOT MALLETS.

4
Getting Hot Is Not the Same Thing as Swinging

The hot manner of playing is not only a means of expression and of creation. The success of jazz comes not only
from the musical emotion that a rich creative thought expresses by means of certain procedures, but also from a kind
of human warmth that is more or less independent of the
musical context and that runs, in a sense, parallel to the
music, even though it springs from it. This indefinable element is the "temperature" of music. Musicians and fans are
in the habit of saying, when a certain degree of excitement
and tension is reached, that the music is "getting hot." The
expression is not inappropriate. To "get hot" is to express
a certain physical state that is distinct from pure emotion
and that usually has some connection with the loudness of
the performance. One doesn't "get hot" by playing pianis-
simo. There can be no doubt that there is a direct relationship between the "temperature" of a piece and the hot
manner of playing. It may even be said that only a performance which "gets hot" achieves to a perfect extent the
element of tension that we have identified as one of the two
principal poles of jazz.

This may be a good place to pause for a glance at a
related problem that will throw new light on the question
of handling sound. I mean the problem of perceiving swing.
It would seem logical to expect every jazz fan to be sensitive

to the expression of this phenomenon. But I have been very frequently disappointed in the many contacts I have had with people who, like me, look to jazz for a large part (or even the essential part) of their artistic satisfactions. In a number of cases, I have been obliged to realize that the pleasure we seemed to share when listening to good jazz recordings was not actually the same at all. Pieces that were still in an embryonic stage as far as swing is concerned brought them a satisfaction that showed their ear to be as weak as the music. They were probably sensitive to vital drive and sometimes to the quality of the tempo, but much less so to relaxation, and they were not at all disturbed even when both the rhythmic conception of phrases and their enunciation were so defective that it was hard to make out any swing impulse underneath. I have had to make the best of this semi-incomprehension afflicting a public that was nevertheless fervent. The perception of swing, which is a natural gift just as much as the perception of jazz or of music in general, can be developed in a listener only by means of ear training that a young Negro gets from his environment but that a European almost invariably lacks. The European, therefore, appreciates certain aspects of swing but misses others that are equally essential. It cannot be said that swing is a dead letter for the average jazz fan—the average I refer to is a very high one—but he has only an incomplete and distorted perception of it.

If the element of relaxation, which finds its expression in swing, scarcely gets across to the great majority of jazz fans, the element of tension is, on the contrary, very highly appreciated by them. Thousands of young people who remain unaffected by the extraordinary swing of James Moody stamp with enthusiasm when Flip Phillips[6] cleverly builds up ten-

[6] Those who heard the concert given at the Salle Pleyel by the "Jazz at the Philharmonic" group during the 1952 Salon du Jazz will not contradict what I say here. For that matter, Phillips is also an excellent swingman.

sion by using procedures that it would be easy to catalogue. "Getting hot" is relatively easy; a student band can do it as well as anybody. Exasperated, distorted sonorities played fortissimo are generally sufficient. On the other hand, only a few people can express swing of a certain quality.

Unfortunately, as a result of hazy definitions, the average fan still confuses relaxation and tension, swing and the hot manner of playing. "Swinging" and "getting hot" are nonetheless two separate acts, and they do not always complement each other. This duality, which all the jazzmen I know are aware of, has been pinned down by Pierre Gérardot, who deserves the credit (unless I am mistaken) of having been the first to note in writing the purely rhythmic character of swing.[7] It has been observed that colored musicians have never called the public's attention to this fact. The reason is that professional jazzmen do not like to emphasize their colleagues' shortcomings. Besides, the good musician associates with others like himself and is unaware of bad jazz, or would like to be. I am convinced that every good musician recognizes the swing-hot duality as self-evident, requiring no commentary. There is no need to talk about what can be taken for granted. Such is not the case, as we have seen, for the French fan. An example will clarify what I mean. Simply compare Eddie Vinson's JUMP AND GRINT and Teddy Wilson's I FEEL LIKE A FEATHER IN THE BREEZE. I had occasion to play these two records in the course of some public talks. The first is an orchestral blues in which everything is done to get the "temperature" as high as possible; the second is a very simply played piano solo. JUMP AND GRINT, it is true, might have been hallucinating if deplorable drumwork didn't sup-

---

[7] P. Gérardot: "Le problème de la section rythmique," in *Jazz-Hot*, March, 1948, p. 12: "Generally this word [swing] is confused with atmosphere, and frequently, after a rhythmically deplorable performance, people will say, 'That really got hot, what swing!' Now, the term atmosphere (that is, violent accentuation of musical color, intense production of heat) does not necessarily imply that there was any swing."

press all real swing in it; the rhythmic quality of I FEEL, a piece that is hardly hot at all, is irreproachable. After hearing both, the public invariably revealed that, for it, Eddie Vinson's record was the one that had more swing.

In regard to swing, the average fan is in the situation of that character Rabelais writes about as eating his bread in the smoke of roast beef. The elementary rhythmic obsession that any jazz performance creates, even though it may lack several of the characteristics we have regarded as necessary, and the heat (artificial or spontaneous) that any instrumentalist who is up on hot procedures can generate take the place of swing for him. That explains his liking for oldtime jazz, his distrust of complex bebop rhythms, which disconcert him, and his aversion for the cool style, which is perfectly logical inasmuch as cool musicians refuse just what such an amateur finds most estimable in jazz.

It is certainly true that the hot manner of playing—and the element of tension that comes from it—is the most accessible side of jazz. But the manifestation of swing can give a great deal more joy to the person who is no longer insensitive to it than the most torrid performance. Thanks to swing, jazz has marvelously transcended its rhythmic monotony. What might have been a hopeless weakness has become its fundamental strength. There is in swing a portion of that admirable madness that can be glimpsed behind the loftiest attainments of contemporary art.

Chapter XV

THE ESSENCE

1
What Is Not Essential

We have looked over the conceptions of rhythm and the handling of sound as they apply to the jazz musician. Our search for what is essential to this music now obliges us to ask a series of questions concerning other factors that appear to be equally important. What we have to do is distinguish between the vital center of jazz and the part that is just connected with it. African holdovers, the spirit and form of the blues, the repertory, improvisation, arrangements, melody, harmony—are these simply elements of jazz? Do they constitute its essence? The importance of these questions is obvious. We shall regard as essential only those characteristics that are at once specific and constant.[1] For instance, the growl is part of the language of jazz. It arose from a need to express certain sensations that do not exist outside this music. However, the growl is not essential, since innumerable works that are undeniably jazz make no use

[1] In "Où il le fallait, quand il le fallait" (in *Jazz-Hot*, December, 1949), Lucien Malson put the problem in these Husserl-like terms: "The essence of a thing consists of the elements that it would be impossible to suppose absent without destroying the thing itself." So it is in the case of jazz. This would seem to be the only way to state the question.

whatsoever of this effect. With a few exceptions, jazz uses only a two- and four-beat meter. But this meter is not specific; it existed long before the first Negro slaves set foot in America. Nevertheless, both the growl and the 2/2 or 4/4 bar are part of larger conceptions (sound and rhythm) that we may be obliged to regard as essential.

Melodic holdovers from Africa are not essential to jazz. There is, for example, no trace of them in Coleman Hawkins' BODY AND SOUL. This same piece authorizes us to disqualify, as essential characteristics, the language and spirit of the blues, which played a great role in the gestation of jazz but do not seem to be constant and necessary elements. The form of the blues is even less important than the style. The principle of the four-bar unit of construction, which was introduced into Negro-American folklore at an undetermined epoch[2] and subsequently adopted by jazzmen as an unchangeable rule, is called into question in certain modern works. This observation brings us to a consideration of the twofold problem of repertory and form. The pieces that are referred to, in a regrettable misuse of the term, as "jazz classics" are not at all an essential part of this music. André Kostelanetz has produced a version of TIGER RAG that is completely outside the realm of jazz. On the other hand, any piece that lends itself to the conditions of infrastructure that jazz requires can be assimilated. Jazzmen have borrowed innumerable themes from different repertories and have treated them with great liberty without thereby altering the essence of their art. Again, the example of CONCERTO FOR COOTIE shows that jazz can very well get away from the theme-and-

[2] There can be no question that this acquisition was borrowed, since this kind of construction had been at the base of all European dance music for centuries. Besides, it is not certain that the original blues did not have a much freer form to begin with. A vestige of such liberty appears in the lack of concern a minstrel like Big Bill Broonzy has for such construction and even for the unity of the measure. Doesn't he have some bar-and-a-half interludes in BLACK, BROWN AND WHITE?

variations form that almost all its works follow. Improvisation, whether individual or collective, is not essential either. We have seen that jazz can be expressed by means of arrangements. And arrangements themselves are merely a device the jazz musician uses as the need arises. Counterpoint is a form of thought and of expression that is found in a small number of works, especially if the word is taken in a strict sense. The same thing is not true, of course, in the case of harmony and melody, which figure in virtually all recorded works. It might be claimed that both disappear in certain drum solos, but such solos are only an episodical part of jazz. Melody and harmony would therefore be essential if they didn't have, in jazz, a non-specific character that is not completely offset by the phrase-chorus idea and the blues mode, which are, as we have seen, the only real contributions of the Negro-American genius in this domain. In both cases, borrowings are more numerous if not more evident than innovations.

Our study of rhythm and sound brought out the existence of two phenomena, swing and the hot manner of playing. Are these two elements constant and specific enough to satisfy the criteria for what is essential? As to whether they are sufficiently specific, there can be no doubt about the answer. Sometimes one of the two elements is enough by itself to place a musical fragment in the world of jazz. Byas' initial inflection in LAURA identifies the performance as being jazz even before rhythmic values and the infrastructure produce the sensation of swing. Inversely, a slow piano solo by John Lewis or Erroll Garner may be made up of sounds that could figure in a European composition, but its pulsation will show that it is jazz. But doesn't this twofold example suggest that a careful examination of how constant these swing and hot phenomena are might lead to unexpected conclusions?

2

Historic Persistence of the Swing and Hot Phenomena

It seems certain that the solution to the problem we are considering—what constitutes the essence of jazz—lies in the tension-relaxation duality. What remains to be seen is whether these two elements have always existed side by side in equal proportions or whether one has been more important than the other at different times.

Reconstitutions of primitive jazz seem to show clearly not only that the Louisiana pioneers had very little swing but also that their rhythmic conceptions made it impossible for swing to appear in more than an embryonic stage. The jazzmen who did honor to the New Orleans style between 1920 and 1928 represented a definite advance over their predecessors, as we have seen; but frequent slips in performance and certain backward rhythmic conceptions prevented most of them from matching the fullness of swing achieved by Armstrong and his disciples. The element of relaxation is accordingly much weaker in the primitive and oldtime styles than the element of tension, which reaches a level of paroxysm. At least during the primitive period, hot language may be said to outweigh swing in a proportion of nine to one. But as time went on, this proportion continued to change in favor of swing. An equilibrium was established between 1935 and 1940, at the beginning of the classical period. Jazz lost some of its early savageness; it became organized and polished, its violence was put under control. At the same time, conceptions and means of execution were modified, and both the soloist and the accompanist were able to express a more intense swing. That was when thousands of young pianists, white and colored, took Teddy Wilson as an example. People began to be less interested in playing hot than in swinging. However, two opposing trends were in the process of being born. The first was a reaction and included a whole series of screaming tenor saxophonists like Illinois Jacquet. These musicians re-emphasized the elements of tension, but without sacrificing the quality of swing that the preceding generation had acquired. Still, their dynamism was more often than not expressed at the expense of the strictly musical quality of their solos. At the other extreme, Lester Young took over the element of relaxation at the high degree of perfection to which Armstrong and Hodges had brought it and carried it even further by developing muscular relaxation and suitable rhythmic conceptions. This step forward may, however, have been accompanied by a certain weakening of vital drive. The type of swing created by Young is what cool musicians identify themselves with. But the price paid by the followers of this movement for their adherence to these conceptions and their legitimate desire to go beyond them has been an almost total abandonment—a necessary abandonment, freely consented to and even solicited—of the element of tension. The same elements are to be found in ultramodern as in primitive jazz, but the proportions are reversed. The element of relaxation is now very much in evidence, whereas the element of tension is considerably subdued.

3
Must Jazz Be Divided into Compartments?

Is it reasonable to give the name of jazz to successive musical conceptions in which the proportions of the two elements we have regarded as essential are so variable? Wouldn't it be better to dissociate them? If 1952 jazz had almost nothing in common with 1917 jazz, the reason may be that there had been a change of essence between those two dates. If we consider only the hot manner of playing as essential, certain solos of Lester Young lose almost all title to being called jazz; but the same thing is true of the greater part of New Orleans jazz if we consider swing as the essential element. Certain theoreticians have crossed this Rubicon. They affirm that New Orleans music (which they call "jazz") is essentially different from classical jazz (which they call "swing"), just as the latter is absolutely different from modern jazz (which they refer to as "bebop"). According to their way of seeing things, Ella Fitzgerald is not a jazz singer, she is a "swingwoman"; Charlie Parker and Miles Davis are no more related than she is to such "real jazzmen" as King Oliver and Johnny Dodds. The weakness of this theory is immediately aparent in the superpositions it involves. Where does Louis Armstrong come? Is he a jazzman or a swingman? Thanks to him, doesn't the phenomenon of swing, which the pioneers felt only vaguely, appear at the height of the New Orleans period? In our introduction, we wondered whether it was legitimate to divide the history of jazz into several distinct periods. A procedure that may be acceptable in the interest of clarifying an explanation ceases to be valid when used as the starting point for what is supposed to be a demonstration of historical truth. Under such circumstances, the arbitrariness of making radical separations between styles that obviously intermingle becomes evident.

4
Toward a Change of Essence?

We have observed that the elements of relaxation and tension, which we consider conjointly essential, exist permanently side by side, but that the element of tension has grown smaller as the other element increased. In works belonging to the cool movement, tension is very weak. There is reason, then, to consider the possibility that one of the two poles between which the electricity of jazz is concentrated may disappear. The public, as we have seen, is more sensitive to tension than to relaxation, and its current attitude might incline us to pessimistic considerations. But quite apart from those, it behooves us to wonder whether such a total effacement of one of its major components would not entail the effacement of all jazz. In other words, can it be that we are witnessing a change of essence? Probably so. If the curve of its two elements were to continue bending in the same direction, the evolution of jazz would find a logical conclusion in its own disappearance. Bernard Heuvelmans would be closer to the truth than Boris Vian. Jazz would seem to have been just a lucky accident. But doesn't European musical thought itself, considered at a distance, have the appearance of an accident without parallel in history? The important thing would be for jazz to have a successor in some kind of Negro-American music that would offer as much as jazz without actually being the same thing. Some people believe that this has happened, and that what we call cool jazz is nothing other than the new art that has come to take the place of the old form, which is about to disappear. Considering all the great jazzmen who are still alive—some of them hardly over thirty—talk of this imminent demise strikes me as premature.

By our definition, jazz consists essentially of *an inseparable but extremely variable mixture of relaxation and tension* (that is, of swing and the hot manner of playing). Defined in this way, jazz has an incredibly rich past, considering the briefness of its history. It has involved the most varied forms of expression—vocal and instrumental, monodic and polyphonic, individual and collective, improvised and worked out. After remaining a music of the common people for a long time, some of Ellington's works put it in the ranks of highbrow music; Armstrong gave it mystical overtones, and Miles Davis added to it a chamber music character that it had lacked before. It has something to offer to every mood and can be sometimes light, sometimes serious. There is nothing like it for dancing, but it is also at home in the concert hall. Although it is the music of the American Negro, its universality has long since been established. Its disappearance would be deplorable unless a worthy successor arose to take its place. For it is doubtful that recordings made in our time will be enough to give men in later centuries an adequate idea of its beauty. Of course, richer and nobler art forms have died out over the centuries, leaving only meager hints of their greatness. It is only natural to hope that a more favorable destiny awaits one of the most vital musical manifestations of our time. Or could it be that this enormous vitality is precisely what makes it so hard to imagine its ever being dead? In any case, the only answer to this question, as to any other question about the future, is a large interrogation point. Tomorrow's music will be whatever tomorrow's men are.

V

JAZZ AND EUROPE

Chapter XVI

THE INFLUENCE OF JAZZ
ON EUROPEAN MUSIC

Around 1930, it was commonly claimed, in so-called advanced circles, that the major contribution of jazz had been to stimulate European music by supplying it with new ideas about rhythm, melody, and sound, and also perhaps by showing it how to be simple. This notion would have become fixed in many minds if it hadn't been seriously contested. Admittedly, as an example of the triumph of primitivism over the European tradition, it was well designed to appeal to people with a passion for the exotic. Much was being made of the influence of Negro sculpture on Picasso, and there was no end of commentary based on analogies and the inevitability of correspondences between the arts. On top of everything, wasn't this thesis supported by the declarations of the very composers who had been "inspired by jazz"?

It may seem rash to question a thesis that even Stravinsky has supported. Still, certain chronological facts call for a closer examination of an historical situation that has perhaps been somewhat embroidered on. Thirty years later, it is possible for us to establish with some certainty what jazz had to offer from 1920 to 1925. For that matter, a glance at contemporary accounts is enough to show that the music generally referred to as "jazz" at that time did not owe much to the New Orleans tradition. True, some European artists

may have gone to the real source (we shall see that at least
one of them was certainly not unacquainted with it), and
it may also be that these artists grasped some of the elements
of authentic jazz behind the distortions and degradations
of commercial versions. What we shall try to tell from a few
brief analyses is how they used these elements and what
importance this contribution had.

One fact stands out immediately: Not all European music
was "influenced" by jazz. Of the five great contemporary
masters whose superiority is gradually being recognized—
Schoenberg, Berg, Webern, Bartók, and Stravinsky—only the
last was affected by this music from the other side of the
Atlantic. If the criteria are kept reasonably strict, a catalogue
of works in which this influence is apparent would include
only three musicians—Stravinsky, Ravel, and Milhaud. All
three lived at the time either in France or where French
was spoken (Stravinsky composed his *Histoire du Soldat* and
Ragtime in French Switzerland). This observation, which
limits the range of the topic we are discussing, will simplify
our task, for we shall confine ourselves to these three
musicians.

1
Jazz and Ravel, Stravinsky, and Milhaud

The first questions to ask are, naturally, "How did Ravel,
Milhaud, and Stravinsky get acquainted with jazz?" and
"What kind of jazz did they know?" As for Ravel, the answer
is difficult, because we must rely on what other people have
reported. It is easy to imagine the composer of *Daphnis*
jumping on the "latest thing," regardless of where it came
from, eager to exploit this novelty, slightly shopworn though
it may have been, after he had followed Debussy and flirted
a moment with Schoenberg. There is no dearth of anecdotes,

in some of which he is shown applauding Jimmie Noone, in others the orchestra at the Moulin Rouge. But we have learned to take anecdotes with a grain of salt.

What Stravinsky tells us in *Chroniques de ma vie* has much more weight. "I must draw attention," he writes, "to a work that I composed just after finishing the score of my *Soldat* and that is significant, in spite of its modest dimensions, because of the appetite I had then for jazz, which sprang up in such a startling way as soon as the war was over. At my request, I had been sent a whole pile of this music . . . "[1] Stravinsky had very probably heard ragtimes (but played by whom and under what conditions?). Did he depend on scores for a better acquaintance with this kind of music? This hypothesis, which seems very likely, would explain certain errors that we will have to take into consideration. If we accept it, we must admit all the restrictions inherent in such an approach to a phenomenon that cannot be reduced to a musical text, however faithful the score may seem.

Of these three musicians, Darius Milhaud is undoubtedly the one who had the most direct contact with jazz. His abundant testimony will serve to show us how a European composer in the twenties was able to hear and assimilate this music. Perhaps we should call attention once more to the fact that, for a European, the word jazz evoked small colored bands, large white orchestras like Paul Whiteman's, and even whimsical ensembles in which car horns competed for the spotlight with musical saws. It seems that Milhaud first ran into the well-trained white orchestra; does he not cite, as responsible for his "first contact with jazz," "Billy Arnold's orchestra, fresh from New York"?[2] Was Milhaud captivated by the spruce "novelty" of the rhythms and timbres Billy Arnold showed off? No doubt he was; and no

1 Igor Stravinsky: *Chroniques de ma vie*, I, p. 168.
2 Darius Milhaud: *Notes sans musique*, p. 133.

doubt many of his contemporaries would have reacted in the same way. "I had the idea," he wrote later, "of using these rhythms and timbres in a piece of chamber music, but first I had to dig a little deeper into the mysteries of this new musical form, whose technique tormented me."[3]

He had a chance to do this in 1922, during his first trip to the United States. After hearing some "excellent jazz" (*sic*) at the Hotel Brunswick in Boston, the composer of *l'Homme et son désir* discovered in Harlem "music completely different" from the kind he was acquainted with: " . . . the melodic lines, set off by the percussion, overlapped contrapuntally in a throbbing mixture of broken, twisted rhythms."[4] From this picturesque description, it might be thought that Milhaud had suddenly come across real jazz. On the other hand, when he describes certain performances in which "the singers were accompanied by a flute, a clarinet, two trumpets, a trombone, a complicated group of drums for one player, a piano, and a string quintet,"[5] it seems clear that the French musician is referring to theaters where operettas and musical revues were given. The very composition of the orchestra shows that jazz had no more of a role there than it has today at the Folies-Bergère, even though good jazzmen often played in the pit (such as Louis Armstrong, for instance, at the Vendome Theatre in Chicago). Nonetheless, that is the kind of orchestra he must have known before composing *La Création du Monde*. This work, he writes, "gave me at last a chance to use the elements of jazz that I had studied so carefully; my orchestra, *like those of Harlem*, was made up of seventeen soloists and I used the jazz style *without reserve*, blending it with a classical feeling."[6]

Four years later, Darius Milhaud made another trip to

[3] *Ibid.*, p. 134.
[4] *Ibid.*, p. 154.
[5] *Ibid.*, p. 154.
[6] *Ibid.*, p. 167. The italics are ours.

the United States. When he was there before, he had told
newspapermen who asked him about American music that
jazz was the most interesting thing it had turned out. (Let
us note, in passing, that he had not yet had the revelation
of Negro jazz at that time.) In 1926, his attitude had changed
radically: "I disappointed the American newspapermen
again," he reports, "by declaring that jazz no longer interested
me."[7] What did he hold responsible for this quick disillu-
sionment? Jazz itself? No. "Snobs, whites, people who were
looking for exotic effects." Does he not show a little resent-
ment in the observation that, after him, other "tourists of
Negro music" had "dug into its innermost recesses"? (The
statement is quite an exaggeration, in any case.) What is
more important, coming to the United States with such a
preconception, how could he have failed to remain outside
jazz at the very moment when it was undergoing the most
prodigious of evolutions? The French composer was not
even curious enough to investigate a certain Louis Armstrong, though people were beginning to talk about him
at that time.

The following year, Darius Milhaud published a volume
of musical esthetics entitled *Etudes*. The famous influence
of jazz was no longer anything but a souvenir for him then:
"The influence of jazz has already passed by, like a salutary
storm after which the sky is purer, the weather more re-
liable," he comments. "Little by little, renascent classicism
is replacing the broken throbbings of syncopation."[8] Nevertheless, Milhaud is willing to cast a tender glance back at
this music which preserves an "extraordinary variety of
expression."[9] "In order to get a good idea of it," he adds, "it
is naturally necessary to hear a really serious [*sic*] jazzband,
made up of sound musicians . . . and using orchestrations

[7] *Ibid.*, p. 215.
[8] Darius Milhaud: *Etudes*, p. 22.
[9] *Ibid.*, p. 52.

of unquestioned value, on the order of Irving Berlin's." For the reader's information, let us point out that Irving Berlin is the untrained musician (it seems that he did not even know how to read the treble clef) whose deathless memory is assured by such masterpieces as A FELLA WITH AN UMBRELLA and ALEXANDER'S RAGTIME BAND.

Darius Milhaud has one final scruple: "To one side, we find a kind of music that came from the same source but has evolved in a completely different way, among the Negroes."[20] But we can no longer rely completely on the composer's discernment, since on a previous page he makes this bewildering statement (written several years after his Harlem experience): "In 1920-21, it was enough to hear Jean Wiener at the piano and Vance Lowry on saxophone and banjo, at the Gaya Bar on Rue Duphot, to become acquainted with jazz played in an *absolutely complete, pure, and intact* way."[21] For us of the following generation, Vance Lowry has remained one of those legendary geniuses in which, for that matter, the "prehistoric" era of jazz abounds; but we have had many chances to hear Jean Wiener, alone or with Clément Doucet, make a brave effort to "play jazz" in his all too personal way! So there we have a good idea of the carelessness—I almost wrote deafness—of a composer who, upon hearing three kinds of music that are *essentially different*, was not able to avoid a confusion that other, less gifted musicians fortunately cleared up a few years later.

The statements of Darius Milhaud, the rarer ones of Stravinsky, and the attitude of Ravel show pretty well that not one of them grasped the real meaning of jazz. Such mistakes of interpretation and judgment can be explained—especially in the case of the last two, who were great musicians—only by an insufficient acquaintance with authentic jazz. We now realize that what counted in 1923 jazz was King Oliver's

20 *Ibid.,* p. 56.
21 *Ibid.,* p. 51. The italics are ours.

band and others like it, made up of musicians who had, for the most part, come from New Orleans to settle in Chicago. Not one of our composers, we may be sure, had a chance to know them. Did they become acquainted with jazz only on its outer edges, and did they take minor works as typical manifestations of the Negro's genius? Did they let themselves be taken in by commercial counterfeits? This seems rather likely, even in the case of Milhaud, who was acquainted with a more authentic aspect of jazz. The surprising thing is that someone like Ravel was able to take even as much interest as he did in such obvious trash.

2
Melodic Borrowings

Stravinsky's and Milhaud's statements are not confined to emphasizing the esthetic interest of jazz (or of what they took for jazz); they also betray a desire to adapt and stylize it, and some of their works confirm this. Stravinsky's ragtime in *l'Histoire du Soldat, Ragtime pour onze instruments,* and *Piano Rag Music* show the way; Milhaud follows with *La Création du Monde;* and Ravel brings up the rear with the fox trot of *l'Enfant et les Sortilèges* and his two piano concertos. We shall confine our discussion to these pieces, which are the most representative of what has been boldly called the "jazz epoch" in Europe. We shall try to make out in them what the three composers were able to grasp among the elements of authentic jazz and what got across to them by way of commercial jazz; and then we shall try to evaluate the use each of them made of this material.

What did jazz of the primitive and oldtime periods have to offer the European composer melodically? Surely nothing but what it had itself taken over from Negro-American folk-lore—the blues scale. In this respect, the influence of jazz is clear. There are appreciable melodic borrowings from the language of blues and spirituals in the compositions we are considering. Ravel's *Concerto in G,* for example, has melodic lines in which the blue note plays a role. Sometimes this role is apparent, as in the secondary motif that is played, in the part of the score marked 5, by the clarinet and the muted trumpet and that is taken up later by the piccolo; sometimes it lies underneath, as in the theme in triads of the finale, which exploits the analogy between the blues scale and the mode of D. Even more clearly, the melodic theme that develops in the *Concerto pour la main gauche* beginning at number 28 borrows its elements from Negro blues. On a bass in the form of a pedal point that supports a C major chord with appoggiaturas, the theme is announced in two successive parts, which are dominated by a blue note (third degree for the first, seventh degree for the second) and which resolve on the tonic and the dominant, which we have already identified as the poles toward which these blue notes are attracted. Taken in descending order, the combination of these two parts produces, by elision of the fourth degree, one of the melodic lines most frequently used by oldtime singers and players of the blues (fig. 27).

FIG. 27

Other examples of such faithfulness to the letter, if not to the spirit, of the blues are to be found in *La Création du Monde.* Milhaud's piece abounds in passages that take their melodic inspiration from the blues scale. The subject of the Fugue not only is based on the same defective scale, but also includes the *changeable third.* F♮ alternates with F♯, one exercising on the other an attraction that is first descending and then ascending (fig. 28). It seems that the composer got close here to the true significance of the blue note—its in-

FIG. 28
LA CRÉATION DU MONDE (Max Eschig, publisher)

stability. The true feeling of the blue note is expressed by a slide, and the way this subject is written permits such a slide if it does not actually indicate one. On the other hand, the clash between the blue note and the major third at number 32 in the transition motif played by the oboe (fig. 29)

FIG. 29
LA CRÉATION DU MONDE (Max Eschig, publisher)

has a non-sliding character that is accentuated by the octave jump. This takes us away from jazz, which offers no similar example, to the best of our knowledge.

The variability of the blue note is again highlighted in the very design of the countersubject of the Fugue (fig. 30),

FIG. 30
LA CRÉATION DU MONDE (Max Eschig, publisher)

in which the seventh and the third degrees are alternately affected by a chromatic slide. One thing to note is that this countersubject contains (element *a*) the initial motif of the most celebrated of all jazz themes, the *St. Louis Blues.* Further, the principal motif of the composition (fig. 28) is typical of the blues. This four-note figure seems to be particularly prized by composers "inspired" by jazz. Doesn't George Gershwin also use it in his *Rhapsody in Blue?*

The harmonic climate and evolution of the blues do not depend solely on the more or less frequent use of blue notes. They result above all from a perpetual interplay between the tonic and the subdominant. Darius Milhaud seems to have understood this perfectly. The tail of the subject of the Fugue begins the traditional subdominant modulation. True, this direction is changed almost as soon as it is suggested, since the new tonality immediately imposed by the second voice is not the one expected; but perhaps this is just a surprise effect.

The harmonization of the melodic theme introduced by the oboe at number 20 in the score is more convincing. First, the composer harmonizes the blue note on the third degree (E♭) by means of a subdominant chord that resolves naturally to the tonic, which is embellished by an altered seventh (another blue note). It is by an extension of this procedure that Milhaud achieves the most interesting result from a musical point of view. Taking up the same theme one tone higher a little further on (number 23), he causes it to be heard over different harmonies, intelligently transforming the blue note on the third degree into a blue note on the seventh degree and the subdominant chord into the dominant. He forms a kind of "complex of blue notes" based on the analogy between these degrees that can be taken for one another and then plays around with the resulting tonal ambiguity, which is a phenomenon that jazz musicians exploited hardly at all, as much attached as they were to tonal stability. On the other hand, the superposition in a single cluster of the leading note and the blue note on the seventh degree (F♯ and F♮, in our example) creates an harmonic relationship that Duke Ellington came across on his own several years later and used as one of the bases of his dissonant system.

The first measures of the piece, nevertheless, would make us doubt that Milhaud understood the real meaning of the blue note. To repeat, the blue note is an appoggiatura that has the distinctive feature of resolving, not on a neighboring degree, but a minor third below—that is, on the tonic or the dominant. In the third measure of the score, an F♯ in the bass (third degree of the major scale) and an F♮ in the violin and cello (third degree of the minor scale, or blue note) are superimposed. Is this to be considered as a chance effect of polymodality, or as an intentional use of the blue note? In the first case, wouldn't Milhaud be guilty of a serious error in composition by giving a false sense at the beginning of the piece to a note that plays a key role later on—the kind of fault Mozart would have committed if he had begun his *G minor Symphony* with a magnificent G major chord? In the second case, doesn't Milhaud seem to neglect deliberately the sliding character of the blue note, reducing it to the modest, commonplace role of the third degree in the mode of D? Whichever explanation is accepted, the procedure seems weak and uncertain.

Such criticism cannot be made of Stravinsky in *l'Histoire du Soldat*. The mastery shown almost everywhere throughout this extraordinary stylistic exercise compels admiration. It is to be feared, however, that the section called "Ragtime," the only one in which the "influence" of Negro-American music can be detected, is one of the less brilliant and possibly the least successful of the composer's works. Melodically, it contains no borrowing from the blues, except for a timid and no doubt involuntary allusion during the exposition of the violin theme, where there is some major-minor playing around with the third degree. Some vague blue notes are scattered around in the principal melodic design of *Piano Rag Music,* but they are surrounded by a polytonal accompaniment that robs them of all resemblance to the Negro's music. Finally, in *Ragtime pour onze instruments,* the language is not very melodic and is intentionally insignificant; and though there are traces of a slide from major to minor on the third degree (and vice versa), the ear has a hard time grasping the relationship between blue note and real note that is conveyed so clearly by certain passages in *La Création du Monde.* It is quite possible that, as early as 1918, Stravinsky had assimilated the melodic language of the blues as well as Milhaud and Ravel did later on; but in that case, he showed more reticence than his successors in the use of easy effects. This *Ragtime* is a monstrous stylization, but its ugliness is appealing, like the ugliness of some of Picasso's paintings. There is a world of difference between this voluptuous exploitation of the hideous and the picture-postcard exoticism that the fox trot of *l'Enfant* shows Ravel delighting in. Both pages are caricatures, but they are not of the same kind.

Stravinsky's handling of melody may remain mysterious to us, but there is no secret about Milhaud's and Ravel's. Both were satisfied with introducing into their compositions some melodic lines that appealed to them as having an exotic flavor. There is nothing surprising in this attitude, which so many musicians between the wars had in common. We might even wager that future historians will call this the period of *coloring.*

3

Rhythmic Influence

Was jazz able to contribute more rhythmically? It is not

certain. Our composers made abundant use of syncopation (which jazz did not invent, although in jazz it took on a different meaning) and the resulting rhythmic formulas. Did they find in it a means of getting away from regular metrics and classical accentuation? It is doubtful. The innovations of *Le Sacre du Printemps,* which had quite a different importance, had already supplied an answer to these problems.

Maurice Ravel seems to have assimilated the rhythmic procedures of jazz in a very elementary way. There is nothing in his music that could make anyone think otherwise. It is hard to imagine what aberration has led some commentators to refer to jazz for an explanation of the irregular accents in the *Concerto pour la main gauche,* which are surely much closer to West Indian folklore. Admittedly, the important theme that appears at number 28 of the score is heard against a regular pulsation, but it resembles an *alla marcia* rather than the beat of jazz. The drums, far from contributing to any kind of accentuation, are not heard from after eight bars. When they appear again, behind the trombone solo, their disconnected rhythm is anti-jazz. The melodic theme does use syncopation abundantly, but only to break up the regularity of construction and to make the melody somewhat independent of the accompaniment rhythmically.

La Création du Monde shows a less superficial understanding of jazz rhythm. Milhaud's determination to write in the spirit of jazz is already apparent in his choice of meter. Except for two or three extremely brief changes of measure, the whole piece is in 2/2 regardless of tempo. From the first measures of the Prelude, syncopated formulas appear. At first they are not at all jazz-like. Only in the Fugue is there to be found a rhythmic connection that would be looked for in vain in the preceding part. Rhythmically, the subject of the Fugue is rather stiff, though hardly stiffer than the formulas jazzmen were so addicted to from 1920 to 1925. In the hands of a good jazz musician, it could be swung in spite of the construction of its initial motif (the principal motif of the composition), which scarcely seems amenable to swing. Rhythmically, this motif corresponds to a series of eighth notes forming the anacrusis and leading up to an accented quarter note on the strong beat. Several sections of the subject use this rhythm. By means of accents, the countersubject emphasizes the weak part of the beat and then, by contrast, the beat itself. All these rhythms work against one another or, occasionally, coincide. The resulting impression of disorder is undoubtedly intentional, even though the composer does not always seem to be completely in control of the forces he unleashed.

From the point of view of rhythmic construction, the third movement is undoubtedly the most interesting. Several elements are called into play; first, a motif of three notes (sometimes four) of which the next to the last, an accented half note, is syncopated; next, an irregular rhythm (in 3/8) that is superimposed on the countersubject of the Fugue or on a series of brief syncopations (dotted quarter notes). The fourth movement is almost completely dominated by a rhythmic figure repeated over and over by the piano. The formula is the same as that of the principal motif—three eighth notes leading to a quarter. Not one of these rhythms, syncopated or otherwise, has more than an incidental similarity to good jazz of the period.

Although *Ragtime pour onze instruments* was composed several years before *La Création*, Stravinsky's writing shows a distinctly more highly developed sense of jazz. In places, the formulas used by the Russian master attain a rhythmic flexibility that makes them resemble the riffs of jazzmen (fig. 31). Are they pure products of the imagination or are they based on something else? The chances are that they represent an adaptation of pre-existing elements—the adaptation of a genius, admittedly. It is too bad that Stravinsky,

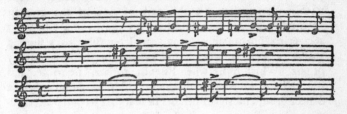

FIG. 31

undoubtedly under the influence of the inexact system followed in the scores that helped him become acquainted with
Negro-American music, uses a misleading notation, putting
a dotted quarter note and a sixteenth when he should have
written a triplet made up of a quarter note and an eighth.
This basic slip, which was also made subsequently by Milhaud, Ravel, and all the other musicians who tried to write
"in the style of jazz," could not help leading to a distortion
of the occasionally very well thought out rhythms of *Ragtime*.

There is not much to learn from an analysis of *Piano Rag
Music* and the ragtime of *l'Histoire du Soldat*. The first
makes cheerful fun of its sources, if we are supposed to be
able to find any trace of the original ragtime and its regular
accentuations in the extremely diverse meters of this piece—
5/4, 3/4, 2/4, 3/8, 5/8. A similar rhythmic capriciousness
animates the ragtime of *l'Histoire du Soldat* after the principal figure—which doesn't come off any better rhythmically
than melodically—has been stated. The 4/8 at the beginning
is followed by 5/16 and 7/16 measures that violate the
metrical unity. One of these asymmetrical episodes is worth
making a remark about. At number 34, the composer notes
in the margin that it is appropriate to "make the rhythm
mechanical and precise." Was this just to avoid an insuf-
ficiently strict performance? Did Stravinsky want to show
that his intention was to caricature jazz? Or did he regard

jazz rhythm as something "precise" but "mechanical"? Such a misunderstanding on the part of one of the greatest rhythmic geniuses the world has ever known would be truly staggering. Fortunately, many years later, Stravinsky showed that he was not completely unaware of the rhythmic duality of jazz. "Which of us, when listening to jazz," he wrote, "has not felt an amusing and almost giddy sensation when a dancer or solo musician persists in marking irregular accentuations but does not succeed in diverting the ear from the regular metrical pulsation beaten out by the percussion?"[12]

This constant affirmation of the meter that is expressed by the unremitting pulsation of jazz is echoed very faintly in *Ragtime pour onze instruments*. Nonetheless, at times, the way the bass and drum parts are written, though traditional, suggests a real jazz beat. At such moments, we are very close to certain jazz scores that came later. At no time does the music of Darius Milhaud give us this impression. The reason is that the composer of *La Création* was set on going jazz rhythms one better. By introducing a certain type of polyrhythm, he destroyed the very bases of jazz rhythm. In the Fugue, the drums express a rhythmic pedal point that divides the four-beat period into four groups of three quarter notes followed by one group of four quarter notes. This may produce an amusing polyrhythmic effect; but what has become of the steadiness of pulsation—or even a suggestion of such steadiness—which is the very lifeblood of jazz rhythm?

4
Incompatibility

We touch here upon the heart of the problem. The rhythms of jazz, which are very simple in themselves, have the "giddy" power Stravinsky refers to only when they are

[12] Igor Stravinsky: *Poétique musicale*, p. 45.

set against a steady beat. By destroying the basic pulsation, our composers killed the principle of attraction on which the phenomenon of swing depends. The positive element of an electric current has no power if it is cut off from the negative element, its opposite; and in the same way, a syncopated rhythm becomes insignificant and loses its Dionysian power when cut off from its invaluable auxiliary. For want of having understood this, our composers got from jazz only a fraction of what it had to offer. Esthetically and technically, the pieces (or parts of pieces) we have cited must be regarded as great failures.

Even if they had been perfectly thought out in the abstract, these works would nonetheless have remained at a stage of half-realized intentions, for between the creator and the listener there is that indispensable intermediary, the interpreter. Anyone who is acquainted with jazz knows that the best-conceived rhythms remain insignificant unless they are performed with swing. Similarly, jazz sonority cannot be expressed by means of a stereotyped timbre or series of timbres; it must be created anew with each phrase. Neither swing nor the range of sonorities can be written down on paper. If the truly creative role of these two elements is recognized, it must be granted that a work of jazz can be said to exist totally only in performance.

Nevertheless, jazz scores do exist. With a few exceptions, they are necessarily pieces written under special circumstances, composed for a given orchestra by a musician who knows in advance what the group he is writing for is capable of. Duke Ellington's statements show very well that, while a piece is being worked out, the creator remains constantly in touch with the orchestra. His ability to use the band as an instrument is conditioned by what he knows of the players' musical nature. To write a cool arrangement for a band like Lionel Hampton's in 1946 would be as useless as to prescribe cavalry maneuvers for foot soldiers.

Such an absurd thing is nonetheless what European composers wound up trying to do. "To use these rhythms and timbres," as Darius Milhaud proposed to do, presupposes interpreters capable of translating such rhythms and finding such timbres. There is a twofold impossibility here. However skillful a technician or fine a musician he may be, no classically trained performer can create any illusions in such respects. It takes a long acquaintance with jazz to assimilate its language; what symphony player, what concert soloist, what chamber music specialist has enough time to bring off such an attempt successfully? The failure of so-called *symphonic jazz* orchestras, in which Colonne or National Orchestra musicians try to play "like jazzmen," is significant. There is no need to call attention here to the exaggerated vibratos, the uncontrolled glissandos, and the jostling syncopations that accompany such bastard enterprises. But were Milhaud, Ravel, and Stravinsky concerned about having their works performed by jazzmen?[12]

An adaptation of the language of jazz to European music would be possible only under two conditions. First, the performer would have to be capable of playing the composer's rhythms with at least a certain amount of swing. Second, the composer would have to be acquainted with the performer's special sound effects and adapt his music to them, just as a playwright creates a role with a given actor in mind. But the absurdity of this double requirement is immediately apparent. What essential difference would remain between such "classical" music and a jazz composition? None at all. Such music would be jazz, and all the more authentically jazz because it would require real jazzmen to perform it.

Thus, any real exchange between European music and jazz is seen to be impossible. One of these two arts borrows

---

[12] I have not felt it necessary to include Stravinsky's *Ebony Concerto*, composed in 1945 for the Woody Herman band. Both its date and the composer's intention situate it outside the scope of this study.

elements from the other, but the influence is always in the same direction. Jazz is able to put to good use what it acquires from European music, but the European tradition is incapable of assimilating what jazz has to offer. It is, of course, possible to mute the trumpets, make the trombones slide, pile up clarinet portamentos, add different kinds of drums, and syncopate the rhythmic figures; but the most these elements can contribute is a momentary picturesqueness. What does a wa-wa amount to out of its expressive context? What is a blue note without inflection? What is syncopation without swing? Like the legendary animal that tried to drink the moon in a pond, Stravinsky, Ravel, and Milhaud were dealing with reflections. The compositions that depend for their substance on this hazardous metamorphosis show how vain such an attempt must be.

Moreover, can it be said that this metamorphosis and these borrowings were necessary? The answer is an unqualified no. Stylistic exercises are not what is important at a time when the renewal of a centuries-old tradition is at stake. Stravinsky made history when he wrote *Le Sacre du Printemps;* he placed himself in the margin of history when he wrote *Ragtime*. The profound modifications that European music underwent between the wars were not at all related to jazz, and the compositions we have studied here played no role in them. Thus, our composers' energy was spent in an impossible and useless effort at transplantation.

DISCOGRAPHY
and
INDEX

DISCOGRAPHY

INDEX OF RECORDINGS CITED

What follows is an alphabetical listing of records cited in the text, the group leader's name and usually the label on which the record was originally issued in the U.S. or abroad, the label of its early reissue, or reissues. Following on this index the reader will find some notes on current availability and on jazz discographies.

— M.W.

Any published discussion of the current availability of phonograph recordings in any category of music is a thankless and somewhat useless task, particularly in the more-or-less permanent context of book publication. Recordings, particularly reissues of archival classics, go in and out of print constantly and sometimes rapidly. Properties change hands as well. The American Decca catalogue is currently the property of MCA Records, and Charlie Parker's Dial recordings listed below were last collected on the Warner Brothers label.

Well-stocked record shops in our large cities are always a good place to start, and, with help from a sympathetic clerk, the customer can sometimes discover the availability of specific titles by specific artists in the monthly loose-leaf reference volumes which most large stores keep on hand.

The following are North American shops specializing in current jazz issues, both domestic and imported. They will also undoubtedly be receptive to requests for specific titles and even rare, out-of-print selections:

Jazz Record Mart, 11 West Grand Avenue, Chicago, Illinois 60610.

The Jazz Man Record Shop, 3323 Pico Boulevard, Santa Monica, California 90405.

Ray Avery, Rare Records, 417 East Broadway, P.O. Box 10518, Glendale, California 91205.

Jeff Forsythe, 14 Jason Lane, Mamaroneck, New York 10543.

Coda Publications, P.O. Box 87, Station J, Toronto, Ontario M4J 4X8, Canada.

The following two operations specialize in imports, the second particularly imports from Japan, where interest in jazz and jazz records runs high:

Daybreak Express, P.O. Box 250, Van Brunt Station, Brooklyn, New York 11215.

Dan Serro, 165 William Street, New York, New York 10038.

The reader may want to deal directly with some of the more prominent British and European shops in seeking current Common Market catalogue items. (As always with imports, a high degree of patience is advised.) Here is a sample listing:

Peter Russell's Hot Record Store Ltd., 22-24 Market Avenue, Plymouth PL1 1PJ, England.

James Asman's Record Center, Mail Order Dept., 63 Cannon Street, London E.C.4, England.

Dobell's Jazz Record Shop, 77 Charing Cross Road, London W.C. 2, H OAB England.

Dave Carey, The Swing Shop, 1-B Mitcham Lane, Streatham, London S.W.16, England.

Jazz Bazaar, P.O. Box 1126, 5466 Neustadt, Germany.

Pierre Voran, Pan Musique, 35 rue de France, 06 Nice, France.

The standard discographies in jazz are:
Jazz Records 1897–1942 (two volumes) by Brian Rust, Arlington House, 1978, and
Jazz Records 1942–196– (eleven volumes) by Jorgen Grunnet Jepsen, Karl Emil Knudsen, 1970.

The above-mentioned titles and other jazz books are available from:
Oak Lawn Books, Box 2563, Providence, Rhode Island 02907.

Walter C. Allen of Canada, Box 929 Adelaide Station, Toronto, Ontario, M5C 2K3 Canada.

Finally, I can only wish the reader luck. To cite one example of frustration, as this is written, the Lloyd Scott *Symphonic Screach* which figures so prominently in M. Hodeir's discussion of Dickie Wells, has yet to see a legitimate LP reissue in the U.S.,* and *Dickie Wells Blues* appeared only once (Prestige 7593) and soon became an out-of-the-way item. — M.W.

*Incidentally, the model for that Lloyd Scott performance is Fletcher Henderson's *Gouge of Armour Avenue,* which is included in the Smithsonian Institution's Henderson LP Collection. Write for information on that and other issues to: Smithsonian Customer Services, P.O. Box 10230, Des Moines, Iowa 50336.

INDEX

Selected Grove Press Paperbacks

E487   ABE, KOBO / Friends / $2.45
E237   ALLEN, DONALD M., ed. / The New American Poetry: 1945-1960 / $5.95
B77   ALLEN, DONALD M. and CREELEY, ROBERT, eds. / New American Story / $1.95
E609   ALLEN, DONALD M. and TALLMAN, WARREN, eds. / Poetics of the New American Poetry / $3.95
B334   ANONYMOUS / My Secret Life / $2.95
B415   ARDEN, JOHN / Plays: One (Serjeant Musgrave's Dance, The Workhouse Donkey, Armstrong's Last Goodnight) / $4.95
E711   ARENDT, HANNAH / The Jew As Pariah: Jewish Identity and Politics in the Modern Age, ed. by Ron Feldman / $4.95
E521   ARRABAL, FERNANDO / Garden of Delights / $2.95
B361   ARSAN, EMMANUELLE / Emmanuelle / $1.95
E532   ARTAUD, ANTONIN / The Cenci / $3.95
E127   ARTAUD, ANTONIN / The Theater and Its Double / $3.95
E425   BARAKA, IMAMU AMIRI (LeRoi Jones) / The Baptism and The Toilet: Two Plays / $3.95
E670   BARAKA, IMAMU AMIRI (LeRoi Jones) / The System of Dante's Hell, The Dead Lecturer and Tales / $4.95
E96   BECKETT, SAMUEL / Endgame / $1.95
E692   BECKETT, SAMUEL / I Can't Go On, I'll Go On: A Selection From Samuel Beckett's Work, ed. by Richard Seaver / $6.95
B78   BECKETT, SAMUEL / Three Novels: Molloy, Malone Dies and The Unnamable / $3.95
E33   BECKETT, SAMUEL / Waiting for Godot / $1.95
B411   BEHAN, BRENDAN / The Complete Plays (The Hostage, The Quare Fellow, Richard's Cork Leg, Three One Act Plays for Radio) / $4.95
E531   BERGMAN, INGMAR / Three Films by Ingmar Bergman (Through a Glass Darkly, Winter Light, The Silence) / $4.95
B404   BERNE, ERIC / Beyond Games and Scripts. With Selections from His Major Writings, ed. by Claude Steiner / $2.50
B186   BERNE, ERIC / Games People Play / $2.25
E718   BERNE, ERIC / What Do You Say After You Say Hello? / $8.95
E331   BIELY, ANDREY / St. Petersburg / $6.95

E216	KEENE, DONALD, ed. / Anthology of Japanese Literature: Earliest Era to Mid-19th Century / $5.95
E573	KEENE, DONALD, ed. / Modern Japanese Literature: An Anthology / $7.95
E522	KEROUAC, JACK / Mexico City Blues / $3.95
B300	KEROUAC, JACK / The Subterraneans / $1.95
E705	KERR, CARMEN / Sex For Women Who Want To Have Fun and Loving Relationships With Equals / $3.95
E505	KOCH, KENNETH / The Pleasures of Peace and Other Poems / $1.95
E492	KOLAKOWSKI, LESZEK / Toward a Marxist Humanism / $2.95
B210	KUROSAWA, AKIRA / Roshomon / $4.95
B413	LAVERTY, FRANK / The O.K. Way To Slim / $2.95
B9	LAWRENCE, D. H. / Lady Chatterley's Lover / $1.95
B335	LEGMAN, G. / Rationale of the Dirty Joke / $2.95
B262	LESTER, JULIUS / Black Folktales / $2.95
E163	LEWIS, MATTHEW / The Monk / $4.95
E578	LINSSEN, ROBERT / Living Zen / $3.45
E54	LORCA, FEDERICO / Poet in New York. Bilingual ed. / $4.95
B373	LUCAS, GEORGE / American Graffiti / $2.95
B146	MALCOLM X / The Autobiography of Malcolm X / $1.95
E701	MALRAUX, ANDRE / The Conquerors / $3.95
E719	MALRAUX, ANDRE / Lazarus / $2.95
E697	MAMET, DAVID / American Buffalo / $3.95
E709	MAMET, DAVID / A Life in the Theatre / $3.95
E716	MAMET, DAVID / The Water Engine and Mr. Happiness / $3.95
B326	MILLER, HENRY / Nexus / $3.95
B100	MILLER, HENRY / Plexus / $3.95
B325	MILLER, HENRY / Sexus / $3.95
B10	MILLER, HENRY / Tropic of Cancer / $1.95
B59	MILLER, HENRY / Tropic of Capricorn / $1.95
E583	MISHIMA, YUKIO / Sun and Steel / $2.95
E433	MROZEK, SLAWOMIR / Tango / $3.95
E568	MROZEK, SLAWOMIR / Vatzlav / $1.95
E636	NERUDA, PABLO / Five Decades: Poems 1925-1970. Bilingual ed. / $5.95
E364	NERUDA, PABLO / Selected Poems. Bilingual ed. / $5.95
E650	NICHOLS, PETER / The National Health / $3.95
B385	O'CONNOR, ULICK, ed. / Irish Liberation / $2.45
B199	OE, KENZABURO / A Personal Matter / $3.95
E687	OE, KENZABURO / Teach Us To Outgrow Our Madness / $4.95

GROVE PRESS, INC., 196 West Houston St., New York, N.Y. 10014